THE AA GUIDE TO

Durham &
Northumberland

C000195840

CONTENTS

▶ Finding your way

Use the maps below together with the atlas section and the
town plans throughout the guide to explore Durham and
Northumberland. The A–Z section lists the best of the region,
followed by recommended attractions, activities and places to
eat or drink. The Places Nearby section then lists other points
of interest within a short travelling distance to help you explore
a little further.

Many of the restaurants that we've included carry an AA
Rosette rating, which recognises cooking at different
levels nationwide, from the very best in the local area to the
very best in the UK. Pubs have been selected for their great
atmosphere and good food. You can find more Rosette-rated
places to eat at theAA.com.

We're guessing you probably have your accommodation
sorted already, but for those who like to play it by ear, we've
recommended a few campsites to help you out (see page 46).
Caravan and campsites carry the AA's Pennant rating, with the
very best receiving the coveted gold Pennant award. If your
tastes run more to luxury then theAA.com also lists AA-rated
hotels and B&Bs.

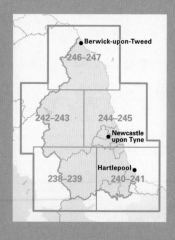

INTRODUCTION

The northeast is one of England's most eccentric regions – and its inhabitants certainly think so. There's a brash but engaging assertiveness to be found here and, as you'll soon discover, Durham and Northumberland have plenty to brag about.

If it's history you're after, you'll find heaps of it. On Hadrian's Wall you can imagine scarlet-cloaked Roman legionaries keeping watch for painted Pictish warriors while cursing the English weather and dreaming of home. Desolate battlefield sites and hulking fortresses such as Alnwick, Dunstanburgh, Bamburgh and Warkworth are reminders that this, until not so very long ago, was a contested border region. The ruins of Lindisfarne and Durham's serene cathedral bear witness to the region's early Christian history. There are places celebrating industrial heritage such as the Killhope Lead Mining Centre (there's a name to conjure with) and the Weardale Railway, while you'll find reminders of a seafaring heritage at places such as Hartlepool's historic quayside.

From the Scottish border south to the Tyne, Northumberland has some of Britain's best beaches. On summer days, and even

in winter, you'll see surfers and other brave souls making the most of the coast. Inland, there are some great walks and bike rides in the dales of the Cheviot Hills and the Simonsides – just hilly enough to be interesting, without being brutally steep. There's dramatic scenery in the High Pennines, where waterfalls plunge into deep valleys, and there are swathes of heather-scented moorland. Northumberland National Park covers over 400 square miles of moorland and valleys with clear streams and and pretty, stone-built villages.

These tracts of hill country and coast are great for wildlife watching. You'll find flocks of puffins, guillemots and other seabirds around the Farne Islands, and seals and dolphins offshore. You may even see red deer on heathery moors.

After a wild day out on land or sea, you'll find plenty of potential for a wild night out in Newcastle, where the Bigg Market is legendary among those who live large – if you can take the pace. Anthony Gormley's colossal Angel of the North is a local icon; nearby in Gateshead the BALTIC Centre has established the region as a hub for edgy art and design.

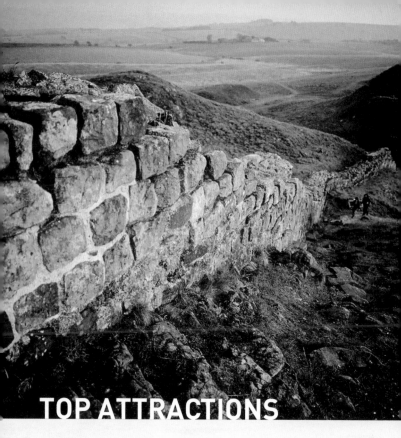

TOP ATTRACTIONS

▲ Hadrian's Wall

Stand on one of the high points of Roman Britain's mighty rampart, look north and imagine you're a legionary, far from home and watching out for Pictish raiders. Explore Housesteads (see page 150), the most complete Roman fort in Britain, and see the home comforts the Empire provided for its soldiers, including hot baths and steam rooms with underfloor heating, and latrines with running water. Other sites on the wall include the milecastle at Gilsland (see page 129), the Mithraic temple at Carrawburgh (see page 88) and remains at Chesters (see page 90).

◄ Durham Cathedral and Durham Castle

Durham's grey-towered Cathedral (see page 112) – resting place of The Venerable Bede and Saint Cuthbert – is one of the great churches of Europe. This Romanesque marvel was begun in 1093 and finished in 1133. Opposite is the castle (see page 111), built not long after William's conquest of England, with a Great Hall added in the 14th century.

◄ Kielder Water and Forest Park

Europe's largest artificial lake and Britain's largest man-made forest are both at Kielder (see page 151). Kielder Water has 27 miles of shoreline, surrounded by over 150,000 acres of woodland. It's not wilderness, but it is one of Britain's biggest nature reserves. The reservoir is ideal for watersports and fishing.

► The Angel of the North

Towering over the A1 outside Gateshead, Antony Gormley's rust-stained, 66ft-tall, steel statue, with its 177ft wingspan is half superhuman, half airliner. Many hated it when it went up in 1998, but it's now a northeast icon, locally known as the Gateshead Flasher. Stop in the car park near the bottom for a look at this huge statue (see page 124).

◄ BALTIC Centre for Contemporary Art

Those who think art should be all bucolic landscapes and royal portraits, may not like the offerings at the BALTIC (see page 126). Like London's Tate Modern, this is art in a converted industrial building – in this case a 1950s flour mill. It prides itself on cutting-edge stuff. Hard work for some, but if you have an open mind, you should feel the benefit.

◀ Beamish

This living museum (see page 72) warmly invokes the spirit of the North from Georgian times up to the early 20th century. Among its delights are re-creations of a typical market town, a country railway station, a colliery and a very evocative pit village. If you get peckish you can fill your boots with authentic old-fashioned fish and chips.

▶ Alnwick Castle

Looking up at Alnwick Castle (see page 55), you may expect to see a Quidditch match in full flow, as it played Hogwarts in the first two Harry Potter movies. Still the home of the Percys (since 1309), Alnwick is in better nick than most of the region's ruined fortifications, with pretty gardens and a treehouse.

◀ Hamsterley Forest

Hamsterley Forest (see page 132) offers more than 30 miles of cycle trails – some adventurous, others are more easy-going – as well as walking and horse riding paths and forest roads in its 5,000 hectares of woodland in the Bedburn and Ayhope valleys. They include the informative Sky Rainforest Discovery Trail.

▲ Lindisfarne (Holy Island)

Lindisfarne's ruined priory (see page 146), built in the 11th century, is one of the most evocative places on the Northumberland coast. The original burial place of seventh-century St Cuthbert, it was rebuilt after Viking attack, but destroyed again by Henry VIII. Dinky 16th-century Lindisfarne Castle (see page 145) was converted into an enviable private house in 1903.

▶ Locomotion: the National Railway Museum

One of the greatest changing railway collections in the UK, with interactive displays, and star attractions that span the decades from 18th century pioneers to 20th hi-tech (see page 100).

◀ Cragside

Set in more than 900 acres of country park and gardens, Cragside (see page 97) was built in the 19th century for the first Lord Armstrong. A whimsical cross between an English manor house and a Bavarian schloss, it was the first house in the world to be lit by hydroelectricity.

HISTORY OF DURHAM & NORTHUMBERLAND

You could say – and you'd be right – that the northeast has produced more history than it really needs. All too often, the story is of bloody conflict – dramatic and exciting to read about now, but tragic and terrifying for those who lived through it. Romans, Anglo-Saxons, Normans, rebel earls, Scots reivers and Viking raiders have all left their mark here.

In the beginning

Some 6,000 years ago, Neolithic and Bronze Age stone-carvers left a clutter of mysteriously carved and sculpted rock art on the hillsides of Northumberland. The swirling spirals and circles engraved into these boulders look spookily like the patterns made by present-day crop circles.

Around 2,000 years ago, Iron Age warlords built dozens of hilltop fortresses high in the Cheviots, like those at Yeavering Bell, Ring Chesters, Great and Little Hetha, North Blackhags and Humbledon Hill. But their massive walls failed to withstand the Romans, who rolled up in the late first century AD. In AD 130, 10,000 legionaries began work on the region's best known historic landmark,

Hadrian's Wall. With typical Roman efficiency, they completed it, and its chain of legionary fortresses, in just eight years. Even today, it's pretty hard not to be gobsmacked by this amazing piece of military engineering. The wall kept the Caledonian tribes out for almost three centuries, but by the beginning of the fifth century AD the Empire was no longer strong enough to resist the assorted barbarian riff-raff – Picts, Scots, Saxons and Angles, not to mention rebellious Britons – who assailed Roman Britain on all sides. The wall was abandoned, the legions left for sunnier climes, and the former Roman province dissolved into chaos.

Interesting times

More than a century after the Roman collapse, Anglo-Saxon chieftains began to carve out their own little kingdoms. One of these was Ida, an Angle leader who spotted Bamburgh's potential as a natural strongpoint, settled there in AD 547 and – aided by six strapping sons – set himself up as ruler of a new state, Bernicia. Around 150 years later Bernicia merged – through a dynastic marriage – with neighbouring Deira, in a union which created the kingdom of Northumbria. Under its first ruler, Aethelfrith, the united kingdom pushed its frontiers all the way from the Humber in the south to the Forth in the north. After Aethelfrith died in combat (an occupational hazard for kings at the time), his nephew, Edwin, expanded Northumbria's borders still further. From humble beginnings, it became top dog among a pack of Dark Age ministates. Edwin's ambitions naturally led to conflict with other ambitious warlords. In AD 633 the Northumbrians clashed with the armies of Penda, king of Mercia, and Cadwallon, prince of Gwynedd, at the battle of Hatfield Chase. They lost, Edwin was killed, and the winners split Northumbria into its two original parts. A year later, Aethelfrith's son Oscar – Edwin's cousin – reappeared on the Northumbrian scene. Oscar had fled into exile following his father's death, probably because he feared Edwin would murder him if he stayed. Ironically, he avenged his cousin's death by whipping Cadwallon at the Battle of Heavenfield and reuniting Northumbria. Oscar's, successor, Ecgfrith, tried to push Northumbria's borders even further north, deep into Pictland. Big mistake: in AD 685, at Nechtansmere in Angus, he was killed and his army wiped out by Pictish king, Bridei mac Bili. That wasn't quite the end of Northumbria, but it was the beginning of the end.

The coming of Christ

Shortly before his fatal appointment with a battleaxe, Edwin was converted to the Christian faith by Paulinus, bishop of York, who

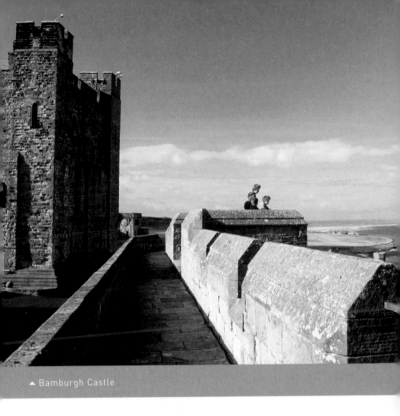

▲ Bamburgh Castle

was busily bible-bashing his way around northern England. In exile among the Christianised Scots of Dalriada, Oswald also became a Christian convert. Back in Northumbria, he invited the Scots missionary Aidan to preach the gospel to his people. Early Christian monks liked islands, and Aidan founded his mission on Lindisfarne, a stone's throw from the great castle of Bamburgh.

The fury of the Northmen

Under a succession of abbots – St Cuthbert is the best known – Lindisfarne became rich and famous thanks to the generosity of pious kings and nobles. But its wealth attracted unwelcome attention. In 794, in the first recorded Viking raid on England, Scandinavian marauders descended on Lindisfarne, murdered its monks and stole its treasures. But the Danes were more than just raiders. They meant to stay. Within a century they had occupied most of eastern England (as well as Ireland and large chunks of Scotland), conquered the southern part of Northumbria, and set up a Viking kingdom with York as its hub.

Welcome to England

In 926, King Aethelstan of Wessex drove the Danish king Olaf Sigtrygsson from York and seized what was left of Northumbria, which became an earldom within Aethelstan's new, united

▲ Battle of Flodden Field Cross

England. But its fortunes continued to wane. In 1018, Malcolm II of Scotland conquered the land north of the river Tweed, pretty much setting the border between Scotland and England where it is today. Not long after his victory at Hastings in 1066, William the Conqueror brought his Norman knights to the region to crush the last English resistance in what became known as 'the harrying of the north'.

The bloody border

So many battles have been fought between Scots and English in this 'debatable land' that you may wonder if there's a patch of ground that hasn't at some time or another been drenched in blood. From the mid-11th century, Scots kings had an annoying habit of invading Northumbria. If you've read Shakespeare's *Macbeth*, you'll remember Malcolm, son of the murdered King Duncan. The real Malcolm III, also known as 'Canmore' – which means 'bighead' – forayed south of the Tweed at least six times between 1061 and 1093. The untimely death of Henry I in 1135 plunged England into anarchy and David I of Scotland seized Norham, Alnwick and Wark. Robert the Bruce laid waste to Northumbria during the Scottish wars of independence. In 1388, a Scottish army led by James, Earl of Douglas, beat a much larger English force led by Henry Percy, Earl of Northumberland –

Shakespeare's 'Hotspur' – at Otterburn. The tide turned against the Scots in 1513 at the Battle of Flodden (actually fought near Branxton), where King James IV of Scotland was killed and his army wiped out. For most of the 16th century, life on Northumbria's northern fringe was precarious. Neither England nor Scotland had full control of the border, and clans of 'reivers' raided churches, burned villages, stole cattle and levied 'black mail' – protection money – pretty much as they chose.

Peace at last

They called James VI and I 'the wisest fool in Christendom'. Despite his wimpish looks and speech impediment, the Scottish king who succeeded Elizabeth I as monarch of England in 1603 was a canny ruler. During his reign over both kingdoms, the Scots and English 'wardens of the marches' managed to bring some tranquillity to the borderlands.

It couldn't last. For the northeast, the Civil Wars of the 17th century started early. Scots invaders opposed to King Charles I crossed the border in the second 'Bishops' War' of 1640 and occupied Durham and Newcastle. In 1644 – now allied with the English parliamentarians and led by a brilliant professional soldier, Alexander Leslie – they captured Newcastle again. But after the total defeat of the Royalist cause in England, Oliver Cromwell's Roundheads marched north to pacify Scotland. Cromwell finished the job within three years. And that seemed to be that – until 1715, when the great men of Durham and Northumberland sided with

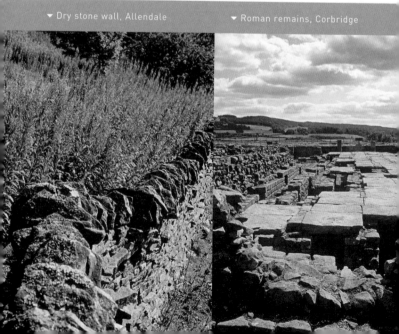

▼ Dry stone wall, Allendale   ▼ Roman remains, Corbridge

James Stuart, the 'Old Pretender', in the Jacobite rising of that year. The rising failed, the ringleaders were executed, and the northeast saw no more battles.

The Industrial Age

Britain plunged into the steam age in the 19th century, and the northeast was transformed. New coal mines opened to fuel new industries. In 1825, the world's first passenger railway opened in County Durham. Tyneside became a centre for shipbuilding, and some of the most famous vessels of the Victorian age came off its slipways. Heavy industry thrived until the slump of the 1920s, when thousands of workers were laid off. Angry Northumbrian miners derailed the *Flying Scotsman* locomotive during the general strike of 1926, and the government sent a gunboat to Newcastle in case the strike turned into a revolution. Ten years later, 200 jobless workers from the shipbuilding town of Jarrow, north of Newcastle, marched to London to protest against poverty and unemployment.

World War II boosted demand for coal, steel and ships, and the northeast's economy recovered. In the 1950s, shipbuilding on Tyneside boomed and Newcastle was the world's biggest coal exporting port. But industrial decline began in the 1960s and continued through the recession of the 1970s. The economic policies of Margaret Thatcher, elected prime minister in 1979, killed off the coal and shipbuilding industries. The effects are still felt – the northeast has the highest unemployment rate in England, and household earnings are 15% lower than the UK average.

▼ The Flying Scotsman

BACK TO NATURE

The landscapes of the northeast range from long, sweeping stretches of sandy coastline to the magnificent high fells of the North Pennines and the dark sandstone ridge of Simonside, heather moorlands and clear streams, craggy cliffs and valley meadows splashed with wild flowers.

A striking natural feature is the Great Whin Sill, a ridge of igneous rock which cuts across the Northumberland National Park. It forms the foundations for the most impressive stretches of Hadrian's Wall and creates the High Force and High Cup Nick waterfalls in the Durham Pennines. Outcrops from beneath the sea form Lindisfarne and the tiny Farne Islands. These varied landscapes are home to an exciting variety of wildlife. Minke whales, white beaked dolphins and harbour porpoises are the most common of the 13 whale and dolphin species found in these waters, but with luck you may also see killer whales and humpbacks. Top spots for onshore whale-watching include Dunstanburgh and Tynemouth Pier, and you really shouldn't miss the opportunity to get up close to dolphins and porpoises on a wildlife-spotting boat trip.

▲ Clockwise from left: Simonside Hills; Gray Wolf in Winter; American Mink

More than 20,000 pairs of puffins nest on the Farne Islands. These colourful clowns of the sea are everyone's favourite, but there are more than 20 other nesting species here, including eider duck, known locally as 'cuddy's chicks', and both of our cormorant species. It's a grand place to spot the first shag of spring.

You'll see peregrine falcons, red kites, ravens, curlews, lapwings and dozens of other bird species in the wide open spaces of the Northumberland National Park, on the grassy moors of the Cheviots, known as the 'White Country' – where grazing white-faced sheep have shaped landscape and vegetation for centuries – and on the heather-clad slopes of the 'Black Country' of the Simonside and Harbottle Hills. One of the best places to see waterfowl is Greenlee Lough, where you can watch whooper swans, greylag and white-fronted geese, and flocks of goldeneye and tufted ducks from the shelter of a purpose-built hide. Bring a flask of tea and a cushion if you like your comforts.

The northeast is one of the emptiest parts of England. Only 2,200 people live in the Northumberland National Park, and wide swathes of the Cheviots and Pennines seem almost as empty. That encourages a whole menagerie of wildlife. This is one of the few places in England where you may see red deer in the wild (though you're more likely to see them in deer parks). In autumn, you may

▶ Lindisfarne Castle

hear the roar of rutting stags (if you've never heard it before, it's quite a scary sound) or even see them clashing antlers in a tussle over territory. You'll almost certainly see hares here, and with a lot of luck you might meet an otter hunting in the clear waters of a valley stream. Otters, once endangered, are making a comeback and are said to be helping to reduce the numbers of a cute but unwelcome invader, the mink. Native to North America, mink have escaped from fur farms and become established across much of England, where they pose a real threat to some of our rarest bird species. The much larger otter happily preys on young and even adult mink. You've a good chance of seeing badgers in and around woodland at twilight – though, with only around 1,500 setts in Durham and Northumberland, they're less common here than elsewhere in England. There are plenty of foxes in the countryside – but because they are often shot by farmers, they're much shyer than their urbanised cousins.

Some enthusiasts have even suggested re-introducing iconic beasts – such as lynx, boar, beaver and even wolf – to the wilds of the northeast, where they once roamed but have been extinct for centuries. There are occasional sightings of wild boars which have escaped from farm herds, but don't expect to see lynx or wolves prowling the Northumberland moors any time soon.

To see some of the world's rarest large mammals, head for Chillingham Castle, where wild white cattle roam the vast castle park. Unique to Northumberland, they have lived there for some 700 years, and are completely untamed. Less than 100 are left.

▼ Staple Island

LORE OF THE LAND

The lore of the northeast chimes with its rugged landscape, crossed by Hadrian's Wall where fairies are believed to cluster, dancing in the moonlight at Housesteads and leaving soot marks from their kitchens on the wall near Chesterholm. Mysterious powers abound here.

Long ago, holes were made in the rocks on the banks of the Hart Burn, near Rothley, when a miller, aggravated by fairies stealing his oats for porridge, dropped a lump of earth down the chimney and splashed hot porridge all over them. Beside Maggie's Dene, a mile north of Newborough, a thorn tree marks the burial site of Old Meg, a witch who was not only burned alive but had a stake thrust through her charcoal heart to prevent her evil soul from straying.

Out on the moors, King's Crag and Queen's Crag, sandstone outcrops northwest of Sewingshields Castle, once home to his court, mark the place where King Arthur, in a quarrel with Queen Guinevere, hurled a rock at her. It then bounced off the comb holding her hair in place and fell between the two crags where it still remains, complete with the marks of the comb's teeth. Arthur and his knights are said to remain sleeping in a cave beneath the castle ruins, awaiting the country's call for help. They were discovered there by a knitting shepherd who dropped his ball of wool and, on chasing it, stumbled on a secret passage – infested with bats, toads, and lizards – that led to the royal dormitory.

Spirit forms

The northeast countryside is alive with spirits that take on animal shapes. The Brag, disguised as a horse or a donkey, tricks unwary travellers into riding on its back – then throws its victim into a bush or pool of water before running off laughing loudly. It works its mischief in other bizarre forms too, from a calf wearing a neckerchief to a naked headless man. The Dunnie also appears as a horse, famously in Hazlerigg. It disappears when ridden, dumping its rider in the mud. Some think it is the ghost of a reiver (a border raider) who still guards his loot out on the fells.

They may look more benign, dressed in moleskin trousers and shoes, lambskin coats and mossy hats topped with a feather, but the Simonside Dwarfs (also called Brownmen or Bogles) take delight at leading travellers to their doom in bogs, the light of their torches flaming like a will-o'-the-wisp. All over Northumberland the Tatty Bogles hide in potato patches, jumping out on unwary farmers and gardeners and causing potato blight. Hedley on the Hill has a spirit all its own, the Hedley Know, able to shift its shape from a pot of gold to a chunk of iron or a lump of rock, confusing anyone who sees it into thinking that their luck has come – only for it to disappear.

▼ Dunstanburgh Castle

Castle tales

Far below Dunstanburgh Castle, the sea froths and rumbles, flinging up massive sprays of spume in a gully known as the Rumble Churn and described as 'ever sounding with the wail of malignant spirits'. One night Sir Guy, seeking shelter from a storm, was met at the castle gateway by a wizard and told that a beautiful lady was imprisoned within. Braving the defences of serpent guards and gigantic skeletons he reached her, barely alive and laid out in a crystal tomb. But still she could not be freed. Now Guy was asked by the wizard to choose between drawing a sword and blowing a horn. Fatefully he chose the horn, fell into a faint and woke back at the castle entrance. Whenever the wind whistles loudly around the castle, local people swear that it is the moaning of Sir Guy, still wishing that he had chosen the sword.

At Bamburgh Castle there lived a wicked queen, stepmother to the daughter of the king of Northumbria. Out of hatred and jealousy she turned the girl into a loathsome creature, the Laidley Worm, which terrorised the region, laying waste to farmland. Word of the disaster reached the king's son, the Childe of Wynde, who, banished from the land by the witch queen, was unaware of his sister's fate. As he approached in his ship the witch thought she still had him under her spell, but he was protected by a branch of rowan, a tree miraculously able to neutralise her powers. He confronted the Worm but the creature refused to engage him in battle and, when she revealed her identity and kissed her brother, returned to her human form. In retribution, the evil queen was changed into a toad and compelled to dwell in a cave beneath the castle with the Childe of Wynde's sword. She is destined to remain there until rescued by a hero who unsheaths the sword three times and kisses her.

Lambton Castle had a Worm, too, this one caught by the heir to the estate who threw it into the well. Abandoning his misspent youth he became a Crusader, but while he was away the Worm became a gigantic menace, curling himself each night around Lambton Hill. When the son returned a witch advised him to cover his armour with razors, and (the price of her remedy) to kill the first creature he saw once the Worm was dead. But when his father – not the planned greyhound – ran to greet his triumphant son the warrior refused to destroy him. Their penance? A permanent curse on a family thereafter beset with disasters, even, some would argue, until the present day.

Underground spooks

Mining in the northeast – often deep under the sea and fraught with danger – brought a host of superstitions. Underground disasters were the work of the Devil or his henchmen, who dwelt at

▶ Hadrian's Wall from Highshield Crags

the foot of every mine in every pit and could even be disguised as pigs or women met on the way to a shift. Even mouthing the word 'pig' was a fearful omen, as were bad deeds, particularly robbing robins' nests. To quell their fears on dark nights or early mornings, Geordie miners sang 'The Collier's Rant' which began:

> As me an' me marra was gannin' to wark,
> We met wi' the devil, it was I' the dark;
> Aw up wi' mi pick, it being I' the neet,
> Aw knock't off his horns, likewise his club-feet.

Between each verse was the chorus:

> Foller the horses, Johnny me laddie,
> Foller them through, me canny lad, oh!
> Foller the horses, Johnny me laddie,
> Oh lad lye away, me canny lad, oh!

Down at the seams, small blue lights reveal the presence of Bluecaps, fairies whose presence ensured the continued supply of rich coal and mineral deposits – as long as they were treated with respect. They expected to be paid at full rate for their labours, and each week would be left a pile of money in a secluded corner. To mock or ignore them was to court disaster, even death.

Island tales

As they built the now ruined priory on Holy Island (Lindisfarne) workers were fed, so the story goes, on bread fashioned from the air, which they consumed accompanied by wine drunk from a bottomless cup. The miracle of the island took place when, attempting to return the body of St Cuthbert to its resting place, the wild December sea in full tide suddenly receded to allow the body bearers to pass through. For good luck and fertility in their new lives, brides marrying at St Mary's church on the island still jump over the Petting Stone in the churchyard, believed to be the socket of St Cuthbert's cross, erected in the seventh century.

St Cuthbert's influence stretched beyond Holy Island to the other Farne Islands, where he exerted his holy powers to banish evil spirits – dwarfs dressed in black cowls who rode on she-goats, brandishing lances and screaming at the tops of their voices. Perhaps they are the wraiths of drowned sailors, their lives lost on the treacherous seas.

HADRIAN'S WALL

Stand on Hadrian's Wall at Housesteads and look north across lough-spattered rolling moors that have hardly changed since Roman times, and it's not hard to put yourself in the sandals of a Roman auxiliary, guarding the Empire's northernmost frontier against the savage tribes of Caledonia.

Rise and fall

Stand below the wall on its north side and look up, and you'll get some sense of how a northern tribesman might have felt on seeing this potent symbol of the power of Rome for the first time.

Almost 2,000 years after it was built, the wall is still the most awesome relic of the Roman Empire in Britain, perhaps in the world. And it was, of course, built to impress.

Writers of historical fiction from Rudyard Kipling to Rosemary Sutcliffe have depicted the wall as a line of defence. It's romantic to imagine it that way, as a frontier where armoured legionaries met howling, blue-painted savages in hand to hand combat.

That did happen. On more than one occasion, the northern tribes came over the frontier to wreak havoc over Roman Britain – sometimes in cahoots with rebellious Britons who resented the Roman yoke. But the true story is a little more complicated.

For starters, the natives of Valentia – as the Romans called the region from north from the Wall to the Firth of Clyde – weren't Picts. The Romans called them Votadini. They called themselves Gododdin, and their language was more like Welsh than the Pictish tongue, of which we know little. They seem to have lived quite amicably with their Roman neighbours – most of the time, anyway.

Archaeologists now think that the wall was built to control movement to and fro across the frontier. Every Roman mile along the wall was a milecastle, with a garrison of eight men to guard a gate through the wall. It's hard to believe that the Romans would have built so many places where people could pass through if the wall's main purpose was to keep them out.

The wall was never held strongly enough to hold every section against a full-on assault from the north, but it was a base from which the Romans could project power north of the border by land or sea. The fort at Chesters – which the Romans called Cilurnum – in the North Tyne Valley near Chollerford was the base of the Second Cavalry Regiment of Asturians for some 200 years, so you can easily imagine cavalry patrols ranging northward across Valentia to nip any invasion in the bud.

Chesters was built around AD 213 – almost a century after the wall itself – to defend the bridge over the North Tyne. The stretch of the Hadrian's Wall National Trail between here and Walltown is the most spectacular part of the trail.

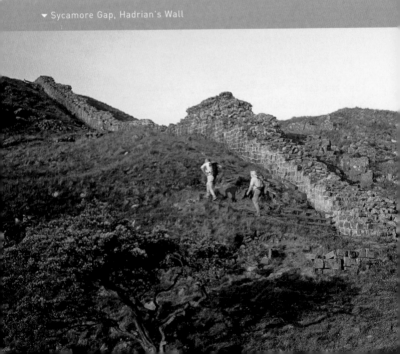

▼ Sycamore Gap, Hadrian's Wall

Work began on the building of the wall around AD 120 on the orders of the Emperor Hadrian. He was keen on big projects – you can still see examples of temples and theatres built at his behest all over the former Empire, from Tunisia to Turkey. Eight years later, a force of some 10,000 legionaries had completed 73 miles of stone and turf ramparts between the Tyne in the east and the Solway in the west, taking advantage of natural features such as the rocky outcrop of the Great Whin Sill. Turrets, milecastles and forts were dotted along it at regular intervals. Just south, a military road allowed the legions to move briskly from one point to another. Moving at the Roman military pace of 20 miles a day, an infantry cohort would have taken around four days to march from one end to the other. The modern B6318 follows the line of the Roman road, so you can now travel the same route in around two hours.

But you should really allow a full day to take in everything there is to see along the wall, and to savour the landscapes on either side, which in many ways have changed little since Roman times. A legion sentry would certainly have been familiar with the call of curlews on the loughs or the honking of greylag geese flying over in winter – though he might also have heard the howling of wolves, which have been extinct in Northumberland for more than five centuries.

You should make time to stop at Chesters, where the remains of a bathhouse – one of the best preserved buildings in Roman Britain – show that the soldiers based here lived quite comfortably. The changing rooms, warm and cold bathing areas, steam rooms and latrines are all visible, and the sophisticated underfloor heating system must have been very welcoming to a saddle-sore cavalryman back from a winter patrol. A thriving civilian settlement next to the fort supplied all a soldier's needs, from barber shops to taverns, gambling houses and warm female companionship.

Corbridge – the Roman Corstopitum – is the oldest site along the line of the wall. Here, you can imagine how a basic military outpost grew into the biggest arsenal and supply depot of the eastern part of the frontier. Around the fort, the northernmost town in the Empire grew up. Extending over 30 acres, it was one of the most populous and important settlements along the wall, and you can imagine that in its heyday it must have been a bustling, colourful bazaar at the crossroads of two Roman highways, where half a dozen languages were spoken – not just Latin and British, but the native tongues of legionaries from as far away as Iberia, Thrace and Illyria – and where tribesmen from the other side of the wall haggled with Romanised British traders, buying and selling trinkets, beads, furs, cloth and weapons.

Much of Corstopitum is buried beneath present-day Corbridge, but at Vindolanda you can see the substantial remains of another civilian settlement, including an inn for travellers – complete with bathhouse – shops, and houses.

In 1973, archaeologist Robin Birley unearthed the first 'Vindolanda tablets' from a drainage pit. Amazingly, soil conditions had preserved these thin leaves of wood, used as notepads by Roman record keepers, and the ink writing on them. They tell us a great deal about everyday life in a Roman garrison town – what people ate and drank, what they wore, and even what they thought of their fellow-officers. You can find out more at the museum at Housesteads – the must-see fort on the wall, and the most complete example of a Roman fort in Britain. Here, you can see the remains of the hospital, complete with operating theatre, the granaries, the remains of Roman buildings by the South Gate – and the communal, multi-seater latrine where legionaries would have perched companionably above a sewer channel fed by running water. In a separate, smaller channel they washed the communal sponges that they used instead of toilet paper.

Rome's first big push to the north was led by Julius Agricola, who around AD 80 led a major expedition deep into Caledonia. At the battle of Mons Graupius (somewhere north of the River Tay) the legions wiped out the combined Caledonian forces. But having taught the tribes a lesson, Agricola then fell back on the line that eventually became the wall. Around 60 years later, during the reign of Emperor Antoninus Pius, the Romans pushed north again, this time building a defensive rampart between the Firth of Forth and the Clyde – the Antonine Wall. But this was a step too far. The Antonine Wall was too easy to outflank by sea, and too remote to be easily reinforced. It was abandoned after only 20 years, and its garrisons fell back on Hadrian's Wall.

In AD 208 Emperor Septimius Severus again led the legions into Caledonia, this time striking deep into what's now Tayside, where a line of small fortresses show his line of march. He ordered the reconstruction of the Antonine Wall, but it was again abandoned only a few years later.

The fall of the wall came not with a bang, but a whimper. There wasn't any desperate last stand against the barbarians. Instead, the legions trickled away. Sometimes, they went to defend the shores of southern Britain against Saxon raiders. Sometimes they marched off behind ambitious commanders to fight in the Empire's endless civil wars. By the beginning of the fifth century AD, Rome had abandoned Britain to its fate, and the wall was left to crumble.

Later settlers found it a handy source of free building materials, and stone dressed by Roman masons found its way into castles, farmhouses, abbeys and cathedrals. At least one of the wall's milecastles was taken over during the Middle Ages by a clan of cattle raiders who used it as a ready-made fortress.

During the 19th century, local landowner John Clayton (1792–1890) bought long stretches of the wall and some of its forts – including Housesteads and Chesters – to prevent further destruction by local people looting its ancient stones. The fascinating museum at Chesters is a memorial to him – and without his work, there would be far less for you see here today.

▼ Housesteads Fort

NORTHUMBRIAN PIPES

If you go to one of Northumbria's many folk music festivals, you're bound to hear the distinctive sound of the northeast's most distinctive instrument.

One musicologist has called the Northumbrian smallpipes 'the most civilised of bagpipes', and in the hands of a maestro such as Kathryn Tickell or Alistair Anderson its melodies are a million miles from the bellicose bray of the better-known Scottish pipes. Unlike the Scottish instrument, the Northumbrian instrument is filled with air by a bellows, which is pumped by the player's arm. Four drones provide the background 'drone' while a chanter with between seven and seventeen keys controls the melody.

The tight fingering, with each note played by either the left pinkie or the right thumb, makes it a tricky instrument to master, but when well played it's a delight to hear. No one knows for sure where these pipes originated. It's even been suggested that they may have been brought to the region by Roman soldiers – similar pipes are still played in Spain, Bulgaria and northern Greece, and legionaries from all these places served on Hadrian's Wall for centuries, so it's not a totally incredible yarn. But the first descriptions of the pipes are in a manuscript dated 1695, and some musicologists suggest the Northumbrian pipes are descendants of a German version of the instrument. That's not unlikely – there was plenty of commerce between the northeast and Germany from the Middle Ages onwards.

Like Scottish clan chieftains, some of the aristocrats of the northeast kept a pet piper and you can see an 18th-century portrait of the Duchess of Northumberland's piper, Joseph Turnbull, with his pipes, at Alnwick Castle. The Dukes of

▲ Stone carving, Hexham Abbey   ▲ Kathryn Tickell

Northumberland kept an official piper for centuries – one of them, Jack Armstrong, played a big part in keeping the pipes alive into the 20th century.

Like a lot of traditional instruments, the smallpipes almost died out during the 19th century, but the folk music revival of the 1960s saved them from extinction. Today, there are at least a dozen virtuoso professional players, as well as dozens of keen amateurs, and at least half a dozen skilled artisan craftsmen are kept busy making new instruments and restoring old ones.

It's a lively instrument, well suited to playing versions of fiddle tunes, jigs, reels and hornpipes – music to dance and tap your feet to, not for marching into battle. The city of Newcastle maintained official 'waits' to patrol its streets to the sound of the smallpipes, and in 1800 the last of these musical watchmen, John Peacock, published a collection of tunes for the pipes, ranging from lively dance tunes to long virtuoso suites such as *Cut and Dry Dolly*. In the 20th century, masters of the smallpipes have included Tom Clough – you can hear three early recordings of his music on a CD, *The Northumbrian Smallpipes* – and Billy Pigg, whose music you can listen to on another CD, The Border Minstrel. Kathryn Tickell must be the best known present-day player of the instrument, not only as a solo musician but in concert with others. Playing with everyone from Sting to the Boys of the Lough and the Nash Ensemble, her music shows that the Northumbrian smallpipes can do jazz and classical as well as traditional jigs and reels. With luck, you can catch her and other exponents of the Northumbrian smallpipes playing live at traditional music venues or traditional music venues such as the Alnwick International Music Festival.

BORDER REIVERS

To go is to gang. To ride is to raid. And blackmail –
meaning 'black rent' – is what's now known as protection
money, paid to gangsters and raiders to persuade them
not to fire your thatch, lift your cattle or molest your
daughters. You could say the hard men known as the
Border Reivers invented organised crime.

Original gangsters

If you lived in the borderlands of Northumberland and Scotland
between the late 13th century and the beginning of the 17th
century, you were in constant peril of a visit from the 'riding
surnames', whose fastnesses in the wasteland were simply beyond
the reach of the law. They were partly the product of the ebb and
flow of almost constant wars, which turned a vast swathe of
territory on either side of the frontier into a lawless no-man's land.
The border moorlands were bad for crops, but excellent for grazing
flocks, which were easy for canny riders to 'lift' and drive off into
their own territory under cover of darkness. The favourite time for
such raids was early winter, when beasts were plump from
summer grazing.

    Mounted on a sturdy pony called a hobelar, a typical reiver
clanked with weapons. At the very least, he carried a lance, sword,
shield and dagger. He might carry a longbow or a crossbow too,
and these never quite went out of fashion even in the 16th century.
By then, the reiver had added flintlock pistols to his arsenal – but
on a dark, wet, winter night, such new-fangled weapons can't have
been very reliable. For protection, the reiver wore a sleeveless
leather doublet, or 'jack', sometimes sewn with small metal plates,
and a plain steel helmet. The governments in London and

Edinburgh appointed March Wardens whose job was nominally to keep the peace and dispense justice, but it was an impossible task. On the English side, the Wardens were often southern gentry who didn't know much about this wild frontier. On the Scots side, the Wardens often had blood ties with the very families they were meant to be policing. In time of war between England and Scotland, the reivers were reckoned to be superb light cavalry and skirmishers, serving on either side at battles such as Flodden. They were also notoriously ill-disciplined and changed sides when it suited them.

If you were a prosperous border dweller, your best protection against the reivers was a fortified bastle house, a sturdy two-storey building with walls up to three feet thick. You and your family lived on the upper floor, which was reached by a ladder that could be pulled up in times of danger. Your most valuable beasts were kept on the ground floor, and the house was surrounded by a stone barmekin wall in which livestock were corraled overnight. These mini-fortresses weren't impregnable – if raiders gained the ground floor, they could set fires to smoke you out – but since their main aim was to ride off with your cattle, they might not bother.

The border had its own laws. The victim of a raid had the right to set off on 'hot trod' across the border on the trail of the raiders, carrying a smouldering turf on a spearpoint as a signal, and recruiting anyone he met to the posse. More formally, the March Wardens might mount a Warden Road to recover stolen goods and punish the most excessive offences, and on 'Truce Days' the English and Scots Wardens met to try to settle cross-border grievances. For many, truce days were an occasion for socialising – sometimes with men they had been trying to kill just days before. Deadly feuds between Border families were common.

The golden age of the reivers was towards the end of their long reign of terror. For most of the 16th century, the rulers of England and Scotland were too busy with civil and foreign wars to pay much attention to the Borders, and they raided almost with impunity. When Queen Elizabeth I died in 1603 the reivers went on a rampage which came to be known as 'Ill Week', claiming that the kingdom's laws were in abeyance until a new monarch took the throne. Unfortunately for them, that monarch was James VI of Scotland, who became James I of England. With both nations under his control, James swiftly filled the lethal power vacuum in which the reivers had flourished. Royal troops moved against the 'riding surnames' from both sides of the frontier. James had a few of the more notorious leaders hanged as an example, and gave others the option of migrating to Ulster – where some of their descendants remain to this day. It would be a while before the Borders were truly at peace, but the great days of the reivers were over.

MADE IN THE NORTHEAST

Newcastle Brown has been an emblem of the northeast for almost a century, since it was launched by local brewer James Porter. It's one of Britain's favourite ales, and is exported all over the world – but the brand is now owned by Heineken and brewed in Yorkshire. Brewing is still alive and well in the northeast, though. The Lion Brewery in Hartlepool makes the **Cameron's** range of heritage beers, favoured by local drinkers since the 1860s. The Northumberland Brewery is proud of its range of real ales, including the evocatively named Gateshead Gold, Newcastle Pride, Northumbrian Ale and **Angel of the North**. If you're fed up with bland bottled lagers, these complex beers will tickle your tastebuds, while more eccentrically named beers from the brewery – such as **Bucking Fastard** – will tickle your sense of humour too.

Take it easy on the Durham Brewery's **Diabolus**, a devilishly strong ale with a 10 per cent alcohol content. Durham's oldest brewery also makes a range of beers that pack a less powerful punch, such as Magus, and an innovative range of fruit beers in flavours such as cherry, raspberry and mango. If you're driving, you'll like the Alnwick Brewery's **Canny Bevvy**, with just 2.8 per cent alcohol content. For a more powerful pick-me-up, try the brewery's **Alnwick Rum**, created in the early 1900s, a unique blend of Jamaica and Guyana spirits with a 43 per cent alcohol content.

Early medieval abbeys and monasteries were famous for their mead, a drink made by fermenting a mix of honey and water. St Aidan's Winery on Holy Isle has been making **Lindisfarne Mead** since the 1960s. Ingredients include grape juice, herbs, honey and spirits, and the alcohol content is a modest 14.5 per cent. The winery also makes tasty fruit and berry wines and liqueurs.

In less law-abiding times, the Coquet Valley was well known for illicit distilling. The moonshiners and smugglers have vanished – probably – but Coquet Whisky in Rothbury sells its own-label whisky, **Black Rory**, created by master blender John McDougall. Coquet also makes its own **Myrtle Gin**, which is aged in bourbon whisky casks and infused with Northumberland bog myrtle.

Visit Doddington Dairy, near Wooler, to sample a range of distinctive cheeses made from unpasteurised milk from the dairy's own cows, including their flagship **Doddington** cheese. The dairy also makes delicious ice cream. At her home in Newton Henry, near Durham, Julia Carniss of the Durham Cow Cheese Company makes the equally delicious, award-winning **Durham Blue**, a creamy blue cheese with a piquant edge. At **Wallington Hall**, you can sample mince pies made to an 18th-century recipe discovered in the house's library. which includes ox tongue, brown sugar, sultanas, lemon and orange zest. You'll also find pan haggerty on many menus in the northeast. Made from spuds, cheese, onions and sometimes cabbage too, it makes a hearty breakfast dish with sausages or bacon.

Singin' hinnies get their name from the sizzling sound they make as they cook. These mouth-watering griddle cakes are made from dough mixed with raisins, currants or berries and are traditional favourites at children's birthday parties. For a special treat, a shiny new coin is hidden in each cake.

The Northumberland village of Craster is the home of the 100-year-old L Robson and Sons smokehouse, which produces the **Craster kipper**. Herrings from the North Sea are gutted, split and soaked in brine, then smoked for up to 16 hours over wood chips to produce this fishy delicacy, which is traditionally served in a white bap. The bap is also an essential component of the **chip buttie**. This cholesterol-packed snack isn't unique to Newcastle, but it must be more popular here than anywhere else in England. It can't be good for you in the long term, but when you need a massive burst of calories after a long walk along the coast or over the moors a chip buttie really hits the spot. So does a bowl of **Alnwick stew**, a hearty dish of gammon hock, simmered with potatoes, onions and herbs.

Ultra-hot **curries** are part of Geordieland's peculiar brand of machismo. At Rupali, in Newcastle's Bigg Market, Rukon Latif serves Curry Hell, billed as the world's hottest curry. If you can finish your serving, it's on the house, and you'll be inducted into the Rupali 'Hall of Flame'.

BEFORE YOU GO

READ BEFORE YOU GO

If you like rip-roaring historical drama larded with historical fact, you'll enjoy Bernard Cornwell's Saxon Stories series. *The Last Kingdom, The Pale Horseman, The Lords of the North, Sword Song, The Burning Land* and *The Death of Kings*, with more books to come, are set in the violent world of ninth-century Britain. Told in the first person, they follow Saxon warlord Uhtred of Bebbanburg as he carves his way from Northumbria to Wessex and back, leaving a trail of dead enemies and weeping women. 'On the Great Wall', one of the stories in Rudyard Kipling's *Puck of Pook's Hill* collection of tales for children, is another ripping yarn, told from the point of view of a young legionary officer guarding the Roman frontier.

Catherine Cookson, one of the most prolific authors in the English language, was born in South Shields in 1906. Her poverty-stricken childhood inspired many of the 103 books that she wrote between 1950 and her death in 1998, several of which – including *The Black Velvet Gown* and *The Mallens* – were filmed for TV.

Grace Darling, by Tim Vicary, is the exciting story of the Northumberland heroine who rowed through stormy seas to rescue the passengers and crew of the Forfarshire, which foundered off the Farne Islands in 1838. Also set on Holy Isle are Sheila Quigley's crime thrillers, *Thorn in my Side* and *Nowhere Man*. Quigley – who has been called 'the queen of northeast crime writing' – is also the author of eight crime novels set in Seahills, a fictional housing estate on the outskirts of Sunderland. If you're a fan of gritty noir, you'll also like Martin Waites's Geordie journalist Joe Donovan, hero of *Mercy Seat, Bone Machine, White Riot* and *Speak No Evil*, who prowls the meaner streets of Newcastle. Also set in Newcastle is *The Murder Wall*, by Mari Hannah, which has spawned a TV spinoff. Joe Cornish's lavishly illustrated *The Northumberland Coast* is a collection of eye-catching images which will whet your appetite for a visit to the shores and isles of the northeast.

Finally, for a dip into the bawdier side of Geordie humour, sample *Viz* magazine. Deliberately offensive, surreal, childish, and filthily funny, *Viz* magazine's sense of humour is – to say the least – distinctive. Launched in Newcastle by Chris Donald in 1979, *Viz* has brought the world such notable characters as the Fat Slags, Sid The Sexist, and many more. Grubby as it is, you'll still find it hard to resist a guilty giggle when reading.

WATCH BEFORE YOU GO

Lots of films have been shot in and around the northeast's imposing castles. Bamburgh and Alnwick were backdrops for *Becket* (1964), starring Richard Burton and Elizabeth Taylor. Bamburgh was also a location for Ken Russell's *The Devils* and *Mary Queen of Scots* (both 1971), and for *Elizabeth* (1998), starring Cate Blanchett. But in most of these, the Northumberland locations are stand-ins for the places where the action is set.

You'll find the region and its people in their own right in the iconic *Get Carter* (1971), in which gangster Jack Carter – played by Michael Caine – comes back from London to his native Newcastle to sort out the geezers who topped his brother. Somewhere along the way, hard man Jack seems to have lost his Geordie accent. Caine speaks throughout in his native Cockney, but it's still a British classic. The multi-storey

▼ Alnwick Castle

Gateshead car park which is the backdrop for one of the film's key scenes was torn down in 2012 to make way for a new retail mall and multi-screen cinema and none but a few film buffs and admirers of 1960s brutalist architecture mourned its demise. Look out too for movies from independent Newcastle film-makers 24:25 Films. The psychological horror film *Bloodless* (2013) and the splendidly named schlock-horror flick, *Zombie Women of Satan* (2009) were both shot on a shoestring in Northumberland.

Somewhat sweeter is *Billy Elliot* (2000), starring Jamie Bell as a young boy who wants to become a ballet dancer but struggles with the attitudes of the mining community in which he lives. It was shot in real colliery villages, including Ellington and Lynemouth in Northumberland and Easington Colliery in County Durham. *Purely Belter* (2000) is another touching comedy about the aspirations of two Newcastle teenagers. On a visit to Newcastle, you'll immediately recognise some of the film's locations.

Legendary TV shows set in the northeast – and available on DVD – include *The Likely Lads* and *Whatever Happened to the Likely Lads*, following the ups and downs of two Geordie chancers, Bob and Terry, from their bachelor days in the 1960s to middle age in the 1970s. A film spin-off, *The Likely Lads*, appeared in 1976. In the 1980s, *Auf Wiedersehen Pet* followed the fortunes of a group of expat builders and kick-started the careers of Northumbrian actor Kevin Whately and Geordie thespians Jimmy Nail and Tim Healy.

THINGS TO KNOW

▶ During the Napoleonic Wars, so the story goes, a French frigate went down off Hartlepool. The only survivor was the ship's monkey mascot, which washed up on the shore. Hartlepudlians had heard that the French had tails. Being a credulous lot, they decided the monkey must be one of the enemy. So they hanged the poor creature. H'Angus the Monkey – a man dressed in a monkey costume – is the official mascot of Hartlepool United FC.

▶ Why, you ask, are natives of Newcastle nicknamed 'Geordies'? It's because the city stayed loyal to King George during the Jacobite rising of 1715, when many of the gentry of Durham and Northumberland backed the exiled James Stuart's bid for the throne.

▶ The 66ft Angel of the North is exactly two-thirds as tall as the more famous Colossus of Rhodes, one of the 'seven wonders' of the ancient world. The Angel is expected to stand for more than 100 years. The Colossus, built in 280 BC, stood for just 64 years. But will the Angel still be a legend 2000 years from now?

▶ Not all the troops who manned Hadrian's Wall were Romans from Italy. The garrisons came from Gaul, Belgium, Spain, Thrace and Dacia. Towards the end of its reign, Rome even recruited Saxon mercenaries to defend Britain against Saxon raiders.

▶ The first-ever commercial steam trains started to run on the Stockton and Darlington Railway in 1825. The railway was pioneered by Northumberland-born George Stephenson. Its first locomotives – built at his son Robert's Forth Street Works in Newcastle – hurtled across County Durham at speeds of up to 15mph, and by 1829, Robert Stephenson had designed and built his famous *Rocket*. It reached a terrifying 28mph.

▶ Alnwick Castle is one of Britain's most-filmed castles, appearing in *Harry Potter and the Philosopher's Stone* (2001), *Harry Potter and the Chamber of Secrets* (2002), *Elizabeth* (1998) and *Robin Hood, Prince of Thieves* (1991). But Hadrian's Wall rarely gets to play itself. *The Eagle* (2011), set in the mid-second century, used Hungary and Scotland as stand-ins for the borderlands of Roman

Britain. For *King Arthur* (2004), with Clive Owen playing the king as a post-Roman warlord, the producers built a replica of a kilometre-long stretch of the wall. It was the largest film set ever constructed – and it was built in Ireland.

▶ Ask anyone to name two stars from the northeast and it's a cert that they'll pick Ant and Dec. But, along with Anthony McPartlin and Declan Donnelly, the region has produced entertainers and musicians including Eric Burdon and Chas Chandler of The Animals and their Durham-born keyboard man Alan Price, guitar legend Hank Marvin, stand-up comic Ross Noble, Roxy Music's Bryan Ferry – and let's not forget Sting, born Gordon Sumner in Wallsend.

THINGS TO PACK

To make the most of Durham and Northumberland, you'll need the essentials. Those essentials are: comfortable footwear, a wind and rain-proof outer layer and – depending on season – a warm inner garment. If you plan to explore the Northumberland National Park, you'll need proper walking boots, not just trainers. If you're just planning to take the occasional short country stroll or along the beach, you should still seriously consider slinging a pair of wellies in the boot. For summer beachcombing and rockpooling, take sandals or surf booties.

Wetsuits for kids are key to a happy family holiday on the North Sea coast – not only do they keep your little monsters warm in chilly waters, they also protect them from sunburn and even jellyfish stings. You'll kick yourself for not bringing binoculars, especially if you go on a dolphin-spotting cruise. If you have any interest at all in wildlife, a good guide to British birds is essential.

There's some great fishing to be had on the lakes, rivers and at sea, so keen anglers should pack a rod, reel and tackle. Midges can be a pest in summer around the loughs of the Northumberland National Park and the margins of Kielder Water. Chemical-based mosquito repellent doesn't seem to deter them, but some claim that a coating of baby oil does the business. And finally, a word about the sun: you'd be surprised how easy it is to burn when the sun comes out, especially if you're on the beach, out on the water or on the hills. Pack some sunscreen, and a lip-block too. But if your plans include a night out with the young and beautiful in Newcastle, pack as little as possible. Geordie lads and lasses seem immune to cold, and take pride in exposing as much bare skin as is legal and decent in all weathers. Turning up in the Bigg Market on a Saturday night wearing warm clothes and sensible shoes will expose you to ridicule as a soft southerner.

BASIC INFORMATION

If you come from the traffic-choked southeast, the country roads and highways of the northeast are a terrible temptation to put the pedal to the metal – especially if you're stuck behind a tractor trundling along at 20mph. Be advised: the

fatal accident rate in Northumberland is nearly double London's road toll. Statistically, an average hour on the roads of Northumberland is 40 per cent more dangerous than an hour in London traffic. Take a deep breath, be patient, enjoy the scenery at a slower pace, and wait for that tractor to turn off – he's not going far.

You run out of motorway not long after arriving in the northeast. The A1 (M) ends at Washington, on the southern fringes of Newcastle, and at any time of day you should be prepared for tailbacks as you head for the Tyne bridges and the city centre. If you're making for the wilds of the Northumberland National Park, your best bet is to hook off onto the A68 at junction 58, just north of Darlington. That way, you sneak round Newcastle and its multiple traffic choke points.

Those choke points also lead to driver frustration. Weirdly, country roads are much more dangerous than rammed ring roads and roaring roundabouts. Single carriageway A-roads are the most dangerous in Britain, and most of your travel in Durham and Northumberland will be on just such roads, so stay safe.

You need to think about the weather, too. Severe winters are more frequent, and often harsher, up here than down in the decadent south. North of Newcastle, towns and villages are thin on the ground, so if your vehicle breaks down or gets stranded, help may take a little while longer to arrive than you might expect.

There are special hazards, too. If you plan to take your car across the causeway to Holy Island, check the tide table. A dozen drivers each year have to be rescued by lifeboat or helicopter when their cars are swamped by the incoming tide. Lots more are stupidly stranded on Lindisfarne until the ebb.

In Durham and Northumberland, it can chuck it down at any time of year. Fortunately, there's lots to do under cover when it turns out wet. The Gate in Newcastle (thegatenewcastle.com) shows the latest films for all ages and tastes and has a choice of family-friendly eating places – including Nando's, TGI Friday, Frankie and Benny's and Pizza Hut – under the same roof. In Durham, the Gala Theatre and Cinema (galadurham.co.uk) shows the latest movies and presents theatre for adults and children. XS Superbowl in Newcastle (namcofunscape. com) offers ten-pin bowling, pool and other games. Posher bowling can be found at Newcastle's 'boutique' bowling alley, Lane 7, along with ping-pong, pool, karaoke and better food than run-of-the mill bowling venues. The 11,000-seat Metro Radio Arena, also in Newcastle (metroradioarena. co.uk) is the northeast's biggest venue, presenting world-famous stars and events.

FESTIVALS & EVENTS

MAY

▶ **Evolution Festival**
evolutionfestival.co.uk
May BH weekend
Kicking off in 2002, Evolution
has rocked Newcastle and
Gateshead's Quayside since
2003. The focus is on pop, drum
and bass, and indie music, but
over the years Evolution has
starred stalwarts such as The
Stooges, The Proclaimers, Echo
and the Bunnymen, Joe
Jackson, Richie Havens, and
The Vaccines. Spin-off event
Evolution Emerging showcases
up and coming talent.

▶ **Northumberland County Show**
northcountyshow.co.uk
May BH
This great family event
celebrates the northeast's rural
and farming heritage. See
horses and sheepdogs being
put through their paces. As well
as ponies, Cheviot sheep,
Border terriers and collies, you
can expect quad-bike events
and prize alpacas.

JULY

▶ **Brass Durham
International Festival**
brassfestival.co.uk
You probably know that
brass bands are big in the
northeast, but this annual
celebration is much than
old-style oompah. Embracing
not only music but outdoor
vaudeville, theatre and art
installations, Brass proudly
presents brass-inspired
ensembles from all over
the world.

AUGUST

▶ **Alnwick International Music
Festival**
alnwickmusicfestival.com
early August
One moment, you're listening
to Northumbrian bagpipe music
– the next, you're watching
dancers from Kerala or African
drummers. There's an evening
dedicated to the musical
heritage of Northumberland,
but you can also expect
dancers and musicians from all
over the world.

▶ **Durham Streets Summer
Festival**
durhamstreetsof.co.uk
August BH weekend
Durham's street festival
has spilled over into regional
venues such as Barnard
Castle. You can expect to be
confronted by streets filled
with mimes, jugglers, fire-
eaters, acrobats and
gymnasts over a weekend of
family entertainment.

▶ **EAT! NewcastleGateshead**
newcastlegateshead.com/
eat-festival
late August–September
Enjoy cooking as entertainment
at this 16-day spread of events
celebrating seasonal produce
from the northeast with
masterclasses by master chefs,
tastings and dining. Tasty.

▶ **Newcastle Arts Festival**
newcastlefestival.org
August BH weekend
You'll find events for children, films, live music and all sorts of performances and workshops at this event in Newcastle.

SEPTEMBER

▶ **Alnwick Food Festival**
alnwickfoodfestival.co.uk;
Watch celebrity chefs in action, meet local food producers and sample their cheeses, cakes, ale and sausages – and much more – at this celebration of all things foody at Alnwick Castle.

▶ **Berwick Food and Beer Festival**
berwickfoodfestival.com;
On the banks of the Tweed, this festival is all about food and beer from Northumberland and the Borders. It has embraced the slow food philosophy, so slow down and savour local real ales, hog roasts and more – enlivened by traditional music and tribute bands.

▶ **Hexham Abbey Festival of Music and Arts**
hexhamabbey.org.uk/festival
The Hexham Abbey Festival is a bit more highbrow than some of the region's other musical events, but it's welcoming, eclectic and inclusive. Hexham hosts nine days of classical, choral, sacred and Renaissance music as well as music and jazz, crafts and visual art in and around its historic church.

▶ **Press Play Film Festival**
pressplayfestival.org
September
Newcastle's light-hearted film festival ticks all the boxes. Whether your tastes run to Hollywood classics, action flicks, new offerings from the international festival circuit or heart-warming family entertainment, you'll find something at this accessible and unpretentious event.

OCTOBER

▶ **TUSK**
tuskfestival.com
Launched in 2011, this festival at Newcastle's legendary Star & Shadow aims to showcase regional talents who haven't yet cracked the big time. It brings total unknowns into the limelight, so this is your chance to hear them before they go global – or vanish without trace.

DECEMBER

▶ **Newcastle New Year's Eve**
31 December
Newcastle is a legendary party town and is at its bawdy best on New Year's Eve. The place to be when the bells ring in the New Year is the Quayside, with a belter of a fireworks display. For sophisticates, posh hotels on either side of the river offer Champagne, dinner and dancing. If you'd rather dance until dawn, Newcastle's clubs have great New Year's specials.

▶ **Tar Bar'l, Allendale**
31 December
Allendale's New Year's Eve celebration probably goes all the way back to Viking times. Strong and fearless men walk the streets and lanes of the villages until the New Year's morn, whirling barrels of flaming pitch at arm's length. Seriously, don't try this at home.

CAMPSITES

For more information on these and other campsites, visit theaa.com/self-catering-and-campsites

Pecknell Farm
Caravan Park ▶▶▶
Lartington, Barnard Castle,
DL12 9DF | 01833 638357
Open Apr–Oct
Pecknell Farm is a small, well laid out site on a working farm in beautiful rural meadowland, with spacious marked pitches on level ground. There are many walking opportunities that start directly from this friendly site.

Crimdon Dene
HOLIDAY PARK
park-resorts.com
Coast Road, Blackhall Colliery,
TS27 4BN | 0871 664 9737
Open Apr–Oct
A large, popular coastal holiday park, handily placed for access to Teeside, Durham and Newcastle. The park contains a full range of facilities for both children and their parents. Touring facilities are appointed to a very good standard.

South Meadows
Caravan Park
▶▶▶▶▶
southmeadows.co.uk
South Road, Belford, NE70 7DP
01668 213326 | Open all year
South Meadows is a spacious and very nicely landscaped park set in open countryside. Tree planting on a grand scale has been carried out, grassy areas are expertly mown and all pitches are fully serviced. The solar heated amenity block is ultra modern, and everywhere is spotlessly clean and fresh. There's a new adventure playground complete with a zip-wire, and dogs have two walking areas, one in a bluebell wood.

Ord House
Country Park ▶▶▶▶▶
ordhouse.co.uk
East Ord, Berwick-upon-Tweed,
TD15 2NS | 01289 305288
Open all year

This very well-run park is set in the pleasant grounds of an 18th-century country house. There is an exceptional outdoor leisure shop with a good range of camping and caravanning spares, as well as clothing and equipment, and an attractive licensed club selling bar meals. If you fancy staging a family contest of sporting prowess you can have a try at crazy golf or table tennis.

Bellingham Camping & Caravanning Club Site
►►►►►
Brown Rigg, Bellingham, NE48 2JY | 01434 220175 & 0845 1307633
Open 15 Mar–3 Nov
Bellingham is a beautifully peaceful campsite inside the glorious Northumberland National Park. Exceptionally well managed, it offers high levels of customer care, maintenance and cleanliness. There are four camping pods for hire. This makes a great base for exploring an often underestimated part of England, and it is handily placed for visiting the beautiful Northumberland coast too.

Sandy Bay
HOLIDAY PARK
park-resorts.com
North Seaton, NE63 9YD
0871 6649764 | Open Apr–Oct
Sandy Bay is a beach-side holiday park on the outskirts of the small village of North Seaton, within easy reach of Newcastle. The site is well placed for exploring the magnificent coastline and countryside of Northumberland, but for those who don't feel like going off site, it offers the full range of holiday centre attractions, both for parents and their children.

Lizard Lane Caravan & Camping Site
►►►
lizardlanepark.wix.com/lizardlanepark
Lizard Lane, South Shields, NE34 7AB | 0191 4544982
This site is located in an elevated position with some nice sea views. All touring pitches are fully serviced and the modern smart amenities block is equipped with superb fixtures and fittings. There is also a shop and a nine-hole putting green. Please note that tents are not accepted.

Bobby Shafto Caravan Park ►►►
Cranberry Plantation, Beamish DH9 0RY | 0191 3701776
Open Mar–Oct
A tranquil rural park surrounded by trees, with very clean and well organised facilities. The suntrap touring area has plenty of attractive hanging baskets, and there is a clubhouse with bar, TV and pool tables.

VISIT THE MUSEUMS | GET OUTDOORS | EXPLORE BY BIKE | GO BACK IN TIME | MEET THE WILDLIFE
TAKE IN SOME HISTORY | HIT THE BEACH | EAT AND DRINK | GET INDUSTRIAL | VISIT THE GALLERIES | GO CANOEING | TRY
HORSE-RIDING | PLACES NEARBY | CATCH A PERFORMANCE | GO AROUND THE GARDENS | TAKE A BOAT TRIP

A–Z of Durham & Northumberland

▶ Allendale

When you arrive in Allendale, look out for the sundial set on the village church. It gives the longitude and latitude of this pretty little town, which sits 800 feet up among the spectacular hill country of the Pennines and claims to be the geographical centre of Britain.

Allendale's pretty market place is peaceful for most of the year but be there on New Year's Eve to see it in a different light. This is the time of the annual Tar Barl celebration. Some say this is a hangover from pre-Christian times when pagan folk celebrated the winter solstice with fires which were meant to drive away the darkness of midwinter and mark the turning of the year, but in fact the earliest recorded Tar Barl event was in 1858 – so, like many 'ancient' English customs, it may really be quite a recent invention. Local men known as 'guisers', chosen for their strength and daring, dress in traditional costumes, blacken their faces and walk the streets carrying blazing tar barrels on their heads, and at midnight a huge bonfire is lit.

Easy on the eye, Allendale town sits in the heart of the valley of the same, where two pretty rivers, the East and West Allen, are fed by many tea-coloured, peaty burns that cascade down from the surrounding high hills.

SADDLE UP

Sinderhope Trekking Centre
sinderhopeponytrekking.co.uk
High Sinderhope | 01434 685266
You'll find great riding trails for experienced riders and beginners around Allendale.

SAMPLE REAL ALES

Allendale Brewery
allendaleale.com
Allen Mill, Allendale
01434 618686 | Open all year,
Mon–Fri 9–5
Taste some of the northeast's finest craft brews in a microbrewery housed in a historic lead mill.

PLAY A ROUND

Allendale Golf Club
allendale-golf.co.uk
High Studdon, Allenheads Road,
NE47 9DH | 07005 808246
Contact club for opening details
Challenging and hilly parkland course set 1000ft above sea level with superb views of East Allen Valley.

EAT AND DRINK

Allendale Tearooms
allendaletearooms.co.uk
Market Place, Allendale,
NE47 9BD | 01434 683575
You'll find few better, more atmospheric spots for a cup of tea, a slice of cake or a scone than this classic establishment. Built in the 1840s, it still has its Victorian beamed ceilings. You can also tuck in to more substantial goodies such as steak pies, pasties and specials which change every day. The wholesome Sunday lunch is a

special treat after a morning's walk in the woods, but it's | popular with local people too, so book ahead.

Allenheads

Amazing but true: pastoral Allendale was once Britain's heavy metal capital, and there was once gold in these hills too.

The lead mining industry flourished until the late 19th century, when the East Allen Mine was once the most important source of lead in Europe. Local landowners developed Allenheads as a model village, with a school, a library, a church and a chapel. You can discover more about the area's mining industry at several heritage centres and visitor attractions in and around Allenheads.

VISIT THE MUSEUMS

Allenheads Heritage Centre

NE47 9HN | 01434 685568

Open all year Sun–Thu 9–5

This community-owned heritage centre, with its restored blacksmith's shop is a great place to find out more about the area and its past. Allenheads is home to an historic 19th-century Armstrong water-engine, designed by the industrialist and engineer, William Armstrong, First Baron Armstrong, owner of Cragside.

Killhope, The North of England Lead Mining Museum

killhope.org.uk

Cowshill, DL13 1AR | 01388 537505

Open Apr–Oct 10.30–5

It's an evocative name, and the hard labour and toxic effects of lead mining did kill the hopes of many miners. This restored 1870s lead-crushing mill, with its huge overshot waterwheel, brings the grim history of Victorian mining to life.

It's 2.5 miles southwest of Allenheads, just across the County Durham boundary.

Alnmouth

If you've glimpsed Alnmouth's riverside parade of pastel-coloured houses from a passing train and been tempted to visit, you won't be disappointed when you do. This is one of the prettiest spots in Northumberland, and a super base for beachcombing.

It was founded in 1150, and for almost seven centuries it was a thriving shipbuilding centre and grain port at the mouth of the River Aln, a fine natural harbour for sailing vessels. Then came disaster. In 1806, a great storm lashed the coast, demolished the Norman church, changed the course of the Aln and heaved up a sandbar which closed the river mouth to ships.

▲ Alnmouth

Alnmouth's 18th-century granaries survived, but have now been converted into houses, which jostle for room with the shops and inns in the narrow streets. The hourly-striking church bell reverberates around the village centre.

The beach must be one of the best in the northeast. Stretching as far as the eye can see, it forms part of the 56-mile Northumbrian Heritage Coast and a walk along its windswept sands is guaranteed to blow away the cobwebs.

PLAY A ROUND
Alnmouth Golf Club
alnmouthgolfclub.com
Foxton Hall, NE66 3BE
01665 830231
Open Mon–Thu, Sun
Situated on the magnificent Northumberland coast, the course was established in 1869, and is the fourth oldest in England. It is widely regarded as one of the finest golf courses in the northeast. The 15th green offers amazing views of the Northumberland coast.

▶ Alnwick

Alnwick's big attraction is its castle. If you've seen the Harry Potter films, you'll experience a spot of déjà vu here. Yes, this is Hogwarts, and it has been the location for many more movies and TV productions. Alnwick (pronounced 'Annick') has been the seat of the powerful Percy family – ancestors of the current Duke of Northumberland – since 1309. You can still see the outlines of the original Norman stronghold of Alnwick Castle, though its strong walls and round towers have been altered over the centuries. Its barbican – the best surviving in Britain – and the impressive gateway, with stone figures mimicking an ever-watchful garrison, were added when the Percys arrived. Within, there's little sign of the Castle's medieval past – during

▼ Alnwick Castle

▲ The Alnwick Garden

the 19th century, the fourth Duke transformed it into a much more comfortable and splendid Renaissance-style palace which glows with fine woodwork and marble and is filled with treasures, including paintings by Canaletto, Titian, Van Dyck and Andrea del Sarto. There are two stunning cabinets made for Louis XIV, and two great Meissen dinner services. The park was landscaped by the renowned Northumbrian designer 'Capability' Brown.

But there's more to Alnwick than its castle. The town has a bustling, cobbled marketplace, and the streets around it are full of shops selling local produce, antiques, and arts and crafts. Outside the former railway station (which now houses one of Britain's largest second-hand book shops) is a column which was erected in gratitude by farmers when the third Duke lowered their rents. The fourth Duke raised them again, and the column subsequently became known as Farmers' Folly.

The 15th-century parish church lies near the castle, while at the other end of town is a survivor of the town walls begun in 1434, the narrow Hotspur Gate, named after the most famous member of the Percy family, Shakespeare's Harry Hotspur. From the park gate you can walk to the gateway to Alnwick Abbey and continue beyond to peaceful Hulne Priory, now a stately ruin.

▶ Alnwick Castle

alnwickcastle.com

NE66 1NQ | 01665 510777

Open Easter–Oct daily 10–6 (last admission 4.30)

Alnwick Castle has had its ups and downs since it was founded in the 11th century. Its clustered towers make it a favourite setting for film and TV productions, but this magnificent residential fortress bears little resemblance to the original castle. It has seen plenty of action, and has been extensively strengthened and rebuilt over the centuries. Its position near the border with Scotland made it vulnerable to attack from the Scots, and it played an important role in the Wars of the Roses during the 15th century. In 1172 and 1174 William the Lion, King of Scotland, laid siege to Alnwick, but on the second occasion he was surprised by reinforcements from the south and was himself taken prisoner.

Since the early 14th century, Alnwick has been the seat of the influential Percy family, Dukes of Northumberland. Although Alnwick was said to be well fortified by the 12th century, it was strengthened further in the 14th century by the Percys, who rebuilt the keep and enclosed the castle inside walls with seven semicircular towers. Sturdy gatehouses were added to both the inner and the outer walls.

After the Wars of the Roses, Alnwick began to decline. Restoration work started in the 18th century and in the 19th century it was further restored and embellished – its exterior a recreation of its medieval appearance, its interior a treasure house of works of art in the Italian Renaissance style. The first duke called in the legendary landscape architect 'Capability' Brown to create a gracious setting for his newly stylish home, and Brown transformed rugged Northumberland countryside into an oasis of manicured lawns and leafy copses. Robert Adam's brother John designed the Lion Bridge in 1773, a fake-medieval vision of battlements and lookouts guarded by the Percy's proud lion crest.

GO ROUND THE GARDENS
The Alnwick Garden
alnwickgarden.com
Denwick Lane, NE66 1YU
01665 511350
Open Apr–Sep 10–6, Oct–Mar 10–4

Looking at this amazing, 40-acre landscaped garden, it's hard to imagine that not so long ago it was derelict wasteland. The brainchild of the Duchess of Northumberland, it highlights include a Poison Garden where you'll find some of the world's most toxic plants, a Serpent Garden formed by winding water features, a beautiful cascade and a lovely Rose Garden. Giddy walkways and rope bridges lead to and from one of the world's largest treehouses, a magnificently eccentric structure which will thrill children and charm their parents.

SEE A LOCAL CHURCH
Church of St Michael
alnwickanglican.com
Bailiffgate, just off Canongate,
NE66 1LY | 01665 602797
Open May–Sep afternoons

Look for the arms of the Vesci and Percy families adorning the walls of this handsome church. Along with the design of its arches and some remaining Norman stonework, they indicate that it was first built around 1300. It was rebuilt in the 14th and 15th centuries, and although its tower isn't the highest, its buttresses, battlements and small pinnacles give an impression of strength and majesty. There are more reminders of the Percy connection in the ornate arcades to the chapels, where the 'Hotspur' capital carries a combination of crescent and fetterlocks that was perhaps first used by the fourth Earl of Northumberland (1470–89) in the reign of Henry VI. Inside, look out for an impressively large early 14th-century Flemish chest, decorated with foliage, dragons and a hunting scene, and for two 14th-century

▼ Library, Alnwick Castle

▼ The Alnwick Garden

tombs with effigies. There's some superb stained glass, too, dating from an extensive restoration in the 19th century.

SADDLE UP
Shipley Lane Equestrian Centre
shipleyequestrian.co.uk
NE66 2LS | 01665 579305
If you're an experienced rider you can enjoy a trail ride over the hills and moors (with a picnic) from Shipley Lane Equestrian Centre. For novices, there are easy-going hacks across nearby farmland.

EXPLORE BY BIKE
Adventure Northumberland
10 Oak Drive, NE66 2EU
01665 602925
There are some great cycling trails around Alnwick, including the Alnwick–Berwick trail, which runs for a little more than 30 miles between the two towns, avoiding main roads most of the way. Adventure Northumberland rents

Diamondback mountain and trails bikes for periods of hours or for as long as a week, and they can tell you about the best places to go for a morning, a full day or even longer.

PLAY A ROUND
Alnwick Castle Golf Club
alnwickcastlegolfclub.co.uk
Swansfield Park, NE66 2AB
01665 602632
Contact club for opening details
A mixture of mature parkland, open grassland and gorse bushes with panoramic views out to sea five miles away. Offers a fair test for golfers.

EAT AND DRINK
Grannies
18 Narrowgate, Alnwick, NE66 1JG
01665 602394
You'll find yourself tempted into Grannies by the home-made cakes in the ground floor shop – and you can enjoy them, and more, in the quirky tea room down the narrow stairs. It's like an old-fashioned kitchen,

▼ Fountains, the Alnwick Garden

complete with granny's bloomers drying overhead. Locals love the scones and teacakes – or you could sample the delicious Chocolate Juliette.

The Hog's Head Inn

hogsheadinnalnwick.co.uk
Hawfinch Drive, Alnwick, NE66 2BF
01665 606576

The name's a tribute to the inn in the Harry Potter stories, but the menu here is solid, modern pub grub, with dishes ranging from locally caught kippers and macaroni cheese to pad thai, teriyaki chicken and Moroccan lamb burgers.

▸ **PLACES NEARBY**

Hulne Park

NE66 3JE

When the Duke of Northumberland isn't shooting game inside the walls of his vast walled estate at Hulne Park, two miles from Alnwick, you can stroll through some (but not all) of its thousands of acres of woods, fields and farmland and admire the ruins of the 13th-century Hulne Priory. The gatehouse is all that remains of the former abbey, and you can also see (from the outside only) the Brizlee Tower. Built by Robert Adam in 1781, this Gothic erection is crowned with a large cast-iron basket in which beacons were lit on special occasions, such as Percy family anniversaries.

Edlingham Castle

englishheritage.com
Edlingham, NE66 2BW
0870 3331181
Open any reasonable time

Don't visit Edlingham Castle expecting massive ramparts. This former fortified manor house has seen better days since it stood as a stronghold against Scottish marauders in the 14th century, and one surviving wall leans alarmingly. It's worth a look, if only as a reminder that not all the northeast's castles are on the scale of Alnwick or Bamburgh.

Church of St John the Baptist

Edlingham NE66 2BN
Open any reasonable time
Even older than next-door Edlingham Castle, this 12th-century church is in rather better nick than its neighbour. It stands on the site of one of Northumberland's oldest churches, built in the eighth century. What is most interesting is its foursquare tower, which was added by the de Edlinghams as another defence against the Scots.

▾ The Treehouse, Alnwick Garden

▶ Alwinton

Base yourself in this little village in the in the Upper Coquet Valley (once notorious as a haunt of smugglers of contraband whisky from Scotland) for a spot of walking and exploring in the green Cheviots (see page 92) and the more rugged Harbottle Hills nearby. Before you set out, get a taste of what's in store from Alwinton church, on the hillside south of the Coquet, which has great views from its churchyard.

Alwinton is famous for the Border Shepherds' Show, held each October, with sheepdog trials, livestock awards and fell racing. Sir Walter Scott stayed at the popular Rose and Thistle in 1817 while writing his heroic tale, *Rob Roy* (in which a young Englishman travels from Northumberland into the wilds of Scotland, where he meets the outlaw Rob Roy MacGregor).

EAT AND DRINK

The Rose and Thistle
roseandthistlealwinton.com
NE65 7BQ | 01669 650226
This historic village inn serves up all the reliable pub grub classics, from home-made steak pie and scampi to chicken curry and ploughman's lunch.

▶ PLACES NEARBY

Harbottle
Hike from the pleasant village of Harbottle to see the Drake Stone, perched high up on the hillside (but watch your footing over the last 50 yards, which is a bit of a scramble). It's easy to see why this 30ft-tall lump of sandstone has its own local legends.

It towers, seemingly unnaturally, above its surroundings, but it was glaciation, not some ancient wizardry, that placed it here, and its reputation as a black magic site is down to the Victorian fascination with the Druids of pre-Roman Britain. That said, it's at the epicentre of a cluster of Bronze Age sites, so it could well have been used as a sacred place. In its way, it's more impressive than the scant remains of Harbottle's medieval castle, although from its tumbledown ramparts there's a nice view of the Coquet Valley.

Holystone Burn Nature Reserve
nwt.org.uk
800 yards west of Holystone village
0191 2846885 | Open access
You might spot roe deer on a ramble through Holystone Burn Nature Reserve, where the Holystone Burn chuckles its way through woodlands and grassland. The valley is wooded with oak, birch and juniper, and as well as roe deer, it's home to badgers, red squirrels and birds including the pied flycatcher, green woodpecker and the aptly named dipper, the only British songbird that can swim underwater. You might also see a merlin, Britain's smallest raptor.

▶ Amble

You can't help feeling that Amble, at the mouth of the River Coquet, has seen better days – and its rebranding as 'Amble by the Sea' smacks slightly of desperation. Amble was little more than a fishing village until it was developed as a port for the export of locally mined coal in the 19th century. When the coal industry, and fishing, declined, it fell back into the doldrums.

The main reason to come to this workaday little place is to visit the Northumberland Wildlife Trust's nearby reserves at Cresswell Pond and Hauxley, or to explore the Northumberland Coast Area of Outstanding Natural Beauty, which comes to an abrupt stop at Amble's harbour. Amble folk, understandably, feel a bit slighted by this. An even better reason to come here is to take a boat trip to Coquet Island, a refuge for puffins and other seabirds, a mile offshore. There's also a modern marina.

GO SEABIRD SPOTTING
Puffin Cruises
puffincruises.co.uk
21 Brownhill Street, Amble,
NE65 0AN | 01665 711975
Take a seabird-spotting trip from Amble Harbour to Coquet Island with Puffin Cruises. Look out for puffins, grey seals and rare roseate terns, as well as eider ducks and other fowl.

GO FISHING
Amble Angling Centre
ambleanglingcentre.org.uk
Amble Harbour, NE65 0AQ
01665 711200
Bring home a catch of fresh mackerel after a sea angling trip with a local skipper.

▶ PLACES NEARBY
Druridge Bay Country Park
northumberland.gov.uk
NE61 5BX
More than three miles of sandy beach and dunes beckon you to Druridge Bay Country Park, three miles south of Amble. The freshwater Ladyburn Lake is a haven for wildfowl in winter.

▶ Ashington

During the northeast's 19th-century coal boom years Ashington was one of the world's largest coal mining communities. Its coal mines closed in 1988, but their glory years are remembered at an excellent museum and visitor centre.

VISIT THE MUSEUM
Woodhorn Museum and Northumberland Archives
experiencewoodhorn.com
Woodhorn Road, NE63 9YF
01670 624455 | Open all year,
Wed–Sun and BHs 10–4; Mon–Tue in school hols
The gleaming metal blades which loom over the entrance to this up-to-the-minute museum may put you in mind of

some killer robot from a sci-fi movie, but they are inspired by the giant cutting machines used to extract coal deep underground in Ashington's mining heyday, when the site was a mine employing as many as 2,000 men. Inside, the museum is full of relics of a vanished industrial era, from trade union banners to naïve but evocative paintings by miners themselves. The Colliery Experience brings listed colliery buildings back to life.

TAKE A MINIATURE TRAIN RIDE
Queen Elizabeth II Country Park
woodhornnarrowgaugerailway. weebly.com
Woodhorn Road, NE63 9YF
Open Sat–Sun 10–2.30
Hop aboard the Woodhorn Railway Society's narrow-gauge railway for a (very short) ride through the Queen Elizabeth II Country Park, next to the Woodhorn Museum. The miniature locomotives run on just over half a mile of track, pulling carriages that used to carry miners around the colliery.

▶ **PLACES NEARBY**
Sanctuary Wildlife Care Centre
wildlife-sanctuary.co.uk
Crowden Hill Farm, Ulgham, NE61 3NH | 01670 791778
Open summer Wed–Sat 11–4; all year for guided tours.
Meet resident foxes, owls and hedgehogs at the Sanctuary Wildlife Centre, where injured or orphaned wild creatures are nursed back to health and – whenever possible – returned to the wild. You'd have to have a heart of stone not to want to cuddle them.

▶ Bamburgh

There's not a lot in Bamburgh – except the castle. But the castle is a high-profile attraction, so the village streets are crammed with visitors on summer weekends. Avoid school holidays and bank holiday weekends to dodge the mobs.

You can make a pilgrimage to the grave of tragic heroine Grace Darling (see page 63), who lies in the parish churchyard. It can be hard to find a cafe table in Bamburgh in high season, so on a summer day a picnic on the beach is a good alternative – there are miles of sands, so there's plenty of space for all. It can be on the breezy side, and the sky is often full of rainbow-coloured kites of all shapes and sizes.

The views of Holy Island (see page 143) from the spectacularly sited golf course at Budle Point are enough to put you off your stroke. If you're a birder, there's lots to see among the wildfowl-haunted wetlands of Budle Bay, west of Bamburgh.

▲ Bamburgh Castle

TAKE IN SOME HISTORY
Bamburgh Castle

bamburghcastle.com
NE69 7DF | 01668 214515
Open 8 Feb–2 Nov daily 10–5,
3 Nov–6 Feb Sat–Sun 11–4.30

Don't be fooled. Like so many castles, Bamburgh isn't quite as medieval as it looks. True enough, this forbidding crag has been a stronghold for thousands of years. This is the easternmost outcrop of the ridge of rock known as the Great Whin Sill, and its natural defences – cliffs that loom 150 above the North Sea – made it irresistible to Iron Age chieftains, Saxon thanes, Viking jarls and Norman lords. Author Bernard Cornwell makes it the ancestral home of his bloodthirsty ninth-century warlord Uhtred, and it has starred as the setting for half a dozen swashbucklers and bodice-rippers (see page 38).

Bamburgh's cliffs protect its seaward sides, while to landwards it is protected by grim ramparts built and strengthened by generations of defenders. You wouldn't want to have tried to storm them.

But Bamburgh (like many another impressive castle) was not as impregnable as it looked. It was seized by the Anglian King Ethelfrith in AD 547 and given to his wife Bebba – hence its Anglo-Saxon name, Beddanburh – 'Beddan's Fortress'. Vikings sacked it in 993. The de Mowbray family built a new stronghold in the late 11th century, but in 1095 Robert de Mowbray, Earl of Northumberland, joined a rising against William II. He was taken prisoner, and his wife surrendered the castle after William threatened to poke her husband's eyes out. After that, Bamburgh remained in Royal hands. It stood off various assaults by the Scots, but in 1464 – during the struggle for the throne between the houses of York and Lancaster – it was besieged by the Yorkist Richard Neville, Earl of Warwick. Neville brought out the big guns, and after a nine-month siege Bamburgh became the first English castle to fall to artillery.

VISIT THE MUSEUM
RNLI Grace Darling Museum
rnli.org.uk
Radcliffe Road, NE69 7AE
01668 214910 | Open Easter–Sep daily 10–5, Oct–Easter Tue–Sun 10–4
It's one of the 19th-century's most ripping yarns, and for once it has a heroine not a hero. Grace Darling must have been a tough lady. In 1838 – despite suffering from consumption (tuberculosis) – the Longstone

4 great views

▶ **Seven Castles**
Hike to the top of Ros Castle, just outside Chillingham. From a viewpoint among the ruins of a 3,000 year old hill fort you can see seven historic castles: Alnwick, Bamburgh, Chillingham, Dunstanburgh, Ford, Warkworth and, out to sea, Lindisfarne.

▶ **On the Wall**
From the highest section of the Hadrian's Wall National Trail, between Walltown and Chesters, you can see a long stretch of the wall as it roller-coasters over the ups and downs of the Great Whin Sill.

▶ **Out to Sea**
Looking east and a bit north from the ramparts of Bamburgh Castle, you've a fine panorama of Lindisfarne and the Farne Islands.

▶ **Pretty as a Postcard**
Alnmouth's blue, pink and white riverside houses, seen from the other side of the river, make it the prettiest seaside village in Northumbria.

Lighthouse keeper's daughter rowed with her father to rescue nine people from the wreck of the SS *Forfarshire*, which had gone aground on Big Harcar. You can admire a romanticised portrait of Grace here, and marvel at the sheer guts of anyone who was willing to go to sea in rough weather in a boat as frail as the locally built coble that she used. Just 21ft long, it's on display along with audio-visual displays and a replica of the Longstone Lighthouse.

Grace died four years later, aged 27. That may seem tragically young, but in 1842 the average age of death in England was just over 28.

SEE A LOCAL CHURCH
St Aidan's Church
staidan-bamburgh.co.uk
Church Street, NE69 7DB
01668 214748 | Open daily
You'll find secret histories inside Bamburgh's parish church. It was built during the 13th century, on the site where St Aidan built the first church in Northumbria in AD 635. There's nothing left of Aidan's little wooden chapel, but the forked beam that the saint was leaning on when he died in AD 651 is said to be built into the ceiling of the tower. The post was said to have survived two fires that destroyed the rest of the original church, and was credited with healing powers – people would cut chips of wood off it and soak them in water to make a miracle cure. It seems to have survived the Reformation of the 16th century, when most English holy relics were destroyed – perhaps because the folk of Northumberland were not very zealous Protestants. Inside, there's a gracious 13th-century chancel with a magnificent reredos in Caen stone, imported from Normandy. Look

out for monuments to the Foster family, who were the royal governors of Bamburgh Castle for 400 years, and an effigy of local heroine Grace Darling. Look out too for the 14th-century knight who, it's said, bore the name Sir Lancelot du Lake.

PLAY A ROUND
Bamburgh Castle Golf Club
bamburghcastlegolfclub.co.uk
The Club House, 40 The Wynding, NE69 7DE | 01668 214378 (club)
Open Mon–Fri, Sun and BHs
The fast, true greens of this superb coastal course enjoy plenty of natural hazards – heather and whin bushes abound. Try not to be distracted by magnificent views of the Farne Islands, Holy Island, Lindisfarne Castle, Bamburgh Castle and the Cheviot Hills.

EAT AND DRINK
Waren House Hotel ⊚
warenhousehotel.co.uk
Waren Mill, NE70 7EE
01668 214581
Handily placed for exploring the coast, Bamburgh Castle and Lindisfarne, Waren House is a Georgian mansion set in six acres of landscaped grounds with sea views. Everything cries out classic country-house style, from the grandfather clock and log fires to the oil paintings and soothing blue and gold hues of the restaurant, where burnished tables and gleaming glassware reflect the candlelight at dinner. Tradition is the watchword in the kitchen,

too, starting with diligent sourcing of the region's finest ingredients which are brought together in a broadly modern British style.

Victoria Hotel ◉

victoriahotel.net
Front Street, NE69 7BP
01668 214431
With its position on the village green and views over to the historic castle, the Victoria Hotel is in a plum spot. The Baileys Bar & Restaurant consists of a number of dining areas, some under a glass atrium roof, with a decidedly modish sheen to the decor. There are trendy muted colour tones, some exposed stonework, nicely designed tables and chairs, and some smart fabric-covered banquettes, plus Milburn's bar

which is decorated with black-and white pictures of the Magpies (that's Newcastle United football team) – it's named in honour of the legendary Jackie Milburn. The menu goes in for egalitarian modern Britishness.

Copper Kettle Tea Rooms

copperkettletearooms.com
21 Front Street, NE69 7BW
01668 214315
On the main street that leads from the church to the castle, the Copper Kettle Tea Rooms is a delightful, cosy building, with panelled walls, arched windows and a pretty garden. As well as its famous cream teas, the cafe offers light meals and snacks, including excellent home-made soup.

▶ Bardon Mill

You might think that any village which lists its railway station and the village pub as its key landmarks is struggling a bit, profile-wise. Bardon Mill also boasts the gorge and river scenery of the National Trust's Allen Banks, and the grounds of Ridley Hall, which once belonged to the Bowes-Lyons (relations of Queen Elizabeth the Queen Mother). It's a conference centre now, but you can walk through pretty woodland and along the banks of the River Allen. But it's the Roman sights and outdoor activities nearby that make Bardon Mill and its environs worth a visit. Bardon Mill is close to the northern end of the Pennines, and the 83-mile Hadrian's Wall Way and National Cycle Route 72 – less prosaically known as Hadrian's Cycleway – pass through the village.

At Housesteads Roman Fort and Museum you can step out onto Hadrian's Wall, while at Vindolanda (see page 221), the biggest surviving civilian settlement on the wall, you'll discover that life there wasn't all spit and polish. Don't miss the Roman Army Museum, with its fine collection of finds such as leather shoes, writing tablets, ornaments and a replica of a Roman kitchen, as well as a video show, 'Edge of Empire', which really brings the ancient frontier to life.

GO BACK IN TIME
Housesteads Roman Fort and Museum
english-heritage.org.uk
Haydon Bridge, NE47 6NN
01434 344363 | Open Apr–Sep daily 10–6, Oct–Mar Sat–Sun 10–4, 17–25 Feb daily 10–4

Imagine you're a Roman sentry and stride out along Hadrian's Wall westwards from Housesteads to Milecastle 37, then on as far as Steel Rigg for great views.

Easy access to this impressive stretch of the wall pulls in the crowds, so avoid weekends if you want the place to yourself. You should visit the museum, with its fine collection of treasures and everyday objects, before exploring the remains of the Roman town, including the North and South gates, rows of shops, and streets where deep ruts worn into the stone by cartwheels betray centuries of Roman occupation. (See page 150)

Vindolanda
see page 221

SADDLE UP
Cragside Riding Stables
cragsideridingstables.weebly.com
Low Fogrigg, Westwood, NE47 7JR
01434 344065

Look out for wildlife including roe deer, red squirrels and buzzards on a woodland trail ride with Cragside Riding Stables, which has horses and gentle ponies for all levels of equestrian experience.

WALK IN THE WOODS
Head for Allen Banks, just the other side of the river from Bardon Mill, where beech and oak trees cling to the hillsides on either bank of the river. You've a better chance of seeing a rare red squirrel here than in the pine and fir forests elsewhere in Northumbria, and if you tread quietly there's a good chance of seeing roe deer too, especially in the early morning and at dusk.

A suspension bridge crosses the gorge, and a small tarn in the middle of Morralee Wood is a good spot to sit quietly and watch for wildlife.

EAT AND DRINK
Twice Brewed Inn
twicebrewedinn.co.uk
Bardon Mill, Hexham, NE47 7AN
01434 344534

Not far from both the Roman sites at Vindolanda and Housesteads, this inn is a wonderful place to relax from the rigours of marching up and down Hadrian's Wall. In the bar there is always a great selection of real ales, and you can eat well in the bar and the restaurant. Local produce is to the fore. Leave room for the ice creams.

▸ **PLACES NEARBY**

General Havelock

Ratcliffe Road, Haydon Bridge,
NE47 6ER | 01434 684376

The garden of the General Havelock, a converted barn, overlooks an idyllic stretch of the River South Tyne. There is an interesting range of ales on tap, and the menu has a number of twists on the expected fare.

Langley Castle Hotel ◉◉

langleycastle.com
Langley on Tyne, NE47 5LU
01434 688888

This forbidding castle dates from 1350 and comes complete with crenellations, seven-foot thick walls, and an immaculately preserved interior. Josephine's Restaurant, recently extended and given a more contemporary look under its beamed ceiling, offers a fine-dining experience, which could be a five-course set-price affair including a sorbet or demitasse of soup and a pre-dessert, with plenty of choice at each of the other courses. Don't expect the roast beef of Old England; this is refined modern cooking with ideas culled from around Europe and beyond to add interest. Pan-fried pigeon breast, for instance, comes with almond and raisin polenta, squash purée and sage jus. The balance of flavours is clearly considered, seen in main courses of baked chicken roulade with pesto, courgette mousse spiked with lime, and red pepper purée, and cod fillet baked with cayenne and served with spicy Puy lentils, spinach and cooling coriander yoghurt. End on a homely note with apple crumble and custard.

▸ Barnard Castle

When you arrive in Barnard Castle village, you will find yourself wondering where the castle in fact is. Don't panic. It's there, but unlike most castles, it's out of sight of its vassal village.

In its day, Barnard Castle was an important market town, strategically located midway along a coast-to-coast route. It takes its name from Bernard de Balliol, the 12th-century baron who founded the castle and settlement. Flowing through Barnard Castle, the Tees was the boundary between Yorkshire and County Durham, and lovers who wished to marry without parental approval could wed illicitly in the chapel on the County Bridge – a no-man's land between the jurisdictions of the Bishop of Durham and the Archbishop of York.

The wide Horse Market, the busy Market Place and the Market Cross, a handsome octagon built in 1747, are reminders of the town's mercantile past. Butter sellers sheltered in the Market Place colonnade, while the upper floor served as the town hall. You can still see the bullet holes in its weather vane,

▲ The Bowes Museum

made during a shooting contest in 1804, when the authorities were more relaxed about gun ownership.

Beyond the Market Cross, The Bank was once the foremost shopping street. Its oldest building, Blagroves House, boasts a tall bay window and the jolly figure of a musician over the door. Thorngate and Bridgegate comprised the industrial area of the town in the 18th and 19th centuries – the mill buildings and weavers' cottages, with their long upper windows, survive. East of The Bank is The Demesnes, an area of open land which used to supply the town with water from many springs.

Walk down Newgate to discover Barnard Castle's greatest surprise, the Bowes Museum. In a French-style château, you'll find one of the most remarkable private art collections in the whole of Europe.

TAKE IN SOME HISTORY
Barnard Castle
english-heritage.org.uk
DL12 8PR | 01833 638212
Open Apr–Sep daily 10–6, Oct–Mar, Sat–Sun 10–4

Bits and pieces of Bernard de Balliol's castle still exist, as well as the 14th-century Round Tower and also the 15th-century Great Chamber, where you can see the boar badge of King Richard III (AKA Shakespeare's Richard 'Crookback'), carved into the stonework of one of the windows.

You can see what attracted de Balliol to the site – it is protected by steep cliffs, and as a bonus it has fine views across the River Tees. Embellished by sturdy walls and deep ditches, it was a formidable fortress, on a site covering more than six acres. It was a sought-after prize, and it changed hands many times.

Through the centuries it was claimed by Alexander II of Scotland, the powerful prince-bishops of Durham, the powerful Neville earls of Warwick, and finally Richard III. After his demise at Bosworth in 1485 and the end of the long Wars of the Roses, the castle fell into disrepair.

Egglestone Abbey

english-heritage.org.uk
DL12 8QN | 0870 3331181
Open daily 10–6

Take time to visit Egglestone Abbey, just over a mile to the southeast of Barnard Castle. The White Friars, or Premonstratensian Canons, lived an ascetic life here from around 1196 until they were turfed out by Henry VIII when he dissolved England's great religious foundations. In 1548 the abbey, minus its Canons, was sold to Robert Strelley, who made part of the cloisters into an Elizabethan house – now itself a ruin. The beautiful but scanty ruins are located above a bend in the Tees. You can still see parts of the church, although the Canons' living quarters have survived less well.

VISIT A MUSEUM

The Bowes Museum

thebowesmuseum.org.uk
DL12 8NP
01833 690606
Open all year daily 10–5

You'll be charmed and amazed by this eclectic collection. John and Joséphine Bowes built this magnificent mansion to house their treasury of works of art and artisanry over a century ago. He was the illegitimate son of the 10th Earl of Strathmore, who inherited huge estates in County Durham from his mother, and became a respected MP, industrialist and collector. She was a French actress, Joséphine Coffin-Chevallier. She had superb taste, he had money and organisational skills, and together they amassed the wondeful collection that became the Bowes Museum. Sadly, neither lived to see the museum open to the public.

Exhibits include Roman altars, porcelain, paintings by both Goya and El Greco, costumes, toys, musical instruments, furniture and complete rooms from demolished buildings. Don't miss the Silver Swan, a unique life-size musical automaton which twice a day preens itself and catches the silver fish swimming in its stream.

PLAY A ROUND
Barnard Castle
Golf Club
barnardcastlegolfclub.org
Harmire Rd, DL12 8QN
01833 638355 | Open daily
Flat parkland in open
countryside. Plantations
and natural water add
colour and interest to this
classic course.

EAT AND DRINK
Clarendon's Café and
Restaurant
29 Market Place, DL12 8NE
01833 690110
Set in a superb 17th-century
building, Clarendon's offers a
good choice of salads,
sandwiches and cakes, as well
as more substantial dishes
such as steak and ale pie.

The Morritt
themorritt.co.uk
Greta Bridge, DL12 9SE
01833 627232
Named after a local artist,
Major Morritt, whose paintings
hang in the hotel, this 18th-
century coaching inn turned
country-house hotel has a long
history of feeding travellers
well before sending them on
their way. Nowadays, the
restaurant's dark oak panelling
and herringbone parquet floors
have been jollied up with a
gently contemporary look
involving lively artwork, silk
window blinds and moody
lighting; it all adds up to an
amenable setting for good
French-inspired cooking that
straddles the border between
the classics and more modern
ideas. Charles Dickens stayed
here while writing *Nicholas
Nickleby* in 1839.

Rose & Crown Hotel ◉◉
rose-and-crown.co.uk
Romaldkirk, DL12 9EB
01833 650213
Rubbing shoulders with a
doughty Saxon church known
as the Cathedral of the Dale,
and bracketed by three village
greens, the stone-built
18th-century Rose & Crown is a
haven of sybaritic pleasures
among the fells and meadows
of remote Teesdale. There's
fine hand-pulled ale to quaff by
the crackling log fire in the bar,
and a rather classy oak-
panelled and candlelit dining
room, where the four-course
dinner menus are built on local,
seasonal produce and inspired
by neatly dovetailed classic and
contemporary trends.

▸ **PLACES NEARBY**
Bowes Castle
english-heritage.org.uk
DL12 9LD | 0870 3331181
Open any reasonable time
The massive ruins of Henry II's
three-storey tower keep loom
over the valley of the River
Greta. This was yet another of
the region's natural defensive
sites, and long before Henry
built a stronghold here the
Romans fortified the site. You
can still see traces of their
earthen walls.

▶ Beadnell

Little Beadnell, about a mile south of Seahouses (see page 205), has the only west-facing harbour on England's east coast. Not a big claim to fame, you might think, but it's sheltered from the North Sea gales, so its fisher-folk must have been envied by their neighbours whose anchorages were exposed to the battering of the waves.

There's little to see here, apart from a 19th-century church, St Ebba's, built on the site of a much earlier chapel, and a group of 18th-century lime kilns, in which seashells were burned to make building lime. But the gorgeous two-mile-long sweep of sand that is Beadnell Bay is a good enough reason to come here. It's home to nesting colonies of rare Arctic and little terns, and its waves and winds have made Beadnell a magnet spot for surfers, kiteboarders and windsurfers. You can see what's left of a 16th-century pele tower built into the renowned local pub, the Craster Arms, which also hosts a couple of fun summer festivals (see below).

EAT AND DRINK

The Craster Arms
crasterarms.co.uk
The Wynding, NE67 5AX
01665 720272
In the 15th century, the English in this neck of the woods built small fortified watch towers to warn of Scottish invasions – this was one of them. Since becoming a pub in 1818 its role has widened to offer not just good food, drink and accommodation, but a programme of live entertainment, the Crastonbury music festival, and a beer and cider festival (last weekend in July). Sandwiches, baguettes, paninis, salads and hot meals are available at lunchtime; in the evening there's braised lamb shank; Thai green chicken curry; seasonal blackboard specials; crab fishcake and other local seafood.

▶ Beamish

If you're beginning to suffer from medieval or Roman history fatigue, visit Beamish for a taste of the region's more recent past. It's yet another popular northeast favourite among makers of period TV drama, thanks to the Northern England Open Air Museum, a reconstruction of a northern English town on the cusp of the 19th and 20th centuries.

Once more prosaically known as 'Pit Hill' – which gives you a clue to its mining past – the village is surrounded by Hell Hole Wood. That gives you some idea of how the locals felt about working in the mines.

▶ Beamish, the North of England Open Air Museum

beamish.org.uk

DH9 0RG | 0191 3704000

Open 23 Mar–3 Nov daily 10–5, 4 Nov–22 Mar Tue–Thu, Sat–Sun 10–4

Take your kids to the North of England Open Air Museum to disabuse them of any foolish notions that life might have been more fun in the old days. No, son, it wasn't. You can ride on an electric tram or steam train, buy sweeties from authentically costumed shopkeepers and meet traditional farm breeds at the Home Farm, which used to supply Beamish Hall (think: Downton Abbey for real). Lessons in the village school and prayers in the Methodist Chapel are not so much fun, but it's the dentist's surgery, with its array of pliers and treadle-powered drill – and total lack of anaesthetics – that makes you grateful to be living in the 21st century.

A reconstruction of a northern town from a bygone era, full of buildings transported from other places, Beamish is filled with details of past times. It tells the story of the people of northeast England between 1825 and 1913, and of their very hard lives. Time travel, anyone?

▲ *Puffing Billy*, Beamish Open Air Museum

VISIT THE MUSEUMS
Beamish, the North of England Open Air Museum
see opposite

ENTERTAIN THE FAMILY
Beamish Wild Adventure Park
beamishwild.co.uk
Beamish Hall, DH9 0YB
01207 233733 | Open all year daily 10–4 (reduced times Nov–Feb)
Build a topple tower, climb a giant tree or a slippery pole, build a den or find your way through a woodland maze. As you'll have guessed from the list of activities, this is one for families with kids, and it caters for them very well. It's not all about scrambling and climbing – you watch some of the 70 resident birds of prey in flight or go on an 'owl walk' with a fledgling owl.

Beamish Wild Ropes Course
beamishwild.co.uk
Beamish Hall, DH9 0YB
01207 233733 | Open all year daily 10–4 (pre-booking essential)
Experience the ultimate adrenaline rush in the treetops, climbing through tunnel nets, jumping the 'leap of faith' and free falling on the incredible 65ft power fan. The Ropes Activity Centre at Beamish Hall provides fantastic outdoor fun and adventure for families, school groups, corporate groups and any other thrill-seeking individuals. Visitors can also enjoy free entry to Beamish Wild Adventure Park (see entry above).

PLAY A ROUND
Beamish Park Golf Club
beamishgolf.co.uk
DH9 0RH | 0191 3701382
Open daily
Attractive parkland course with varied and interesting holes. Good greens and stunning views. Well-drained course providing all year play.

▶ PLACES NEARBY
Tanfield Railway
tanfield-railway.co.uk
Old Marley Hill, NE16 5ET
0845 468 4938 | Open Sun end Dec–end Nov
Tanfield's claim to be the world's oldest railway is a bit of a stretcher – there was a railway here in the early 1600s, but it used wooden rails, wheels and wagons to haul coal from the local colliery to the coast. A second coal-hauling 'waggonway' was laid in 1725, but that was horsedrawn too.

EAT AND DRINK
The Moorings Hotel
themooringsdurham.co.uk
Hett Hill, DH2 3JU | 0191 3701597
Handy for Beamish, this thriving hotel bar attracts custom from ramblers and riders enjoying the countryside along the Tees valley. Thirsts are quenched by beers from Mordue or the microbrewery at Beamish. The menu ranges from breaded cod, haddock and crayfish tail fishcakes on ratatouille to sirloin steak with garlic butter tiger prawns, finishing with warm Scotch pancakes with chocolate sauce.

▶ Bellingham

Bellingham makes a good base for ventures into Northumberland National Park and the Kielder area. Its major landmark is the 13th-century St Cuthbert's Church. Inside is 'Cuddy's Well', named after the patron saint whose mummified body rested here for a spell on its century-long wandering from Lindisfarne to Durham. The well water was credited with miraculous powers and is still used for baptisms.

VISIT THE MUSEUM

Bellingham Heritage Centre

bellingham-heritage.org.uk

Station Yard, Woodburn Road,
NE48 2DG | 01434 220050

A volunteer-run local history museum, where you can learn about the Border Counties Railway, which ran between Hexham and Riccarton, from 1862 to 1958. There are displays dealing with the area's mining heritage as well as the Border Reivers, and WP Collier's photographs of rural life in Northumberland between the wars show a world which has vanished forever. There's also a re-creation of the Stannersburn Smithy, which operated locally from the 1830s until the 1970s.

PLAY A ROUND

Bellingham Golf Club

bellinghamgolfclub.com

Boggle Hole, NE48 2DT
01434 220530 (Secretary)

Contact club for opening details

Rolling parkland with many natural hazards. This highly regarded 18-hole course offers a mixture of testing par 3s, long par 5s and tricky par 4s.

EAT AND DRINK

The Cheviot Hotel

thecheviothotel.co.uk

NE48 2AU | 01434 220696

The Cheviot Hotel's menu uses locally sourced ingredients and include traditional dishes, well as sandwiches and snacks

▶ PLACES NEARBY

Black Middens Bastle House

english-heritage.org.uk

NE48 1NE, 7 miles northwest of Bellingham | 0870 3381181

Open any reasonable time

You can see one of only a handful of traditional bastle houses that are open to the public, at Black Middens, northwest of Bellingham in the remote Tarset Burn valley. Better-off border families could not rely on feudal lords for defence during the troubled 15th and 16th centuries, so they fended for themselves by building these two-storey stone houses to protect their families and livestock. Bastles were usually about 35ft by 25ft in area, with two storeys. Animals occupied the windowless ground floor and people reached the upper floor by a removable ladder – the stone stairway at Black Middens was a later addition.

Berwick-upon-Tweed

0   200 m

Holy Trinity CE First School
NORTHUMBERLAND AVENUE
BELL TOWER PARK
BERWICK-UPON-TWEED STATION
HIGH GREENS
LOW GREENS
RAILWAY ST
CASTLEGATE
Berwick Castle (site of)
TWEED STREET
Royal Border Bridge
River Tweed
A1167
SCOTT'S PLACE
Meg's Mount
BANKHILL
GOLDEN SQ
ROYAL TWEED BRIDGE
OLD BRIDGE
RIVERDENE
RIVERSIDE ROAD
GARDENS
TWEED ST
RIVERDENE
WEST END PLACE
BLACKWELL ROAD
WEST END
UNION PARK ROAD
WEST END ROAD
OSBORNE ROAD
ORD DRIVE
A698
OSBORNE CRESCENT
UNION BRAE
MAIN STREET
PRINCE EDWARD ROAD
A1167
OSBORNE PLACE
OSBORNE ROAD
KILN HILL
St Cuthberts RC First School
MAIN STREET
DOCK ROAD
KILN HILL
MILL STRAND
Dock
Tweedmouth West First School
3LC

Magdalen Fields Golf Club
Magdalen Fields
Berwick Infirmary
H
LOW GREENS
WELL CLOSE SQUARE
BRUCEGATE
VIOLET TERRACE
Ramparts
The Stanks
Holy Trinity
St Andrew's
PARADE
Berwick-upon-Tweed Barracks
M
Ramparts
QUAY WALLS
BRIDGE STREET
DEWAR'S LANE
SANDGATE
WOOL MARKET
SILVER STREET
FOUL FORD
OIL MILL LANE
NESS STREET
EASTERN LANE
LOVE LANE
HIDE HILL
BRIDGE TERRACE
PIER ROAD
PALACE STREET EAST
PALACE STREET
PALACE GREEN
Main Guard
M
Police Station
Town Hall
The Maltings
MARYGATE
CHAPEL STREET
CHURCH STREET
RAVENSDOWNE
TA Hall
WALKERGATE
GREENSIDE AVE
COLLEGE PLACE
PARSONS CLOSE
WALLACE GREEN

▶ Berwick-upon-Tweed

Most people zoom past Berwick by train or car, on their way between England and Scotland. But you should pause here, because it has plenty of history to offer.

The tides of war have washed over Berwick-upon-Tweed more often than any town really deserves. It was in Scottish hands until 1174, when William the Lion handed it over to England as part of his royal ransom after being captured in battle. Over the next 300 years it changed hands 11 times. In 1502, under the 'Treaty of Perpetual Peace' between England and Scotland, it became a sort of free city-state within England – and thereby hangs a tale.

When Britain declared war on Russia in 1854, so the story goes, the declaration was signed by Queen Victoria as Queen of the United Kingdom, Ireland…and Berwick-upon-Tweed. By an unfortunate (but understandable) oversight, when Russia and Britain made peace some years later, Berwick wasn't mentioned in the treaty. So the town remained technically at war with the Czar for more than a century. The matter was finally resolved, ironically, at the height of the Cold War. In 1964, the USSR sent a peace delegation to Berwick to make a solemn declaration of friendship between the socialist superpower and the former mini-state. It took another 10 years for Berwick to make its peace with Northumberland, which it didn't legally join until 1974.

In the Middle Ages the town was protected at its north end by the castle, first mentioned in 1160 and rebuilt at the end of the 13th century. Locals call the dangerously steep steps that plunge down to the river from the castle the 'Breakynecks', for obvious reasons. The Constable's Tower is impressive, and a stretch of the medieval town wall lies alongside the cliffs between Meg's Mount and the railway bridge. You'll be more impressed, though, by ramparts built during Elizabeth I's reign, when the Franco-Scottish alliance threatened England as never before. Walk along them to see fortifications that are unique in England. The 22ft-high stone-faced walls are 12ft thick at the base and topped with grassed mounds.

In 1568 a Protestant, anti-French faction seized power in Scotland. Mary, Queen of Scots, fled Scotland for the tender mercies of her cousin Elizabeth, and Scotland and England

▼ Robert Stephenson's Royal Border Bridge

became cautiously friendly. When James VI of Scotland succeeded Elizabeth to become James I of England in 1603, Berwick's defences should have become redundant. But generals are always fighting the last war but one, so the walls continued to be strengthened through the 17th and 18th centuries. As a result, Berwick-upon-Tweed has the most impressive ring of ramparts of any town in England.

Among Berwick's other landmarks are its bridges. Successive early wooden bridges were swept away by the river. Without one for 200 years, Berwick put up another wooden bridge in Tudor times, but it was King James VI, going to London in 1603, who demanded, and eventually paid for, the magnificent 1,164ft long Old Bridge. It remained the only road bridge in the town until the Royal Tweed Bridge was built in 1928, but the most spectacular of Berwick's bridges, Robert Stephenson's Royal Border Bridge, 2,152ft long on 28 high arches, was built for the railway in 1846. They link Berwick with Tweedmouth, on the south bank of the Tweed. True to local form, Tweedmouth quirkily insists on its own identity and refuses to think of itself as part of Berwick.

Neighbouring Spittal has a good beach, and Berwick harbour is busy with both leisure and commercial boats.

5 top bridges

▶ **Millennium Bridge**
Celebrated musically by progressive rockmeisters The Nice in the 1970 album Five Bridges, the five Tyne spans added a sixth sibling when the Millennium Bridge opened in 2000.

▶ **Tyne Bridge**
The great Tyne Bridge is still Newcastle's icon. See it on a river boat trip from the Quayside.

▶ **Royal Border Bridge**
Robert Stephenson's bridge, built in 1846, still carries the railway across the Tweed on 28 high arches spanning 2,152ft.

▶ **Berwick Old Bridge**
King James VI and I ordered the building of this splendid 1,164ft-long bridge in 1603 as a symbol of the union of the crowns of England and Scotland.

▶ **Chesters Roman Bridges**
You can see the remains of the bridges built by the Romans to cross the North Tyne on either bank of the river, between Chesters and Chollerford.

TAKE IN SOME HISTORY
Berwick Castle and Ramparts
english-heritage.org.uk
TD15 1DF | Open any time
There's almost nothing left of the first castle, but the ramparts are another story. From Meg's Mount, walk round a ring of ramparts and artillery emplacements, which were kept reinforced and ready to repel real and imagined enemies for centuries after England and Scotland became one United Kingdom, from rebellious Jacobites to Napoleonic or Russian invasion fleets. And Berwick's battlements must have been a deterrent – after all, the Czar never did invade.

VISIT THE MUSEUMS
Berwick-Upon-Tweed Barracks
english-heritage.org.uk
The Parade, TD15 1DF
01289 304493 | Barracks open Apr–Sep Wed–Sun and BHs 10–5; please call for details of Main Guard
Designed by Nicholas Hawksmoor and begun in 1717, Berwick Barracks were among the first in England to be purpose-built. The Barracks hosts an exhibition on the life of the British infantryman, the King's Own Scottish Borderers Museum, the Berwick Gymnasium Art Gallery and the Berwick Borough Museum. There is also a Georgian Guard House near the quay. It displays 'The Story of a Border Garrison Town' exhibition.

SEE A LOCAL CHURCH
Holy Trinity Church
berwickparishchurch.btck.co.uk
Walkergate, TD15 1EB
01289 302755
The first thing you should notice about England's most northerly parish church is that it has neither a tower nor a steeple. It was one of only six in the country to be built under the

▲ Berwick Castle

Puritan Commonwealth of Oliver Cromwell, when such fripperies were frowned on, and stands on 12th-century foundations. In 1855, it was prettified with a chancel and some of its Gothic features were replaced by Classical windows and arcading. Cromwell would not have approved. Nor would he have liked the 1893 reredos, designed by Edward Lutyens. Parts of the interior contain many fine elements of the Commonwealth church. These include roundels in the west window of 16th- and 17th-century Flemish or Dutch glass, monuments in the north and south aisles, Jacobean-style woodwork in the west gallery, the pulpit and tester, and 17th-century panels in the 19th-century choir stalls.

PLAY A ROUND

Berwick-upon-Tweed (Goswick) Golf Club
goswicklinksgc.co.uk
Goswick, TD15 2RW
01289 387256 | Open daily
A natural seaside championship links course, with undulating

fairways, elevated tees and good greens.

Magdalene Fields Golf Club

magdalene-fields.co.uk
Magdalene Fields, TD15 1NE
01289 306130 | Open daily
Seaside course on a clifftop with natural hazards formed by bays. All holes open to winds. Testing 8th hole over bay (par 3). Scenic views to Holy Island and north to Scotland.

GO TO THE MOVIES

The Maltings Theatre and Cinema

maltingsberwick.co.uk
Eastern Lane, TD15 1AJ
01289 330999
Visit The Maltings for new release films and world-class cinema, theatre, ballet and dance.

EXPLORE BY BIKE

Wilson Cycles

mouthofthetweed.co.uk
17 Bridge Street, TD15 1ES
01289 331476
Hire a bike to discover any of half-a-dozen trails that start and finish in Berwick-upon-Tweed. You can range inland, follow the coast, sneak over the border to Scotland, or follow a specially designed foodie trail.

▶ PLACES NEARBY

Paxton House, Gallery and Country Park

paxtonhouse.co.uk
Paxton, TD15 1SZ | 01289 386291
House and gallery open Apr–Oct, daily 11–5; grounds daily 10–sunset
Make a cross-border raid into Scotland to visit this grand mansion, built in 1758 for the Laird of Wedderburn. The house is a fine example of neo-Palladian architecture, built in red sandstone to the design of the Adam brothers, the greatest architects of Georgian times.

The young laird, Patrick Home, planned it to welcome his fiancée, the Prussian noblewoman Sophie de Brandt – but she jilted him. He consoled himself by amassing a fine collection of Chippendale furniture and paintings by contemporary Scottish artists including Raeburn and Wilkie.

It's not all high art, though. The house is set in 80 acres beside the River Tweed, and the grounds include an adventure playground.

Conundrum Farm

conundrumfarm.com
Loughend Farm, Berwick, TD15 1UT
01289 306092
Open spring to mid-Sep
If you have kids in tow, take them to Conundrum Farm, where they can feed lambs, Highland cattle, sheep, and a pond full of trout. You can also walk over the battlefield of Halidon Hill, a home win for England in 1333.

▶ Bishop Auckland

At first sight, Bishop Auckland is a dour place. But hang in there. Auckland Castle, home of Bishops of Durham since the 12th century, is the town's redeeming feature. Auckland Castle has been the main residence of the Bishop of Durham since Durham Castle was given to the University in 1832. Just off the market place is the toy-like 18th-century gatehouse – now the home of the castle's billionaire owner – but it is the castle and its lovely green parkland that are the main attractions.

TAKE IN SOME HISTORY

Auckland Castle

aucklandcastle.org
Open Wed–Mon 10.30–4;
winter park only
DL14 7NR | 01388 743750

Amazingly, fewer than 1,000 people a year on average visited Auckland Castle in the first decade of the 21st century. That is changing, thanks to a grand project which aims to pull in 100,000 a year. Local economic benefits should be huge.

The principal county residence of the Prince Bishops since the 12th century, Auckland Castle stands on a promontory overlooking the River Wear. The castle has been added to and adapted over the centuries. In their heyday, the Prince Bishops were stinking rich, and able to embellish their seat with fine furniture, superb

▼ Chapel of St Peter, Auckland Castle

architecture and great works of art, including works by Zurbaran that will open your eyes to an utterly different kind of religious painting. They amassed one of the most amazing collections of religious paintings in the world.

By the 21st century, however, the Church of England was finding it hard to pay for the upkeep of the castle, and proposed to start selling off its treasures. Enter financier Jonathan Ruffer. From the northeast, and a devout Anglican, Ruffer offered to put together a rescue package, starting with £25 million of his own money. Almost by accident, he ended up owning Auckland Castle and its collections, and now lives in the pretty gatehouse. Ruffer's grand plan is to create a unique, permanent exhibition called *5000 Years of Faith* which will celebrate every aspect of belief in Britain from the mysteries of Stonehenge up to the complexities of a multi-faith, 21st-century society. Check the Auckland Castle website for the latest developments.

In the meantime, enter the Castle through the Gothic screen that frames the chapel, built in the 12th century as the Great Hall and converted by Bishop Cosin after 1661. Inside, it's dark but sumptuous, and everything – especially the ceiling – is decorated with his badge, a diagonal cross on a diamond. Much of the rest of the castle has a prosperous

▼ Auckland Castle gatehouse

18th-century look, especially the State Rooms, including the Throne Room – proof that Durham's bishops still acted like royalty even as late as this. St Peter's Chapel houses many of the treasures of past Bishops. After all this Anglican pomp, it is pleasant to wander in the 800-acre park, with Bishop Trevor's pretty Gothic deer shelter, mature, majestic trees and spreading lawns.

GO BACK IN TIME
Binchester Roman Fort
durham.gov.uk
1.5 miles north of Bishop Auckland
01388 663089 | Open Easter–Jun & Sept daily 11–5, Jul–Aug 10–5
A 20-minute walk along the banks of the Wear from Bishop Auckland brings you to Binchester, the site of the largest Roman fort in County Durham. For centuries, locals used Roman buildings as handy sources of ready-made building materials. Binchester is no exception. You can see bits of its masonry in the seventh-century Church of St John in Bishop Auckland, where the illiterate Saxon builders built a stone bearing a Roman inscription reading LEG VI (the Sixth Legion) into the north wall – upside down. To them, it was just another chunk of pre-cut masonry. More masonry from the fort was used in the church at Escomb, three miles northwest of Bishop Auckland.

Binchester was garrisoned by Iberian cavalry and Belgic foot-soldiers; they must have enjoyed relaxing in the bathhouse, with its sophisticated underfloor heating, bits of which you can still see.

PLAY A ROUND
Bishop Auckland Golf Club
www.bagc.co.uk
High Plains, Durham Road, DL14 8DL | 01388 661618
Open daily
A parkland course with well-established trees, offering a challenging round. A small ravine adds interest to several holes including the short 7th, from a raised tee to a green surrounded by a stream, gorse and bushes. Pleasant views over the Wear Valley and over the residence of the Bishop of Durham. It has the distinction of having five par 5 holes and five par 3s.

EAT AND DRINK
Ship Inn
shipinnmiddlestone.co.uk
Low Road, Middlestone, DL14 8AB
01388 810904
A bustling local that knows how to generate community loyalty, not least through an ever-changing real ale portfolio. The lounge is all nautical memorabilia (despite being 23 miles from the sea) and walls are festooned with old beer pump clips. Lying 550ft above sea level, the rooftop patio offers excellent views over the Tees Valley and Cleveland Hills. Home-cooked food is served in the bar, using locally reared beef, pork and lamb, with

dishes such as corned beef pie and award-winning pork and leek sausages. Look out for regular themed evenings.

▶ PLACES NEARBY
Witton Castle Lakes
wittoncastlelakes.com
Witton le Wear, DL14 0DE
01388 488691

You'll find some of the northeast's finest fly fishing and coarse fishing on 20 acres of water set amid the parkland of Witton Castle Country Park. If you're a fly fishing purist, three lakes are reserved for your rod and tackle. Devotees of worm fishing have a coarse-fishing lake all to themselves.

▶ Blanchland

Blanchland's stone houses, set in a deep, lush wooded valley among high moorland, glow golden in the sunlight. Most of these cottages were built in the mid-18th century for Lord Crewe, Bishop of Durham, to house the families of workers in his local lead mines. After the mines closed, Blanchland remained in the hands of the Crewe Trustees.

In the centre of the village is the L-shaped square, which may have been the courtyard of the 12th-century Premonstratensian abbey which once stood here. It is reached from the north through the 15th-century gatehouse, complete with battlements, and from the south over the bridge.

Part of the church ruins were well restored in the 18th century – you enter under the tower into the north transept, and turn under the crossing for the rest of the building, tall and light. Notice, on the floor, the grave slabs of the abbots, carved

▼ Blanchland, Northumberland

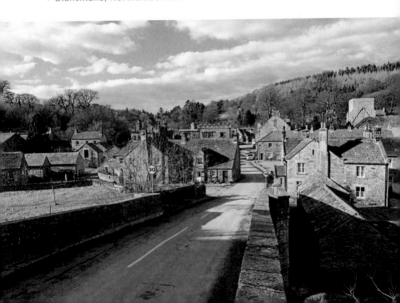

with their mitres, and of foresters with horns. The picturesque Lord Crewe Arms next door was the Abbot's Lodge. Portraits of Lord Crewe, his wife Dorothy Forster and his niece, the other Dorothy, can be found here.

EAT AND DRINK
The White Monk Tearooms
The Old School, Blanchland, DH8 9ST | 01434 675044
Located in the heart of this lovely village, the White Monk Tearooms occupy the former village school. There are two loft rooms and a garden. Home-made scones with cream and jam, as well as delicious cakes (try the coffee-and-walnut) are on the menu. Simple lunches are served.

▶ Brancepeth

You can't go into Brancepeth's castle, which is now a private home. That's no big loss – it may look quaint, with its distinctive 'chess piece' turrets, but it's a 19th-century confection, not the real thing. Although there was a medieval stronghold here, the existing castle was rebuilt from scratch in 1837 by the Edinburgh architect John Patterson for Matthew Patterton, son of a wealthy mine owner. That said, Brancepeth is a pleasant place to wander around, with its pretty Georgian cottages.

SEE A LOCAL CHURCH
Church of St Brandon
stbrandon.co.uk
Brancepeth, DH7 8DZ
0191 3780289
The 12th-century church of St Brandon stands apart, in its own wooded grounds. Although badly damaged by fire in 1998, the building was meticulously restored and contains still more tombs and effigies of the ubiquitous Neville family, who once owned the castle.

▶ Brinkburn Priory

english-heritage.org.uk
NE65 8AF | 01665 570628 | Open Apr–Sep Thu–Mon 11–4
Thanks to a mid-19th century restoration, there's enough left of beautiful Brinkburn Priory to give you some idea of what it looked like when Augustinian canons lived here, between its foundation in 1130 and the dissolution of the monasteries in the mid-16th century. A cross-shaped building with a low central tower, it has perfect proportions and round-headed Norman windows. Very little remains of the rest of the buildings, but the setting among beech woods, within a narrow valley beside the River Coquet, makes it a very pleasant place for a stroll.

▶ **PLACES NEARBY**

The Anglers Arms

anglersarms.com

Weldon Bridge, Longframlington,

NE65 8AX | 01665 570271

Commanding the picturesque Weldon Bridge over the River Coquet since the 1760s, this part-battlemented former coaching inn on the road to Scotland is full of knick-knacks and curios, pictures and fishing memorabilia. The carefully tended half-acre of garden is perfect for alfresco dining and includes a children's play park. You can fish on the pub's own mile of River Coquet. Timothy Taylor Landlord and Theakston Best Bitter are among the real ales to accompany bar meals like Chinese duck salad or traditional cod and chips. An old Pullman railway carriage provides a different dining experience, with silver service as standard, and dishes such as tournedos Flodden, which is prime fillet stuffed with Applewood cheese wrapped in bacon and coated in garlic sauce; grilled fillet of salmon with new potatoes, baby corn, green beans, rocket and chilli sauce; and a tasty stir-fried vegetable sizzler.

Linden Tree

macdonald-hotels.co.uk/lindenhall

Linden Hall, Longhorsley, NE65 8XF

01670 500033

The friendly and informal Linden Tree pub stands within the 450-acres surrounding of Linden Hall, the impressive Georgian mansion that is now a popular golf and country club. A sunny patio makes for a relaxed setting for lunch in summer and the brasserie-style menu makes good use of Scottish beef and lamb. Dishes might include Thai green curry mussels; 21-day aged Scottish beefburger with tomato relish and beef dripping chips; leg of lamb steak; battered haddock with chips and mushy peas or steak-and-ale pie. Round off a long day with a nightcap in the golfers' lounge.

▶ **Cambo**

Cambo village, about 11 miles west of Morpeth (see page 161), is a bit of a throwback to the days when country squires ruled England. It's entirely surrounded by the 13,500 acres of the Wallington Estate (see page 223), for 200 years the domain of the Trevelyan family and now protected by the National Trust. The main attraction is their grand country mansion, but there are plenty of walks exploring the historic landscape, and a walled garden created by the Trevelyan family in the 1920s.

▸ Carrawburgh

Kick your imagination into high gear when you come to Brocolitia, as the Romans called Carrawburgh. The fort is reckoned to be a late addition to Hadrian's Wall. It was added around 130 AD, perhaps because security needed to be beefed up – unlike earlier forts, it did not project beyond the north side of the wall.

The fort is still mostly unexcavated, but nearby are the remains of the most complete Mithraic temple to be found in Britain. Mithraism, a mystery religion which set the forces of light against those of darkness, came from Persia. Members were initiated through a series of grades, and knew each other through secret handshakes, so it was an ancestor of present-day Freemasonry (and, perhaps, even of the early Christian faith). It was very popular with Roman soldiers of all ranks, and remained so even after Constantine I made Christianity the Empire's official religion.

GO BACK IN TIME

Coventina's Well
english-heritage.org.uk
Beside Carrawburgh fort, B6318,
3.75 miles west of Chollerford
0870 3331181
Open all reasonable times

Water deities never quite die. Coventina's Well, an ever-flowing spring beside the fort at Carrawburgh, was dedicated to a Celtic water goddess, whose name is forgotten. When the Romans arrived, they cheerfully renamed her Coventina and inducted her into their belief system. Bronze, brass, silver and even gold coins and other objects were thrown into the spring for luck. In 1876, more than 16,000 coins were recovered from the site. Some, minted to honour Emperor Antoninus Pius's foray beyond the wall in 155 AD, show a defeated Britannia with bowed head and lowered banner, the picture of submission.

Temple of Mithras
english-heritage.org.uk
Carrawburgh, B6318, 3.75 miles
west of Chollerford | 0870 3331181
Open all reasonable times

There's a fascinating whiff of blood and steel in the air here, where three third-century AD altars to Mithras, the enigmatic, bull-slaying deity worshipped by many Roman soldiers, were uncovered by a farmer in 1949.

The temple was built low and dark, representing the cave where Mithras slew the primeval bull and in doing so brought innumerable benefits to mankind. The uninitiated gathered in a small ante-room. Beyond this was the temple, with three altars (those you see today are replicas) and statues of Mithras's attendants, Cautes, with his torch raised to represent light, and Cautopates, torch down for darkness.

One of the altars shows Mithras as the Unconquered Sun. Above the altars there was once a sculpture of Mithras and the Bull – perhaps destroyed by Christians during the fourth century. The seven Mithraic grades of worshippers – Father, Courier of the Sun, Persian, Lion, Soldier, Bridegroom and Raven – would sit or kneel on low wattle and wooden platforms as the mysteries, which included a symbolic meal of bread and water, took place.

To see the original altars and a vivid, full-scale reconstruction of the temple, visit the Great North Museum in Newcastle upon Tyne (see page 171).

▼ The Roman Temple of Mithras

▶ Carvoran

You can still make out the outline of Magnis fort at Carvoran, but the only stones still visible are part of the northwest tower. Next to the fort, which was built before Hadrian's Wall, to guard a strategic road junction, is the Roman Army Museum, with finds from Magnis and other sites along the wall, as well as a model of the fort. The museum brings to life the daily existence of the soldier on the Wall, with full-size figures decked out in authentic uniform and weapons. Find out how much they were paid, what they ate, how they trained – and how they overcame the boredom of life at the edge of the Empire by playing dice, wining, dining and wenching.

East of Carvoran, the wall runs over the Nine Nicks of Thirlwall, where the original nine gaps in the Whin Sill have been reduced over time to five by intense quarrying. Turret 45A was probably a signal post in use while the wall was being constructed – its stones are not keyed into the structure.

Just to the west, there is a fine stretch of the vallum, and further beyond this lies 14th-century Thirlwall Castle, beside Tipalt Burn, and built, as usual, to defend against the marauding Scots. The castle's last inhabitants left in the 18th century, but the ruin is reputedly haunted by a ghostly dwarf who guards an ancestral gold table.

▶ Cherryburn

Thomas Bewick Birthplace Museum

nationaltrust.org.uk

Station Bank, Mickley, Stocksfield, NE43 7DD | 01661 843276

Open Jul–Aug daily, mid-Feb to Jun, Sep–Oct Thu–Tue

Naturalist Thomas Bewick was a countryman born and bred. You can almost feel his deep love of the birds and beasts of his native countryside in the superb illustrations and tailpieces that Britain's greatest wood-engraver – born at Cherryburn in 1753 – created for his books, especially *A General History of Quadrupeds* and *The History of British Birds*. The farmhouse, home to later Bewicks, now houses an exhibition on Thomas. You can see the cottage where he was born, and there are always farm animals around. On demonstration days prints are made in the adjoining barn.

▶ Chesters

Where Hadrian's Wall crossed the North Tyne, the Romans built a wooden bridge guarded by Cilurnum Fort, now called Chesters. Cavalry were stationed here – remains of stables have never been positively identified, but you can see the barrack block. The officers had larger rooms at the river end of the block. In the centre of the fort, the commanding officer sat on a raised platform to dispense justice. The rooms behind were used by clerks and standard bearers, who also looked after the accounts and pay. A stone staircase leads into the strongroom, which still had its iron-sheathed oak door when excavated in the early 19th century. The well-preserved east gate and the west gate have short sections of the wall attached.

Near the river was the garrison's bathhouse. You can still trace its main chambers – the changing room, with niches probably for clothes, the hot dry room, like a sauna, hot steam rooms, hot and cold baths, as well as the latrine, draining to the river. Furnaces and underfloor heating must have made this a popular place in the camp.

Nearby are remains of the bridge, but they are better preserved over on the opposite bank, reached by a footpath from the bridge at Chollerford. In the river you can see an original pier, which carried the wooden pedestrians' bridge, as well as a later stone bridge built in about AD 206 to carry vehicles; two of its piers can still be seen when the river is low.

GO BACK IN TIME
Chesters Roman Fort and Museum
english-heritage.org.uk
Chollerford, NE46 4EU
01434 681379
John Clayton (1792–1890) managed a successful law practice, but his passion was archaeology. To stop local people destroying Hadrian's Wall by hauling away its stones for building material, he bought long stretches of the wall and several of its forts, including Housesteads. He owned the Chesters Estate and fort, and made accessible many of the region's Roman remains. Among the treasures here are statues of a reclining river god, and the (now headless) goddess Juno Dolichena.

▶ **PLACES NEARBY**
Chesters Bridge Abutment
english-heritage.org.uk
On A6079 0.25 miles south of Low Brunton | 0870 3331181
Open any reasonable time
If you're really keen on the Romans and have a very powerful imagination you may like to stop briefly at Chesters Bridge. Here the few remaining stones of a bridge which carried the Roman military road across the North Tyne are testament to the enduring skills of the Empire's military engineers. Built in AD 160 on the site of an earlier bridge which was part of Hadrian's Wall, the second bridge was demolished in AD 670 to provide stones for the construction of St Wilfred's Church in Hexham.

▶ Cheviot Hills

Less than an hour from Newcastle (see page 166), in the north of the Northumberland National Park, the Cheviot Hills mark the border with Scotland. This wild, romantic landscape, with its distinctive rounded hills, formed when lava flowed over the area, is criss-crossed with bridleways which allow horse riders, cyclists and walkers to follow the routes of ancient cattle drovers. The dramatic waterfall of Linhope Spout is worth a visit, or you can ascend to the highest point in Northumberland, Cheviot summit. At 2,674ft (816m), this will give you views of the Lake District on a clear day – or almost as far as Edinburgh.

The Hills cover an area of almost 250 square miles. At the Cheviots' northern edge, you can trace the Iron Age hill-fort at Yeavering Bell (see page 156), one of the best-preserved in the country. Avian moorland residents include red grouse and ravens, and in the summer, curlews and wheatears.

▶ Chillingham

Chillingham village is home to some remarkable survivors. The Earls of Tankerville, related by marriage to the powerful Grey family, built the Tudor village, and its church, where the 15th-century tomb of Sir Ralph Grey has some rare figures of saints that escaped the purges of the Reformation. Chillingham Castle, dynastic seat of the Greys, dates from the 13th and 14th centuries and narrowly escaped being demolished in the second half of the 20th century. And the white cattle which roam wild in the castle's great park are descendants of a herd that has lived here since 1220.

TAKE IN SOME HISTORY
Chillingham Castle
chillingham-castle.com
NE66 5NJ | 01668 215359
Open Apr–Oct Sun–Fri 12–5;
other times by prior arrangement
The 'most haunted castle in England' (check out the 'Ghosts' section of their website for a rundown of their various spectral inhabitants) looks pretty much as it did in the mid-14th century, when Sir Thomas Grey was permitted to crenellate its battlements and add a moat to its defences.

The Greys – one of the great noble families of northern England – seized it in 1245 and held it until the 20th century. In the intervening years, they hosted English monarchs including Henry II and Edward I, played their part in keeping the Scots at bay, and threw the occasional prisoner into the dank and sinister oubliette that you can see today.

Georgian additions were made in 1753, and new state

▲ Chillingham Castle

apartments were built in the East Range after a fire in 1803. The Greys fell on hard times in the 1930s and were forced to sell the castle's contents in 1933. It stood empty until World War II, when it was a billet for soldiers and was again damaged by fire.

Dry rot ravaged its timbers and the castle seemed doomed for demolition until a relation of the Greys, Sir Humphrey Wakefield, bought the castle in the 1980s and began its triumphant restoration. Among other things revealed was a bundle of Tudor documents hidden in a blocked-up fireplace, shedding new light on the secret history of the Greys.

You can now see the splendid Great Hall, with banners and armour, as well as antique furniture, tapestries and restored plaster- and metalwork, and a spine-chilling torture chamber.

Grass was brought up to the castle walls in the 18th century, and the moat is now a huge tunnel under the south lawn. A formal garden was built on the site of the medieval tournament ground, with elaborate plantings that survived until the 1930s. Rescued from near-desolation, it forms a replica of an Elizabethan garden that befits one of the north's most important castles.

Older even than the castle, the 1,000-acre park at Chillingham has been walled since 1220. Uncultivated for more than 650 years, it is still medieval in atmosphere.

MEET THE CATTLE – FROM A SAFE DISTANCE

Chillingham Wild Cattle Park

chillinghamwildcattle.com
NE66 5NP | 01668 215250
Open Easter–Oct Mon–Fri and Sun am; tours at 10, 11, 12, 2, 3, 4
Bring binoculars to be sure of a good look at Chillingham's unique herd of wild white cattle, which have roamed this vast domain for around 700 years. They have white coats; their muzzles and horn tips are black. Only the dominant bull sires calves; when eventually defeated by one of the younger males he is banished to a distant part of the park.

▶ Corbridge

Corbridge was the first big fort on Rome's northern frontier. It was built around AD 90 – more than 30 years before work started on Hadrian's Wall – to guard the Roman roads which crossed the Tyne here.

The town, once Northumbria's capital, suffered from invasion by Danes and Scots. Not surprisingly, there are two defensive pele towers in Corbridge. One, at the end of Main Street, dates from the 13th century. It was converted into a house in about 1675.

The other, the Vicar's Pele, is made from Roman stones and was probably put up in the 14th century. Sitting in the churchyard and little altered over the centuries, it remains one of the best peles to be found in the north.

St Andrew's Church, too, uses some Roman stones – between the tower and the nave is a whole Roman archway. The tower's lower parts were probably built before AD 786, and there is more Saxon work in the walls, as well as a Norman doorway and a 13th-century chancel. Lots of stone cross slabs are built into the walls and floors, and part of the chancel floor is a medieval altar stone.

GO BACK IN TIME

Corbridge Roman Site and Museum

english-heritage.org.uk
NE45 5NT | 01434 632349
Open Apr–Sep daily 10–5.30, Oct daily 10–4, Nov–Mar, Sat–Sun 10–4
The Romans built and rebuilt their fort at Corstopitum over several centuries, and the fort you're looking at now is the fourth version. It was built about AD 140 as a jumping-off point for the pacification of Caledonia. That turned out not to be one of the Empire's brighter ideas, but Corstopitum continued to be an important military base long after the Romans finally gave up on conquering the north at the end of the second century. It changed from a purely military base into a thriving mercantile

▲ Roman remains at Corbridge

community – the most northerly in the Roman Empire. Much of that settlement is still buried, though its stones are found in many Corbridge and Hexham buildings.

The big granaries, with their stone-slabbed floors and walls, give you an idea of the immense logistics of feeding the legions which manned the wall, and the inscriptions and small personal objects – combs, buttons and bronze pins – remind you that the Roman soldiers and the civilians who lived here were people just like us.

The square courtyard to the north of the main street (part of Stanegate) was never finished and no one is quite sure what it was. Opposite are the military compounds, where you can trace the workshops and officers' houses before descending into the former strongroom to see where soldiers and locals worshipped both Roman and local gods.

Pride of place in the museum at Corstopitum goes to the Corbridge Lion. A finely carved, spirited beast with a bushy mane, it is depicted attacking a stag. It is thought that the lion may have started its life on a tomb, but was later moved to ornament the great fountain in the town. You can still see the fountain's large stone tank, which was fed by an aqueduct, between the granaries and the courtyard building. The tank's edges were worn down over centuries as metal blades were sharpened against the stone.

EAT AND DRINK

The Angel of Corbridge

theangelofcorbridge.com
Main Street, NE45 5LA
01434 632119

In the scenic Tyne Valley and handy for Hadrian's Wall, this reinvigorated old coaching inn has made a success in each area of its operation; there's a striking restaurant offering a solid English menu drawing on the producers of Northumbria (including their own lambs) and a traditional locals' bar, where beers from the local Wylam brewery are in evidence; the Angel also has a Martini bar. Typical dishes might include a main course of pan-seared lamb's liver with bacon, champ (mashed potato) and onion gravy. Tempting sandwiches (sliced local ham with home-made pease pudding) and a range of tasty puddings complete the deal.

▸ PLACES NEARBY

Aydon Castle

english-heritage.org.uk
Corbridge, NE45 5RT
01434 632450

Set in a curve of the Cor Burn just north of Corbridge, Aydon Castle is really a very early fortified manor house, built at the end of the 13th century and given its battlements in 1305. Where it was most vulnerable, to the north side, it has an irregular outer bailey, and behind that a small, open courtyard, with the living quarters to one side. Unusually for its early date, there was no keep. Instead there was a hall and a solar with a fine fireplace and some beautifully detailed windows – don't miss the bearded face staring out from above the northern one. Look out, too, for the garderobes – medieval toilets – to be found at the southeast corner of the south range.

Within the walls there was an orchard, so conditions must have been comfortable for this unsettled border country. There were times of excitement. Being captured by the Scots in 1315, and by English rebels in 1317. In the less fraught 17th century it became a farmhouse – which helped to preserve its main features.

Dilston Physic Garden

dilstonphysicgarden.com
Dilston Mill House, Dilston, Corbridge. NE45 5QZ
07879 533875
Open mid-Apr–mid-Oct Wed and Sat 11–4

Discover how age-old herbal remedies still have relevance today, from herbs that can help sleeplessness and anxiety to powerful derivatives that can battle cancer, at this contemporary physic garden.

▶ Cragside

nationaltrust.org.uk

NE65 7PX | 01669 620333 | Opening times vary – check ahead

It may look like a peaceful country mansion, built in the golden years of the British Empire. But Cragside is the product of blood and steel. It was built as a weekend retreat for the first Lord Armstrong, founder of the company which became Vickers Armstrong, the great armourer of the Empire.

William Armstrong, born in Newcastle in 1810, began building hydraulic cranes and lifts at his works at Elswick on the Tyne and went on to patent the breech-loading artillery which caused such huge loss of life in conflicts such as the American Civil War. In retirement he continued experimenting and inventing, giving Cragside not only lamps made by his friend, electrical pioneer Swan, but also hydraulic lifts and kitchen spit, telephones between the rooms and electric gongs. Cragside was also the first house in the world to be lit entirely by electric light.

The drawing room has a double-storey chimney-piece of Italian marble, and the dining room, in Old English style, is one of the finest Victorian domestic rooms in the country. In contrast to all this 'Englishness' is the fashionable print-filled Japanese Room.

▶ Craster

A picturesque village that seems almost to tumble into the sea, Craster became a haven for fishing in the 17th century, although its harbour, today used by pleasure craft and traditional cobles, was given its present form in the 1900s. It was built by the local landowners – the Crasters – in memory of Captain Craster, killed on an expedition to Tibet in 1904. The harbour exported whinstone (used for roads and kerbs), and you can still see the concrete arch that once supported the chipping silos. The quarry is now the National Trust car park, a good starting point for walks to Dunstanburgh Castle.

Howick Gardens, a mile south of Craster, surround a late 18th-century house (not open), which was the home of the second Earl Grey. As Prime Minister, he steered through the 1832 Parliamentary Reform Bill – and gave his name to Earl Grey tea; sample it in the Earl Grey Tea House. There is fine woodland with a network of paths and glades where rare plants and shrubs thrive – don't miss the rhododendron season – as well as lawns, a terrace with urns, and alpine beds.

EAT AND DRINK

The Jolly Fisherman
thejollyfishermancraster.co.uk
Haven Hill, NE66 3TR
01665 576461

Now splendidly refurbished, the charm of this historic stone-flagged, low-beamed pub remains undimmed. When it's cold, relax by an open fire; at any time admire impressive Dunstanburgh Castle from the delightful beer garden.

When the pub opened in 1847, Craster was a thriving fishing village; now only a few East Coast cobles leave harbour, mostly for the herring that, once smoked, become the famous kippers. House specialities are fresh fish stew; whole line-caught sea bass; breast of chicken in Serrano ham; and slow-roasted pepper with butternut squash and celeriac risotto. At the bar you'll find Black Sheep and Mordue's Workie Ticket bitter.

◀ Craster Harbour

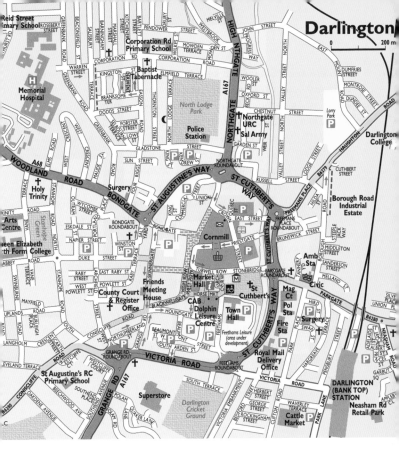

▶ Darlington

Darlington's big claim to fame is that it was at one end of the world's first passenger steam railway. The Stockton and Darlington line opened in 1825, with carriages drawn by locomotives designed by George Stephenson at giddying speeds of more than 20mph. You can see the very first of these revolutionary engines, *Locomotion No. 1*, at the Head of Steam Museum, housed in the former North Road Station. On its maiden trip it hauled a 90-ton train, with Stephenson driving. There are more railway relics at the national Railway Museum's 'Locomotion' museum at nearby Shildon (see overleaf).

Fine 18th- and 19th-century houses reflect Darlington's prosperous past, and there are some most impressive public and commercial buildings, too. Engineering works, attracted by the railways, undertook projects throughout the world, including the renowned Sydney Harbour Bridge. It's not all metal bashing, though. St Cuthbert's, the 12th-century parish church, is one of the best of its date in the north, and has hardly been changed since it was founded about 1192. Its tall spire makes a powerful statement.

▶ Locomotion: the National Railway Museum

www.nrm.org.uk/locomotion

DL4 1PQ | 01388 777999 | Open Apr–Oct daily 10–5, Nov–Mar Wed–Sun 10–4 (limited opening Mon–Tue)

Discover an unsung hero of the dawn of steam, ride on a vintage train and marvel at how far we've come since the days when they thought that travelling at more than 30mph would make your brain explode. Opened in 2004, Locomotion is one of the greatest changing railway collections of the northeast, with interactive displays, free holiday activities for kids and star attractions including many vehicles from the National Railway Museum collection. Pride of place goes to Timothy Hackworth's pioneering locomotive *Sans Pareil*, built in 1829 to compete in the Rainhill Trials. Hackworth (1786–1850) also built *Puffing Billy* for William Hedley, ran Stephenson's Newcastle Works, and became the first superintendent of the Stockton & Darlington Railway. Another highlight is the 1930s art deco engine, *Duchess of Hamilton*, saved from the scrapyard by Billy Butlin.

▼ Replica Rocket steam locomotive and train

VISIT THE MUSEUMS

Head of Steam - Darlington Railway Museum

head-of-steam.co.uk
North Road Station, DL3 6ST
01325 734125 | Open Apr–Sep
Tue–Sun 10–4, Oct–Mar Wed–Sun
11–3.30

Housed in the carefully restored North Road Station, this museum's prize exhibit is *Locomotion No 1*, which pulled the first passenger train on the Stockton–Darlington railway and was built by Robert Stephenson and Co in 1825. Several other steam locomotives are also shown, together with interactive displays, models and other exhibits relating to the Stockton and Darlington Railway and the North Eastern Railway companies. Special event days and temporary exhibitions are also offered.

Friends Meeting House

6 Skinnergate, DL3 7NB

The Quakers – or the Religious Society of Friends, to give them their proper name – built a Meeting House in Darlington in 1678 (when they bought the plot for £35), but the present structure was not completed until about 1846.

Quakers played a large role in establishing Darlington as a major industrial force from the 18th century onwards. Edward Pease, a devout local Quaker known as the 'Father of the Railways', is buried under a simple headstone in the high-walled burial ground behind the Meeting House, which contains trees planted by him.

The Meeting House had two large chambers – one for men and one for women – separated by large sliding shutters that were raised into the roof space by a winding mechanism that still survives. Elegant wooden steps lead up to a gated minister's stand, with a sounding board over the stand which was added later. Great north and south windows under brick arches have delicate glazing bars and margin lights, and the Skinnergate front boasts a grand stone porch with Doric columns.

SEE A LOCAL CHURCH

Church of St Cuthbert

Market Place, Church Row, DL1 5QG

With its cathedral-like proportions and presence, St Cuthbert's epitomises late 12th- to early 13th-century early English style, with extensive use of wall arcading to frame both internal and external windows. In the 14th century the aisle roofs were raised and new windows inserted, and at this time the belfry and impressive octagonal spire were added over the central tower.

The church – also known as the Lady of the North – is richly decorated at the east end but is quite austere, though well proportioned. The masonry is dressed local sandstone, and most of the main roof has medieval oak supports.

Outstanding features include 15th-century chancel stalls with misericords, a 14th-century font with a 17th-century 'Bishop Cosin' canopy, and a fine collection of 19th-century stained glass.

EAT AND DRINK

Rockliffe Hall ⊚⊚⊚
rockliffehall.com
Rockliffe Park, Hurworth-on-Tees, DL2 2DU | 01325 729999
Rockliffe stands in 375 acres by the River Tees, outside the village of Hurworth, near Darlington and offers the full luxury pack, from nuptials to massages to golf, with an elegantly refurbished, ornate dining room in the old orangery, all gilt pillars against an ivory-white background, the walls crowded with little prints and mirrors.

Headlam Hall ⊚⊚
headlamhall.co.uk
Headlam, Gainford, DL2 3HA
01325 730238
With its partly creeper-covered facade and elegant period detailing within, Headlam Hall is a rather grand old girl. The main building dates from the 17th century but has moved with the times: there's a swish spa to deliver 21st-century levels of pampering, and a smart restaurant serving up some sparky modern food. The eating takes place in a series of rooms: the Panelled Room is as described, the Orangery a warm and luminous space with well-chosen neutral colours and well-spaced, linen-clad tables. The suppliers of what is to come are listed on the menu – good quality local stuff – and much is produced on their own farm, or comes from the hotel's own garden.

The County
thecountyaycliffevillage.com
13 The Green, Aycliffe Village, DL5 6LX | 01325 312273
The smart restaurant and terrace is a lovely place to eat, as is the homely bar where you can sup a pint of Black Sheep or the County's own brew. With superb local produce on the doorstep, expect the likes of warm caramelised red onion and Mordon Farm feta cheese tartlet, followed by roast pheasant, roast garlic and thyme mashed potato, sautéed cep mushrooms and jus, with spiced treacle sponge with custard to finish.

▶ PLACES NEARBY
Church of St Mary, Gainford
Low Green, Gainford, DL2 3EN
Though erected in the 13th century, the present structure is believed to occupy a Saxon site. It is recorded that Edwine, a Northumbrian chief who became a monk, died in AD 801 and was buried in the monastery of Gainford 'in the church'.

St Mary's consists of a nave, aisles, chancels and a square west tower that is open to the nave and supported by pointed arches, similar to the ones, resting on cylindrical pillars, that separate the nave and aisles. This graceful arch is repeated in the opening to the chancel and in the three stained-glass lancet windows at the east end.

During much-needed repairs in 1864, a number of pre-Conquest sculptured stones were found and placed under cover. Several fragments of fine Saxon crosses are also preserved, some of which are beautifully carved. Among the collection of ancient stones there is a Roman altar. Various grave covers, and other stones of a later date, are built into the walls of the north porch. Look

also for the 13th-century font with a tall wooden Jacobean-style cover, and three medieval brasses in the chancel.

George Hotel
george-ontees.co.uk
Piercebridge-on-Tees, DL2 3SW
01325 374576
The George, where the original 'Grandfather's Clock' is located, is a 16th-century coaching inn on the banks of the Tees. It has comfortable lounges and bars, with roaring fires in the winter and a great garden for the warmer weather. You can eat in the bar or dine in the riverside restaurant, where well-cooked local food is available.

▶ Derwent Reservoir

This artificial lake is one of the biggest bodies of water in England. Around 3.5 miles long and almost 100ft deep at its deepest point, it's a favourite with dinghy sailors and windsurfers.

The dam to create the reservoir was begun in 1902 and the reservoir started to be filled in 1914, so 2014 might see some watery celebrations. Derwent was also used for practice flights by 617 'Dambusters' Squadron during the run up to the bombings of German hydroelectric dams in 1943.

The dam itself has some pretty cool castellated towers, which make it look a lot older than it is.

▶ PLACES NEARBY
Pow Hill Country Park
thisisdurham.com
Edmundbyers, DH8 9ND
03000 264589
Bring your wellies to properly explore and enjoy this damp area of marsh and bogland on the verge of the Derwent Reservoir. You'll find

it is home to bog ashphodel, bog bean and other bog plants, and to adders, slow-worms and common lizards.

▶ Dunstanburgh Castle

english-heritage.org.uk

Craster, NE66 3TT | 01665 576231

Open Jan–16 Feb and 22 Feb–Mar Sat–Sun 10–4, 17–21 Feb daily 10–4
(times may change, check ahead)

It'll take you 20–30 minutes to trek all the way out to this
castle from the nearby village of Craster (see page 98), but
that trek just adds to the feeling of timelessness here. Low
walls hug the rocky coastline, and only the cries of gulls and
the roar of the waves disturb the silence. Remote, isolated,
lonely and ruined, Dunstanburgh is one of the most dramatic
and atmospheric castles in the north of England.

Dunstanburgh, unlike many other castles, was built from
scratch by Thomas, Earl of Lancaster, a powerful member of

the aristocracy in the reign of Edward II. Lancaster and Edward were constantly at loggerheads, especially over the favouritism shown by Edward to certain members of his court – and, in particular, to Piers Gaveston. Lancaster ordered Gaveston's brutal murder. In the turmoil that followed, the Scots seized the opportunity to begin a series of raids in northern England, and Lancaster built Dunstanburgh ostensibly as a stronghold against a Scottish invasion but really as a retreat for from the wrath of the King.

The site occupied by Dunstanburgh is large, and there would have been plenty of space for local people and their livestock to take refuge from Scottish raids within the great, thick walls that swept around the site. The sea and steep cliffs provided further

▼ Dunstanburgh Castle

protection from attack on two sides. Lancaster's impressive gatehouse was built between 1313 and 1325, and even in its ruinous state it exudes a sense of power and impregnability. It had three floors, and all the building materials appear to have been of the finest quality.

Dunstanburgh is unusual in that it acquired a second gatehouse about 60 years later. By this time, the castle had come into the hands of another duke of Lancaster, the powerful John of Gaunt, third son of Edward III. Active in negotiations with the Scots, he doubtless saw the need for his castle to be strengthened, and as a man of influence, he travelled with a sizeable entourage, all of whom would have required accommodation. Dunstanburgh was besieged by Yorkist armies during the Wars of the Roses, but by the 17th century it had become redundant and events since then have passed it by.

PLAY A ROUND
**Dunstanburgh Castle
Golf Club**
dunstanburgh.com
NE66 3XQ | 01665 576562
Contact club for details
Rolling links designed by James Braid, adjacent to the beautiful Embleton Bay. Dunstansburgh Castle is at one end of the course and a National Trust lake and bird sanctuary at the other. Superb views along the way.

▼ View of Dunstanburgh Castle

10 ancient strongholds

▶ **Alnwick Castle**
Seat of the Percy clan since 1309, Alnwick Castle stands amid breathtaking gardens.

▶ **Auckland Castle**
Stroll through the dinky gatehouse and through the gardens to enter this opulent ecclesiastical residence and you'll be forcibly reminded of the power and pomp of the Anglican church at its zenith.

▶ **Bamburgh**
Let your imagination run wild in this great medieval keep. Gazing out over the North Sea, Bamburgh is pure 'dungeons and dragons' territory.

▶ **Chillingham Castle**
Begun in the 13th century, Chillingham fell into ruin in the 1940s but has been splendidly restored. Wild white cattle roam in its park.

▶ **Dunstanburgh Castle**
Northumberland's largest and most spectacularly sited castle is – reputedly – haunted by a lovelorn knight.

▶ **Durham Castle**
Durham's impressive Norman stronghold is the heart of the city's university quarter.

▶ **Housesteads**
If you have time to see just one of the forts along Hadrian's Wall, it has to be Housesteads. Spectacularly located and well preserved, it's a reminder of the power of ancient Rome.

▶ **Warkworth Castle**
Ancient, awesome Warkworth, standing on a loop of River Coquet, has been knocked about a bit over centuries. It was given a facelift by its owner, the Duke of Northumberland, in the 19th century.

▶ **Lindisfarne Castle**
The little stronghold built to guard Holy Island's harbour in Henry VIII's reign was turned into a charming home in the early 20th century.

▶ **Preston Tower**
This tough little 14th century pele tower – once the home of a hardbitten family of borderers, the Harbottles – makes an interesting contrast to the region's bigger, grander castles.

▼ The gardens of Chillingham Castle

▷ Durham

If the prince-bishops of Durham had set out to make their cathedral the greatest tourist attraction in the northeast, they couldn't have done better. In a sense, that's exactly what they did set out to do. For some five centuries, until the Protestant Reformation, pilgrimages were big business. The lovely bones of St Cuthbert and the skull of St Oswald attracted the halt (disabled), the lame and the old to Durham in hopes of miraculous healing.

The cathedral and the castle were what Durham was all about, from the early Middle Ages onwards. But even without these landmarks the city of Durham would be spectacular. From whichever side you approach, Durham is a magnificent sight. Here, the Wear does a huge loop, in a deep ravine, coming almost to meet itself. From this superb defensive position the city grew over the centuries, down the hill and then outwards.

This is a city that needs to be explored the hard way – on foot. Gently climbing from the market place up Saddler Street you'll see elegant Georgian houses. Owengate leads into Palace Green, dominated by the cathedral's north side and surrounded by fine university buildings, with the castle to your right.

The castle, begun in 1072, now houses University College, and its 18th-century gatehouse has a Norman core, as does the massive keep, which was rebuilt in 1840. Bishop Cosin's ornate Black Staircase leads from the medieval Great Hall to the 18th-century State Rooms and the College Chapel. The real highlight of a tour around the castle, though, is a visit to the splendid Norman gallery and the Norman chapel.

College buildings cluster in the streets around the castle and cathedral, though the university has expanded into several modern buildings to the south of the city. Elsewhere, the city becomes more work-a-day, though the churches – particularly St Oswald's, near the elegant Kingsgate Bridge – are worth exploring. The Heritage Centre at St Mary-le-Bow, North Bailey, vividly tells the history of Durham, while Durham University Oriental Museum, off Elvet Hill Road, is full of wonderful Chinese porcelain and jade. The Durham Light Infantry Museum reflects the military past of the regiment and the city, and houses the art gallery.

A good way to see the best the city has to offer is to take this 2.5-mile walk. Start in the Market Place, and from the statue of Lord Londonderry on his horse, walk along Silver Street to descend to Framwellgate Bridge, built by Bishop Flambard in

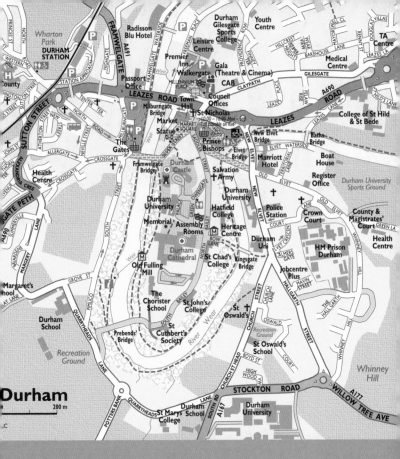

Durham

200 m

about 1128 and rebuilt after a flood in 1401. Immediately at the end of the bridge turn left down the steps by the Coach and Eight pub to reach the riverbank, going ahead with the castle and cathedral across the river. Now walk behind the riverside buildings to Prebends' Bridge, begun in 1772 with funds from the Canons (Prebendaries) of the cathedral. Do not cross the bridge, but continue alongside the river. On the opposite bank you will see the charming Grecian-style Count's House.

For centuries – until 1836 – the Bishops of Durham were a law unto themselves. William the Conqueror created them Earls – later they became the Prince-Bishops – to protect this remote part of his kingdom. Like some German bishops, but uniquely in Britain, they held absolute power in their very extensive lands. Bishops had their own parliament, they made the law, they minted coins and controlled the army. It was they, not the king, who granted permission for the nobles of the north to build castles, and even the king had to ask permission to enter the Palatinate. The defence of the bishopric is still symbolised by the ceremonial presentation of a fearsome knife – the 13th-century Conyers Falchion, now in the Cathedral

Treasury – as a new Bishop enters the diocese for the first time at Croft on the Tees.

It was in Durham that St Cuthbert's bones finally ended their century-long journey from Holy Island (see page 143) in 995, but the present cathedral building, with its three massive towers, dates from 1093. Enter by the north door with its replica sanctuary ring (a 12th-century door-knocker). The original is in the Treasury.

The main effect of the interior is of enormous strength. Huge columns, alternate ones patterned with bold geometric incisions – spirals, zig-zags and diamonds – hold up the earliest Gothic roof anywhere. Not far from the font, with its riotous canopy given in 1663 by Bishop Cosin, a black stone line in the floor shows how far women were allowed into the monastic church. The east wall is dominated by a rose window, and below it is the Neville Screen, made from creamy stone. Beyond this is the 13th-century Chapel of the Nine Altars, with its tall lancet windows, overlooked by St Cuthbert's tomb which has just a simple stone slab. In the choir, the Bishop's throne is the highest in Britain.

When monks tried to build a Lady Chapel near Cuthbert's tomb, it is said that the misogynist saint supernaturally interfered with the work, causing it to be abandoned. Instead, in about 1170, they built a Galilee Chapel at the west end (well away from St Cuthbert), perched precariously over the ravine. The Venerable Bede's tomb is here.

Off the cloisters, try not to miss the Monks' Dormitory, with its huge wooden roof, and the Treasury, full of fine silver, gorgeous and amazing pre-Conquest embroidery and manuscripts, and relics of St Cuthbert, including his cross and coffin. To get the classic cathedral view, go to Prebends' Bridge, reached from South Bailey.

▸ Durham Castle

dur.ac.uk/university.college

Palace Green, DH1 3RW

0191 3343800 | Open for guided tours only: term time Mon–Fri 2, 3, 4;
school holidays 10, 11, noon; subject to events

Castle and cathedral stand shoulder to shoulder on their rock base above the winding River Wear. In the whole of England, there is no better architectural metaphor for the union of church and state that still dominates Britain.

Durham was already a place of pilgrimage when the Normans rolled up in the second half of the 11th century. The bishopric of Durham was a prestigious religious office, but under Norman rule it became a mighty secular power too. The powerful prince-bishops of Durham built the medieval parts of the castle on foundations that started as a simple defensive mound thrown up around 1072, at a time when William and his Norman sidekicks in the northeast only felt safe behind stockade walls. A stone-walled castle built in the 12th century was demolished in 1340, to be replaced by a grander castle, in keeping with the rising status of the bishops of Durham. This was a place that celebrated their Christian pomp, but which was also built as a reminder that the prince-bishops wielded secular power too. They rode, with the cross in one hand and the sword of the Lord in the other. Meek, they were not.

Some of the earliest work that has survived includes the beautiful chapel crypt, and one of the finest Norman archways in Britain. Between 1494 and 1500, the Bishop of Durham had enormous kitchens installed; amazingly, these are still functional, and now provide meals for students at the University of Durham. There are also signs of some Victorian remodelling.

▲ Durham Castle at night

▶ Durham Cathedral

durhamcathedral.co.uk

DH1 3EH | 0191 3864266 | Open Mon–Sat 9.30–5, Sun, 12.30–5 (school summer holidays open to 8). Access restricted during services and events

This is Durham's iconic sight. Founded in 1093 as a shrine to St Cuthbert, the cathedral is a remarkable example of Norman architecture, set in an impressive position high above the River Wear.

A full programme of concerts and events takes place throughout the year, and there is a St Cuthbert's Day Procession in March (phone for details).

TAKE IN SOME HISTORY
See **Durham Castle**, page 111

VISIT THE MUSEUM AND GALLERY
Durham Light Infantry Museum and Durham Art Gallery
durham.gov.uk
Aykley Heads, DH1 5TU
03000 266590 | Open daily Apr–Oct 10–5, Nov–Mar 10–4
'You'll aim low, lads. Aim low and give them a bellyful.' The Durhams were among the best of the best. They served with Wellington in Spain and Portugal and their battle honours include the Crimea, Afghanistan, and most of the key engagements of World War I and World War II. The history of the 'Dirty Little Imps' is told in displays of artefacts, medals, uniforms and vehicles.

GET KARTING
TopGear Karting
durhamkarting.co.uk
Unit 13, Renny's Lane Industrial Estate, DH1 2RS | 0191 3860999
Open Mon–Fri 12–8, Sat 9–9, Sun 10–6.
Get behind the wheel at Top Gear Karting. The 656-ft indoor all-weather track is open to all ages from 8 years up (minimum height 4ft 7in).

PLAY A ROUND
Ramside Hall Hotel and Golf Club
ramsidehallhotel.co.uk
Carrville, DH1 1TD | 0191 3869514
Open daily
Parkland course consisting of three loops of nine holes, Princes, Bishops, and Cathedral – with 14 lakes and great views surrounding an impressive hotel. Golf academy and driving range on site.

EAT AND DRINK
Ramside Hall Hotel ◉
ramsidehallhotel.co.uk
Carrville, DH1 1TD
0191 3865282
A grand house has stood on the site of Ramside Hall since Elizabethan times, but the sprawling complex you see today has at its heart a largely Victorian house, beefed up in the late 20th century with lots more rooms and three loops of nine holes to set the emphasis firmly on the pursuit of golf. The culinary options run from straightforward carvery and rôtisserie dishes, to the menu in the brasserie-style Rib Room, which majors in slabs of locally reared 28-day-aged beef. Just choose your cut and it arrives with roasted mushrooms, braised onions and a choice of classic sauces; alternatively go for grilled lobster or halibut.

Victoria Inn
victoriainn-durhamcity.co.uk
86 Hallgarth Street, DH1 3AS
0191 3865269
This unique listed inn has scarcely changed since it was built in 1899 – not a jukebox, pool table or TV to be found. Just five minutes' walk from the cathedral, it has been carefully nurtured by the

▲ Durham Cathedral and the River Wear

Webster family for over three decades. Small rooms warmed by coal fires and a congenial atmosphere include the tiny snug, where a portrait of Queen Victoria still hangs above the piano. You'll find a few simple snacks to tickle the taste buds, but it's the well-kept local ales, single malts, and over 40 Irish whiskies that are the main attraction.

▶ **PLACES NEARBY**

Diggerland

diggerland.com
Langley Park, DH7 9TT
0871 2277007 | Open Feb–Nov
(check ahead for exact dates)
Diggerland is an adventure park with a difference, where kids of all ages can experience driving real earth-moving equipment. Choose from various types of diggers and dumpers ranging from 1 ton to 8.5 tons. Supervised by an instructor, complete the Dumper Truck Challenge or dig for buried treasure.

▶ Elsdon

Looking at this quiet village now, you may find it hard to imagine that this was, in its heyday, the headquarters of some of the most expert and hard-handed wardens of the troubled borderland between England and Scotland. Elsdon, on the River Rede, was the capital of the English Middle March, holding the central section of the border. The large and attractive triangular green, surrounded by mainly 18th- and 19th-century houses, was once used to pen up the stock to keep it safe during border attacks. From the early 12th century the village was guarded by Elsdon Castle, built on the Mote Hills to the north by the De Umfravilles. It lasted only until 1160, when they moved to Harbottle Castle. The motte-and-bailey earthworks are the best preserved in Northumbria.

The 14th-century Elsdon Tower, once a defensive pele for the vicars of Elsdon, stands near the church. More than 1,000 skulls, and other bones, were found here in the 19th century – bodies of soldiers who fell at the Battle of Otterburn in 1388.

EAT AND DRINK
Bird in Bush
birdinbushelsdon.co.uk
Elsdon, NE19 1AA | 01830 520804
The Bird in Bush occupies a corner of Elsdon's wide, triangular green. A traditional Northumberland pub, it provides real ales and excellent, wholesome, home-cooked food in its comfortable restaurant and from the bar.

▶ Etal & Ford

Etal's main street is a pretty mix of thatched and stone-tiled cottages, and leads to Etal Castle, the ruins of a border tower-house of the early 14th century. Ford, which has merged with the original village, is a typical 'model village' of the 19th century, devised by the philanthropist Marchioness of Waterford. While many of her Victorian contemporaries were busy swooning and worrying about their complexions, Louisa Anne, Marchioness of Waterford and owner of the Ford Estate, was busy endowing her community with a village school which over many years she embellished with her own paintings of scenes from the Bible – intended, obviously, to enlighten the young minds of Etal and Ford. The school is now the village hall, and her works can still be seen.

TAKE IN SOME HISTORY
Etal Castle
english-heritage.org.uk
Cornhill on Tweed, TD12 4TN
01890 820332 | Check ahead for opening details
When they weren't fighting the Scots, the lords of Etal Castle

If you're looking to get away from the daily grind, you've come to the wrong place. Driven by a 16ft waterwheel, the great millstones of this 19th-century mill keep on turning, producing wholemeal wheat flour that you can buy to take home after watching it being made. There's been a mill here for more than 700 years.

Lady Waterford Hall
ford-and-etal.co.uk
Ford | 01890 820338 | Visits for groups by prior arrangement only
The school built and decorated by the Marchioness of Waterford is now the village hall. Louisa Anne's paintings of biblical scenes still adorn the walls.

▲ Heatherslaw Corn Mill

TAKE A TRAIN RIDE
Heatherslaw Light Railway
heatherslawlightrailway.co.uk
Ford Forge, Cornhill on Tweed
TD12 4TJ | 01890 820317
Open late Mar to early Nov daily; trains leave hourly 11–3
You've got to love Britain's miniature railways, and this five-mile stretch of 15-inch gauge track is one of the best. The little steam locomotive takes 50 minutes to haul its train of pretty blue-painted carriages from Etal to Heatherslaw (or vice versa) – at not much more than walking pace, and a lot slower than it would take to cover the same distance by bike. But that's not the point. The point is that it's a fun way to travel through the countryside.

spent their time feuding with the Heron family, masters of neighbouring Ford. By the 15th century, the de Manners had married into the de Ros dynasty and were able to move out of Etal into posher digs, leaving the castle to be garrisoned by a bunch of men-at-arms. Etal fell to James IV of Scotland when he invaded the northeast in 1413. It's an atmospheric enough little stronghold, but not a patch on the great castles of the region.

Heatherslaw Corn Mill
ford-and-etal.co.uk
Ford Forge, Cornhill on Tweed, TD12 4TJ | 01890 820488
Open Apr–Oct daily 11–4

▷ Farne Islands

Keep your head down if you visit the Farne Islands in tern season. You're quite likely to be dive-bombed by Arctic terns jealously guarding their nesting sites, and they've been known to draw blood. The terns aren't alone. Puffins are, as always, top of the bill here, but you may also see fulmars, petrels, razorbills, ringed plovers, rock pipits, eider ducks – locally known as 'Cuddy's chicks' – kittiwakes, guillemots, cormorants, oystercatchers and, of course, gulls of all kinds. Grey seals breed on the beaches, too.

Of the 30 or so bits of sea-lapped dolerite rock with their stacks and cliffs, only Inner Farne and Staple Island can be reached by boat from Seahouses (see page 205) in April and the summer season when it's not too rough. The National Trust has owned the islands since 1925, and permits to land on them must be bought from the wardens. Check that your boatman is licensed to land his passengers. During the breeding season, from May to July, landing is restricted – and if the weather's bad you may not be able to land at all.

St Aidan used to come to the islands from Lindisfarne for lonely prayer and meditation, and St Cuthbert, the Northumbrian shepherd boy who became the north of England's most admired saint, lived a solitary life for a time on Inner Farne. He built himself a hut, and there are stories of him reproving the greedy and thoughtless birds and bringing them to conduct themselves in a more Christian manner. He died on the island in AD 687. A chapel there survives, built in his memory in the 14th century.

▾ Puffins, the Farne Islands

St Aidan spent each Lent on Inner Farne, one of the 28 Farne Islands (or 15, if you count at high tide), and St Cuthbert lived here from AD 676 to AD 685. His cell on Inner Farne was surrounded by an embankment so that all he could see was heaven above. The present St Cuthbert's Church on Inner Farne, near the site of his hermitage, dates mostly from about 1370 and has 17th-century woodwork which was brought here from Durham Cathedral (see page 112) in the 19th century.

To the west is Prior Castell's Tower, which may have held a lighthouse from the days when there were Benedictine monks on the island. Today's white-painted lighthouse, which is open to visitors, was built in 1809. Further out, beyond Staple, is Longstone, a rather uninviting, low, bare rock with a red-and-white striped lighthouse, built in 1826. This was where the Darling family lived, and from where Grace and her father set out on their rescue mission.

For many visitors though, the main attraction of the Farne Islands is that wildlife. Egg collectors caused unprecedented damage in the 19th century, and the Farne Islands Association, set up in 1880, employed watchers to protect the breeding birds. There are nature walks on both these islands.

The great dolerite rocks that form the Farne Islands are the easternmost part of the Great Whin Sill, and the rocks are home to at least 17 species of bird, which perch precariously on the cliffs or wheel noisily overhead – always wear a hat when visiting these islands!

▼ Cormorant and chick ▶ The coastline of Inner Farne

STRIKE A LIGHT
**Farne Islands and
Longstone Lighthouse**
trinityhouse.co.uk
Inner Farne and Staple Island
01665 721099

You think you've got it tough? Then imagine being a lighthouse keeper (or his wife or child) on this lump of windswept rock six miles offshore. The red and white tower with its brilliant lights was built in 1826, and cost almost £5,000 – a truly enormous sum at the time. The keeper was required to keep the oil-fuelled lamps lit at all times. Winter gales sometimes swept right over the rock, forcing the inhabitants to take shelter in the upper storeys of the lighthouse tower.

Amazingly, the light here wasn't converted to electrical power until 1952, and the last lighthouse keeper left as recently as 1990, when the beacon was finally automated.

▼ Grey seals by the Longstone Lighthouse

10 northeastern birds & beasts

▶ **Red kite**
Once extinct in the northeast, red kites were reintroduced in 2004. These spectacular raptors now breed in the region, with more than 40 known nesting sites.

▶ **Curlew**
The haunting cry of the curlew is one of the distinctive sounds of the Northumbrian moors and North Sea coast.

▶ **Puffin**
Everybody's favourite seabird nests in large numbers on the Farne Islands.

▶ **Guillemot**
You can see these elegantly plumaged seabirds nesting next to puffins on the Farne Islands and at sea.

▶ **Hen harrier**
One of Britain's rarest raptors is on the verge of extinction in England, but if you're lucky you may still spot a hen harrier over Northumberland, as a few still breed just across the border in Scotland.

▶ **Red deer**
Britain's largest land mammal can be seen in deer parks all year round and may be heard bellowing in the wild in the autumn rutting season.

▶ **Otter**
Otters are very elusive, but are making a comeback on some of the region's remoter streams and river banks.

▶ **Minke whale**
If you take a North Sea wildlife cruise, look out for these spectacular sea mammals in waters around Seahouses and off Sunderland.

▶ **Harbour porpoise**
You can see our smallest cetacean on stretches of the North Sea coast, especially around Seahouses.

▶ **Grey seal**
Grey seals are numerous around the Farne Islands, where you'll see them basking onshore at low tide.

▶ Flodden

Flodden is the forgotten battle that decided the fate of
Britain. Because of William Wallace, everyone remembers
Bannockburn, fought in 1314. Because of the 'damned
cowardly Italian' Charles Edward Stuart, everyone remembers
Culloden, fought in 1746.But Flodden was the greatest battle
ever fought between the royal forces of Scotland and England.
It wasn't, in fact, fought at Flodden, but rather at Branxton,
some four miles west of Ford (see page 115). The battlefield is
marked today with a modern cross dedicated to 'the brave of
both nations' who fell here.

   In September 1513, James IV of Scotland invaded England at
the behest of his ally, Louis XII of France. Big mistake. For
once, the Scots outnumbered the English, but the Earl of
Surrey nevertheless inflicted on them the bloodiest defeat in
the long, bloody history of the border. The English victory was
down to Surrey's infantry, who were equipped with the bill, a
short-shafted polearm which proved better at close quarters
than the pikes used by the Scots. These 15ft-long weapons
were cutting-edge stuff. James was a keen student of the latest
trends in military technology – and that, perhaps, was his
downfall. Scottish foot-soldiers were used to fighting with the
spear, and James's army had not been properly trained to use
the long pike. And James placed too much faith in another
16th-century super-weapon: artillery.

   His cannon banged away at Surrey's ranks to no effect, and
when the Scots eventually came downhill to meet the English
infantry the battle became an old-fashioned mess of blood and
steel. It is said that almost every family in lowland Scotland lost
a son in the battle. Among the dead were James and his son
Alexander Stewart, 12 earls, 15 clan chiefs, a bishop and 2
abbots – as well as 5,000 English fighting men. Scotland, as an
independent state, never really recovered from Flodden.

GO BACK IN TIME
**Flodden Battlefield
Trail**
flodden.net
4 miles west of Ford | Open at
all times
From the cross that marks the
epicentre of the battle, you can
follow the movements of the
cold, wet, frightened foot
soldiers of both sides who
fought and died here.

EAT AND DRINK
The Red Lion Inn
redlionmilfield.co.uk
Main Road, Milfield, NE71 6JD
01668 216224
Dating back to the 1700s, sheep
drovers from the northern
counties stayed at this stone
building before it was used as a
stopover for the mail
stagecoach en route from
Edinburgh and London. Well

placed for salmon and trout fishing on the River Tweed and for shooting on the Northumberland estates, the Red Lion offers a relaxing atmosphere, good guest beers and wholesome food. Start with veal, wild mushroom and chorizo broth with potato dumplings before enjoying pan-fried breast of chicken, borders haggis, peppercorn sauce, creamed potato and vegetables; for pudding choose baked stuffed bramley apple, toffee sauce and vanilla ice cream. There's also a beer festival in June.

▶ Gateshead

You should go to Gateshead if only to be rocked by Antony Gormley's *Angel of the North*. Like it or loathe it, you can't ignore the huge steel figure, airplane-style wings outstretched, standing on the edge of Gateshead at the junction of the A1 and A167. Together with two other key projects, it has pulled Gateshead out the dumps, out of the shadow of Newcastle (see page 166), and into the limelight.

The Millennium Bridge linking Gateshead with its northern neighbour, and the BALTIC Centre for Contemporary Art have also done a lot to put Gateshead on the map. A former grain warehouse, this world-class arts venue houses art galleries, restaurants, live performance spaces, a cinema and a library. There's more culture next door, where performance venues, educational areas, studios, bars and cafes are housed inside the gleaming curves of the Norman Foster-designed Sage Centre. Elsewhere, there's the huge MetroCentre – more than just a shopper's paradise, and the Gateshead International Stadium is a renowned sports venue.

VISIT THE MUSEUMS AND GALLERIES
BALTIC Centre for Contemporary Art
see page 126

Shipley Art Gallery
twmuseums.org.uk
Prince Consort Road, NE8 4JB
0191 4771495
Open Tue–Fri 10–4, Sat 10–5
If your tastes in art run to paintings of cows in fields, hay wains, woodland scenes and portraits of sleek Dutch burghers and their wives, you'll probably prefer Shipley Art Gallery to the edgy BALTIC. The core of this collection was given to the people of Gateshead by a 19th-century lawyer, Joseph Shipley, and it has expended to include more than 800 Dutch and Flemish paintings from the 16th and 17th centuries, as well as an important Victorian collection and hundreds of other *objets d'art*.

▶ Angel of the North

Towering over the A1 just outside Gateshead, Antony Gormley's rust-stained, 66ft tall steel statue with its 177ft wingspan is half superhuman, half airliner. Controversial when it went up in 1998, it has since become an icon of the northeast, seen countless times in film and photo montages of memorable sights around the British Isles. Locally it is affectionately nicknamed 'the Gateshead Flasher', a typical example of the area's iconoclastic humour.

Gormley's art is all about the human figure, either on its own or in conjunction with its surroundings, and the *Angel* is probably his

most striking piece mainly due to its size. Gormley's model, as usual, was himself, a process which involving being covered in clingfilm and plaster of paris. The statue cost around £1 million pounds – mainly provided by the National Lottery – and took four years to complete.

Ironically in 2008, a smaller (but still life-size) version of the *Angel*, used by Gormley during the design process, was the first item to be valued at over £1 million pounds by experts on the BBC's Antiques Roadshow. It seems they were aiming a bit low, as two other models have sold at auction for over £3 million.

There's a car park near the bottom of it, so you can really get a proper look at this mammoth statue.

▶ BALTIC Centre for Contemporary Art

balticmill.com

South Shore Road, Gateshead Quays, NE8 3BA | 0191 4781810

Open Wed–Mon 10–6, Tue 10.30–6

You'll find plenty to challenge your perceptions of what art really is in this former 1950s grain warehouse, once part of the old BALTIC Flour Mills. BALTIC Centre for Contemporary Art sometimes seems to go out of its way to present exhibitions that are calculated to have those with conservative tastes frothing with rage. Its project space, BALTIC 39, often manages to go one step beyond, with its choice of installations and video work. But it's not all about shocking the viewer. BALTIC also hosts family-friendly activities such as necklace-making and, at Hallowe'en, pumpkin carving.

LISTEN TO ALL THAT JAZZ
The Sage
thesagegateshead.org
St Mary's Square, Gateshead Quays,
NE8 2JR | 0191 4434661
The Sage, Gateshead's superb
arts venue, hosts the annual
Gateshead International
Jazz Festival and an array of
concerts and performances by
world-class folk, rock, classical
and jazz musicians.

TAKE A WALK IN THE PARK
Derwent Walk Country Park
Rowlands Gill, NE39 1AU
01207 545212 | Open access
The park enfolds woodland and
water-meadows, and at Bill
Quay Community Farm you can
take the family to admire rare
heritage breeds such as
Gloucester Old Spot and

Saddleback pigs, Longhorn
cattle and Jacob's sheep. You
can choose from a selection of
short and long waymarked
walking, cycling and riding
trails, and you might even see
foxes, roe deer or badgers.

GO SKIING
**Whickham Thorns
Activity Centre**
gateshead.gov.uk
Market Lane, Dunston, NE11 9NX
0191 4335767 | Open Mon, Wed
and Thu 9.30–4, Tues 9.30–3.30,
Sat–Sun 10–6.30
You can go skiing on a year-
round dry slope, practise
archery or hire a bike for the
day at Whickham Thorns
Activity Centre.

▶ Gibside & Gibside Chapel
nationaltrust.org.uk | Rowlands Gill, Burnopfield, NE16 6BG
01207 541820 | Open see website
The Gibside Estate was the brainchild of George Bowes, an
ancestor of the late Queen Mother. The great house and
most of the buildings are in ruins but the chapel, framed
by a shady avenue of Turkey oaks, is carefully tended by the
National Trust. Designed by Paine in 1760, it was only
completed in 1812.

The interior is reached through a columned entrance
beneath a central dome and six fine urns. It is not as ornate as
Paine intended – he wanted more elaborate plasterwork and
statues. The three-decker pulpit, with a cover like a pagoda
roof, dominates the interior, while the small altar seems to be
an afterthought.

This impressive Palladian chapel stands in the grounds of
Gibside House, which was once owned by the Bowes-Lyon
family, relations of the late Queen Mother. Originally intended
as a mausoleum for George Bowes, the chapel was built
between 1760 and 1812, and he was eventually buried in the
crypt along with other family members. Protected by double

▲ Gibside Chapel

iron doors at the rear of the chapel, the crypt is usually open to the public only on Heritage Days.

Inspired by the Pantheon in Rome, the chapel combines the form of a Greek cross with a porticoed dome that is raised on a high drum and decorated with festoons. It is constructed of local sandstone, with cherrywood interior furnishings.

The entrance to the chapel is, unusually, on the east side behind the altar. Under the dome visitors will find a rare mahogany three-tiered pulpit, as well as two sets of box pews: one for the Bowes-Lyon family, the other for the chaplain, dignitaries and tenant farmers; servants sat in the stone seats.

▶ Gilsland

You'll find one of the best-preserved milecastles on Hadrian's Wall, with remains of its north and south gates, walls and two barrack blocks. It's near the railway bridge. The wall passes through the village – the most westerly in Northumberland – and there's a section of it in the vicarage garden.

▶ Greenhead

There has been a river crossing at Greenhead since at least Roman times. The A69 is the latest of a series of important routes crossing the Tipalt Burn, following both the Maiden Way and the Stanegate Roman road, which served Hadrian's Wall. The village lies in a small hollow beside the burn, and to the north are the picturesque ruins of medieval Thirlwall Castle, where Edward I is reputed to have stayed on one of his many brutal campaigns against the Scots.

Walk half a mile or east of Greenhead village to find one of the highest standing sections of Hadrian's Wall. Next to it is the site of the Roman fort of Carvoran (see page 90). It has not yet been excavated, but next to it the Roman Army Museum depicts the life and times of the Roman soldier (see Vindolanda, page 221).

▶ Haltwhistle

You can use Haltwhistle as a base for exploring the north Pennines, but don't neglect the attractive town centre, with its stone streets radiating from the market place. Haltwhistle Burn flows into the South Tyne east of town and there are pleasant walks alongside the burn up to Hadrian's Wall.

Some of its Victorian station buildings, including the stationmaster's house, waiting room and ticket office, date from as early as 1838. The Red Lion Inn is based on a defensive tower, probably of the 17th century, when Haltwhistle was still at the mercy of Scottish raiders. It was under the protection of the powerful Ridley family, and the tomb of John Ridley, brother-in-law to Nicholas Ridley, the Protestant martyr burned at the stake in 1555, is in Holy Cross Church. Don't miss the village church, either. Its exterior isn't much to look at, but inside it's one of the finest in Northumberland. Mostly Early English, it has long, thin lancet windows, restored in 1870.

Two miles away you can see what's left of Great Chesters fort, including a blocked gateway and the remains of an aqueduct. It was called Aesica by the Romans, built around AD 128 to guard the Caw Gap.

EAT AND DRINK

Milecastle Inn

milecastle-inn.co.uk

Military Road, Cawfields, NE49 9NN

01434 321372

A traditional pub decorated with horse brasses and local pictures, the Milecastle occupies a wonderfully remote and peaceful location high on the moorland edge. One horizon is serrated by the line of Hadrian's Wall and there are easy walks up the lane past Roman camps to reach Milecastle 42 beside the wall at Cawfield Crags. Tasty beers from Newcastle's Big Lamp Brewery are your reward for a breezy stroll, accompanied perhaps by game pâté with toast; chicken curry with rice and chips; or a choice of pies. A roaring winter fire warms, or you could sit outside in the curlew-haunted countryside.

▶ **PLACES NEARBY**

Vindolanda and Roman Army Museum

see page 221

Walltown Crags and Turret

On B6318, 1 mile northeast of Greenhead | Open at any reasonable time

You can see a miles-long stretch of Hadrian's Wall from here as it switchbacks up and down along the rocky ridge of the Great Whin Sill.

The Wallace Arms

Rowfoot, Featherstone, NE49 0JF

01434 321872

This traditional place serves good, simple food. There is plenty of fresh fish, like haddock in beer batter, as well as steaks and pies. Snacks and sandwiches, vegetarian dishes and a children's menu are available.

▶ **Harthope Moor**

If you like high, wild country then you'll love Harthope Moor, one of the biggest swathes of wilderness in England. The highest classified road in England cuts across this windswept expanse of heather and moorland, where sheep graze and curlews call.

▶ **PLACES NEARBY**

St John's Chapel

The village of St John's Chapel in Weardale can be reached by the highest classified road in England, over Harthope Moor from Teesdale. The church, overlooking the small square with its diminutive Town Hall, was rebuilt in 1752 with impressive classical columns to be seen inside. There are pleasant footpaths all around, and access across a footbridge to the Weardale Way. At Ireshopeburn, one mile west, is the Weardale Museum, in a former manse, with reconstructions of Dale life around 1870. Next door is the 18th-century chapel where John Wesley preached and a room in the museum is dedicated to him and his work.

Weardale Museum
weardalemuseum.co.uk
Ireshopeburn, DL13 1HD
01388 517433
Open May–Oct daily 2–5
The northeast clung to the Catholic faith much longer than most of the rest of England. But in the industrialising 19th century, it became a hotbed of Wesleyanism, a stern faith which was adopted by many of the region's working-class communities.

John Wesley, founder of Methodism, preached at High House Chapel in Weardale, and the former minister's house next door is now the Weardale Museum. It depicts life in the Durham Dales in the 19th century, and has a strong Wesleyan connection, with possibly the largest collection

of Methodist memorabilia in the region.

High House Methodist Chapel
weardalemuseum.co.uk
Ireshopeburn, DL13 1HD
Open May–Oct daily 2–5
High House Chapel was built in 1760 as 'a preaching house for Divine worship' and is the oldest Methodist Chapel in the world to have been in continuous weekly use since then. Wesley himself preached in the small village in 1752, and a plaque outside the chapel marks the site.

Nestled by the side of the road in rolling countryside, the sandstone building has a Welsh slate roof and 19th-century sash windows. The interior is tall, split by galleries running around the walls, and dominated by the large and imposing pulpit.

▸ Hamsterley Forest

Hamsterley Forest offers more than 30 miles of cycle trails – some adventurous, others easy-going – as well as walking and horse riding paths and forest roads in its 5,000 acres of woodland in the Bedburn and Ayhope valleys. They include the informative Sky Rainforest Discovery Trail.

SEE A LOCAL CHURCH
Church of St James
hamsterleyvillage.com
0.5 miles east of Hamsterley village
01388 488257 | Contact churchwarden for opening times
Nobody seems to know why this 12th-century church is located well outside the village that it serves. It dates from 1180, with

a number of later additions, including 13th-century windows and a 17th-century chapel. Norman features include an elegant doorway. Inside, there are carvings of the coats of arms of local notables, including the 19th-century novelist Robert Surtees.

▶ Hamsterley Forest

The Grove, sited in a clearing by the confluence of the Euden and Spurlswood becks, and surrounded by some of the oldest trees in Hamsterley, was home to the Surtees family, who farmed here and used the estate for hunting. The Forestry Commission purchased the estate in 1927, and began planting the area with commercial timber, filling the Bedburn and Ayhope valleys and extending across the high moorland separating the two becks. Hamsterley Forest is now Durham's single largest plantation and extends over more than 5,000 acres. Sitka spruce, larch and Scots pine climb the steep hillsides, but among the plantations are some 62 acres of oak wood, partly planted to commemorate the coronation of George VI in 1937.

The cycle of planting, re-growth and harvesting of different tree types has created a mix of environments that wild plants, insects and animals can thrive in. Bat boxes have been placed in some areas to encourage them to nest. Keep a look out for kingfishers, or in autumn, you may see salmon as they migrate upstream. You may see red squirrels or roe deer – but sadly, no hamsters.

EXPLORE BY BIKE
Wood n Wheels
woodnwheels.org.uk
Hamsterley Forest, Redford,
DL13 3NL | 0333 8008222
Open daily 10–6

You can rent all kinds
of bikes – from top-
spec mountain and
trail cycles to child-friendly
models – at Wood n
Wheels cycle hire.

▶ Hartlepool

You'll search in vain for Hartepool's Saxon roots. Only the ancient graveyard remains of Hartlepool Abbey, built in the mid-seventh century, although archaeologists have had fun fossicking among its tombs in search of Anglo-Saxon artefacts and holy bones. It seems that the abbey was trashed by Viking raiders less than two centuries after it was built. After that the village that had grown up around it dropped off the map.

Hartlepudlians have always had a healthy suspicion of outsiders. During the Napoleonic Wars, they famously (allegedly) lynched an unfortunate monkey mascot which was washed ashore from a wrecked French warship. It was common knowledge that Frenchmen had tails, so they strung the poor beastie up.

Hartlepool became County Durham's main fishing port during the early Middle Ages, and after the Norman Conquest its lords were the de Brus family, ancestors of Robert the Bruce, victor of Bannockburn and eventual King of Scotland. Edward I of England seized the town during Scotland's War of Independence, and in 1315 it was sacked by Bruce's sidekick, Sir James Douglas. Scots allies of the Parliamentary side occupied Hartlepool for a while during the Civil Wars.

Hartlepool's defences were strengthened during the late 18th century (to keep out any more of those French monkeys) and again in 1860 and 1900. Some of its gun emplacements are still in place, but their cannon failed to deter the German navy from turning up to bombard the port in 1914, killing 117 people.

Hartlepool thrived as a fishing harbour and a coal port, but the town fell on hard times with the decline of heavy industry in the second half of the 20th century, and has struggled to bootstrap itself back to prosperity. Attracting tourism to its rejuvenated waterfront is a key part of its strategy.

VISIT THE MUSEUMS AND GALLERIES

Hartlepool's Maritime Experience

hartlepoolsmaritimeexperience.com
Maritime Avenue, TS24 0XZ
01429 860077 | Open daily summer
10–5, winter 10.30–4

The oldest warship still afloat in Europe, HMS *Trincomalee*, is the big attraction here. You'll find a Maritime Adventure Centre for children, who will also love the regular displays of swordsmanship and firepower. You'll experience the sights and sounds – but, happily, not the smells – of an 1800s quayside as you learn about the birth of the Royal Navy and visit the Quayside shops and the admiral's house.

You'll also find a historic paddle steamer, PSS *Wingfield Castle*. Built in Hartlepool in 1934, she served as a Humber river ferry until 1974, when the forthcoming opening of the Humber Bridge made the ferry redundant.

The free Museum of Hartlepool is also part of the Maritime Experience, and has a collection of archaeological finds and memorabilia spanning some 5,000 years.

Christ Church (Hartlepool Art Gallery)

hartlepool.gov.uk
Church Square, TS24 7EQ
01429 890000
Open Tue–Sat 10–5

The best bit of this historic church, which now houses a changing calendar of art exhibitions, is the view from its 100ft clock tower.

Heugh Battery

heughbattery.com
Moor Terrace, TS24 0PS
01429 270746
Open Thu–Sun 10–4

Mighty cannon were first installed at this sea-facing emplacement in 1859. In 1900 they were replaced with the new six-inch guns, with a range of more than seven miles. They fired in anger for the first and only time in December 1914, when three German warships bombarded the town, but the battery was manned right up until 1956. You can still see some of the original guns and earthworks, and a World War I trench exhibit spine-chillingly recreates the experience of manning a trench on the Western Front.

SEE A LOCAL CHURCH

St Hilda's Church

Church Close, TS24 0PW
01429 267030 | Open Oct–Easter
Sat 2–4, Easter–Sep Wed–Sun 2–4

Built in the late 12th century by the Fourth Lord of Annadale, Robert de Brus, St Hilda's is a gracious building which was extensively restored in the 1930s.

◄ *HMS Trincomalee*, Hartlepool

PLAY A ROUND

Castle Eden Golf Club

castleedengolfclub.co.uk

Castle Eden, TS27 4SS

01429 836510

Beautiful parkland course alongside a nature reserve. Hard walking but trees provide wind shelter.

Hartlepool Golf Club

hartlepoolgolfclub.co.uk

Hart Warren, TS24 9QF

01429 274398 | Open Mon–Sat and BHs

A seaside course, half links, overlooking the North Sea. A good test and equally enjoyable to players of all handicaps. The 10th, par 4, demands a precise second shot over a ridge and between sand dunes to a green down near the edge of the beach, alongside which several holes are played.

Seaton Carew Golf Club

seatoncarewgolfclub.co.uk

Tees Road, Seaton Carew, TS25 1DE

01429 266249

Open daily

A championship links course taking full advantage of its dunes and gorse. Renowned for its par 4 17th; just enough fairway for an accurate drive followed by another precise shot to a pear-shape sloping green that is severely trapped.

▶ Herterton House

rhs.org.uk

Two miles north of Cambo, Hartington, NE61 4BN | 01670 774278

Open Apr–Sep Mon, Wed, Fri–Sun 1.30–5.30

The most amazing thing about Herterton House is that a garden of such romance and beauty can be created 700 feet above sea level in such a seemingly unlikely, windswept environment. It's a tribute to the gardening skills of Frank and Marjorie Lawley, who took over a near-derelict Tudor house and its grounds in 1976. They took a disused farmyard, littered with broken farm implements and waist high in stinging nettles, and turned it into a complex of delightful, individual gardens including the Nursery Garden, a formal garden and a lovely green and gold evergreen garden. The house is draped with jasmines, honeysuckles and fragrant clematis. Box-edged beds contain lilies, crown imperials and dicentras.

A gravel path bordered with cream and white fumitory leads into a physic garden laid out as a knot. This charming garden has geometric beds of medicinal herbs including tansy, camphor and hyssop, and a weeping pear in the centre. Roses in this enclosure, together with the honeysuckle that covers the surrounding walls, give off a heady fragrance in summer.

Behind the house is the largest of the enclosures, a walled flower garden. Regular beds separated by gravel paths have

been planted in accordance with an overall colour scheme. Here there is a profusion of old-fashioned daisies, with pinks, wallflowers, campions and buttercups, while campanulas, violas, geraniums, avens and Jacob's Ladder give the impression of a cottage garden deep in the countryside but, surely, in a more southerly climate.

The Fancy Garden is a parterre of miniature box and beyond it on a low terrace, there is a gazebo where Marjorie Lawley's planting plans of the garden are displayed. From an upper room there are wide and contrasting views of the landscape to the north, and the house and a panorama of the gardens – evidence of the planting plans come to fruition – to the south.

▶ Hexham

Before visiting Hexham's famous priory, take time to stroll through the town centre with its fine houses and charming Victorian shopfronts.

In 1761, the market place, with its stone-columned Shambles, saw the deaths of around 50 people, when militiamen opened fire on a crowd protesting against conscription into the army to fight the French.

Be sure to visit 14th-century Moot Hall, a miniature castle with an archway tunnelling through it, which now houses the Art Gallery. Through the arch, in Hallgate, is another fearsome tower, the Archbishops' Gaol. Built about 1330, it houses the Border History Museum and Library.

Hexham's other attraction is its racecourse, one of the area's best-loved. Tyne Green is a riverside country park and Hexham Race Course lies to the south of town.

Nearby, Chesters Roman Fort (see page 90) is the best-preserved Roman cavalry fort in Britain, with a museum which holds interesting displays of carved stones, altars and sculptures from all along Hadrian's Wall.

TAKE IN SOME HISTORY
Hexham Abbey
hexhamabbey.org.uk
Beaumont Street, NE46 3NB
01434 602031 | Open daily 9.30–5, services and events permitting; crypt 11 and 3.30
In its day, Hexham was a marvel. According to the biographer of its founder, Wilfred, there was nothing like it anywhere in Europe north of the Alps. Wilfrid was spiritual adviser to St Etheldreda, who gave him the manor in return for his support against her husband King Ecgfrith. The pious Etheldreda – a princess in her own right – had vowed to remain a virgin. Her husband was understandably miffed, and to escape his lust she fled to

Ely, in East Anglia. Ecgfrith later remarried, and in AD 678 he got his own back by exiling Wilfrid from Northumbria.

Wilfrid founded his priory in about AD 674 and his biography, written around 700, describes its stately columns, crypts of beautifully finished stone, and 'walls of wonderful height and length'.

However, the church that you see today is based mainly on the Augustinian priory built between 1170 and 1250 in the Early English style. The choir, north and south transepts and the cloisters, where canons studied and meditated, date from this period. The east end was rebuilt in 1860. In 1996 St Wilfrid's Chapel was created to honour the seventh-century founder.

The greatest treasure of all is the Anglo-Saxon crypt, built of Roman stones from Corstopitum (Corbridge), many with carvings. This is all that remains of Wilfrid's original church. From the nave, a steep stone stair takes you down into rooms and passages left intact for more than 1,300 years.

The rest of the priory is impressive, too, especially the early 13th-century choir, the north transept with fine lancet windows and, in the south transept, the Night Stair for the Augustinian canons to descend from their dormitory for night prayers. Look out for the nearby Roman tombstone of standard-

5 top churches & cathedrals

▶ **Alnwick Abbey**
The impressive gatehouse is all the remains of this 12th century abbey.

▶ **Durham Cathedral**
The three massive towers of Durham's 11th century cathedral loom over the city. Inside, this is one of the most impressive churches in England.

▶ **Hexham Abbey**
Founded in AD 674 by St Wilfrid, this gracious church was in fact a priory, not an abbey. Inside is the ornamented stone chair known as Wilfrid's Seat.

▶ **Lindisfarne Priory**
The deeply weathered red sandstone ruins of Lindisfarne Priory evoke Holy Island's long Christian heritage.

▶ **St Cuthbert's, Darlington**
Darlington's 12th century parish church is one of the region's finest. Founded in 1192, it has survived almost unchanged.

bearer Flavius. The stalls in the choir have nicely carved misericords, while Prior Leschman's Chantry contains carvings of unlikely subjects like a bagpiper, a fox preaching to geese and a lady combing her hair. In the chancel of Hexham Abbey is one of its treasures, the stone chair called Wilfrid's Seat or the Frith

◀ Hexham Abbey

Stool – frith means 'sanctuary', and those who sat on it claimed the protection of the Church. Dating from the time St Wilfrid built the church, the chair had a place of honour in the Saxon building, and is ornamented with plait and knot patterns. It's also cracked right across – thanks to the workmen who dropped it in 1860.

VISIT THE MUSEUMS
The Old Gaol

tynedaleheritage.org
Hallgate, NE46 3NH | 01434 652351
Open Feb and Nov Mon–Tue,
Sat, Mar-Oct daily 10–4.30;
closed except by appointment
Dec–Jan

Complete with tales of jailbreaks, banditry and torture, this is the kind of attraction that small boys (and plenty of girls too) really enjoy. Built in 1330, it's the oldest purpose-built nick in England. Authentically costumed guides impersonate the gaoler, the expert border lawman Sir Robert Carey, warden of the West March in the 16th century, and other characters, and a glass lift takes you down to a convincingly grim dungeon where hostages accused of anything from murder to cattle-thieving were held until the families paid their fines.

Not all of them stayed put – in 1538, a gang of Armstrongs and Charltons raided the gaol to free Robert More – suspected of being a Catholic priest and spy – and a bunch of their own clansmen.

▼ Hexham

Moot Hall

tynedaleheritage.org

Market Place, NE46

The Moot Hall, opposite the Abbey, was the home of the Archbishop of York's bailff, who administered the prelate's justice in his jurisdiction of Hexhamshire. It had its own courtroom, and was still used as a lockup in the 19th century.

HAVE A FLUTTER
Hexham Racecourse

hexham-racecourse.co.uk

Yarridge Road, NE46 2JP

01434 606881 | Open 14 race meetings annually, spring–autumn

You'll find Northumberland's only racecourse just south of town, in pretty countryside. Grassy slopes below the stands mean a great view of the action. Go on Ladies' Day to be amazed by flamboyant female headgear.

SADDLE UP
Plover Hill Riding School

Dipton Mill Road, NE46 1YA

01434 607196

Saddle up a sturdy Austrian pony for a ride through woodland or over moors around Hexham. Rides can be as short as one hour or as long as a full day, and maximum group size is five people.

PLAY A ROUND
Hexham Golf Club

hexhamgolf.co.uk

Spital Park, NE46 3RZ

01434 603072

Open Mon–Fri, Sun and BHs

This is a very pretty, well-drained course with interesting natural contours. Exquisite views from parts of the course of the Tyne Valley below. As good a parkland course as any in the north of England.

EAT AND DRINK
The General Havelock Inn

generalhavelock.co.uk

Ratcliffe Road, Haydon Bridge, NE47 6ER | 01434 684376

Built in the 1760s, this riverside inn is named after a 19th-century British Army officer. The pub, with its restaurant in a converted stone barn, is a favourite with local showbusiness personalities. The real ales are all sourced from a 15-mile radius: Mordue Workie Ticket and Big Lamp Bitter are but two. Owner/chef Gary Thompson makes everything by hand, including the bread and ice cream. Local ingredients are the foundation of his dishes, which include steamed lemon sole in a crisp pasty pillow; chicken and mushroom pie; and warm walnut tart. In summer, the patio area is covered by a marquee.

Rat Inn

theratinn.com

NE46 4LN

01434 602814

An attractive, ivy-clad sandstone building, this former drovers' inn catered to farmers from the Borders on their way to the market in Hexham, which just up the road. Just how the Rat came by its name is shrouded in mystery – why not ask the locals for their theories? On sunny days soak up the spectacular views of the Tyne Valley from the glorious hillside garden. On cooler days retreat into the classic bar, where you'll find crackling log fires, a flagstone floor, old pews and benches and an impressive oak bar dispensing six guest ales, perhaps local Wylam Gold Tankard. Blackboard special wines are matched to seasonal dishes. Order from an interesting daily menu that bristles with locally sourced ingredients – meat, game and cheese are exclusively Northumbrian. In addition, herbs are grown in the garden, fish is cured in the pub, and everything is made from scratch, including pickles and puddings. Typically, tuck into pan-fried coley or roast rib of beef for two.

Dipton Mill Inn

www.diptonmill.co.uk
Dipton Mill Road, NE46 1YA
01434 606577

Rebuilt some 400 years ago, this former farmhouse has a pretty millstream running right through the gardens. The Dipton Mill is home to Hexhamshire Brewery ales, which include Devil's Water and Old Humbug. All dishes are freshly prepared from local produce where possible. Try the steak-and-kidney pie; chicken in sherry sauce or braised beef steak with tomato and peppers. A decent selection of vegetarian options includes tagliatelle with creamy basil sauce and fresh parmesan; cheese and tomato flan with salad; and ratatouille with couscous. Dessert brings a number of comforting favourites such as chocolate brownie with ice cream or bread and butter pudding plus a good cheese selection. Salads, sandwiches and ploughman's are also always available.

Miners Arms Inn

theminersacomb.com
Main Street, Acomb, NE46 4PW
01434 603909

The Greenwell family took over this 18th-century village pub near Hadrian's Wall in 2012 and it's very much a family business with David and Elwyn helped by their two daughters. Among the choice of ales, local Wylam Gold Tankard is always available, with guest beers available every week. Mainly locally sourced dishes, including haggis and black pudding with peppercorn sauce; and home-made steak and ale pie typify the traditional food. Visitors can enjoy the open-hearth fire, the sunny beer garden, or simply sit out front soaking up life in this peaceful village. Beer festivals are held occasionally.

▶ Holy Island (Lindisfarne)

Plan your trip to Holy Island with care. Get your timings wrong, and you could end up stuck here until the tide ebbs and exposes the causeway that links Lindisfarne to the mainland – or, at worst, you could be trapped on the causeway by a rising tide. Before crossing the causeway, check the tide tables which are displayed at either end or look up high and low tide times at local tourist information offices or online. The old pilgrims' route from the mainland is marked by posts leading almost directly to the village.

Holy Island was one of the earliest Christian centres in England, and has been known by this name since the 11th century, although its Celtic name, Lindisfarne, is just as familiar. St Aidan came here in AD 635, invited by the King of Northumbria, and his religious foundation became famous throughout Christendom. After Aidan came St Cuthbert, who was buried here in 687. Lindisfarne's wealth and fame attracted

▼ Lindisfarne Castle, Holy Island

Danish raiders, who sacked it in AD 875, after which the
surviving monks dug up the saint's bones and fled with them.
He wandered around the northeast for more than 100 years
before coming to rest in Durham.

Bare, windswept and flat, Lindisfarne seems the perfect
place for the ascetic life of prayer and contemplation favoured
by early monastic communities. Perhaps it was this daily
encroachment by the sea that attracted the early Christians to
the island, for Lindisfarne has a rich history that dates back to
the saints of the seventh century. In the 11th century, the
Benedictines founded a monastery here, the remains of which
can still be visited.

▶ Lindisfarne Castle

nationaltrust.org.uk

TD15 2SH | 01289 389244 | Open Aug daily, 8 Feb–Jul and Sep–Oct Tue–Sun (open alternate weekends in winter); opening times will vary depending on tides: 10–3 or 12–5

A fort was built on the rocky outcrop of Beblowe in the 1540s, when raids by the Scots were a serious problem. Stones from the Benedictine monastery were used in the building. In the event the little stronghold saw no action, when James I of England and VI of Scotland united the two countries, the need for border defences declined and Lindisfarne was allowed to fall into disrepair.

In 1903 Lindisfarne was lovingly restored for Edward Hudson (the founder of *Country Life* magazine) by the leading country-house architect Sir Edwin Lutyens. Lutyens changed very little of the structure, but used his considerable skills to convert austere stone-vaulted ammunition rooms into comfortable living quarters. The castle is a labyrinth of small tunnels and bizarrely shaped rooms, all decorated in the style of a 17th-century Dutch mansion, with an abundance of sturdy oak furniture, brass candlesticks and attractive blue-and-white pottery.

Many of the bedrooms are tiny, and are dwarfed by the great four-poster beds that Lutyens chose. The many living rooms, most with splendid views out to sea or down the coast, have handsome, arched fireplaces and a wealth of nooks and crannies in which Lutyens inserted small window seats. There are three floors: the upper gallery, and the upper and lower batteries. Lutyens made use of these different levels to create an impression of size, so that the little stairways, numerous rooms and narrow passageways make the castle seem more extensive than it actually is.

▼ The Ship Room, Lindisfarne Castle

TAKE IN SOME HISTORY
Lindisfarne Castle
see page 145

Lindisfarne Priory
english-heritage.org.uk
TD15 2RX | 01289 389200
Open Apr–Sep daily 9.30–5, Oct daily 9.30–4, 4 Nov–16 Feb and 25 Feb–Mar Sat–Sun 10–4; 17–21 Feb Mon–Fri 10–4. Please check high tide times before visiting

You may take the claim that St Cuthbert's body still remained miraculously undecayed 11 years after his death with a pinch of salt, but this was his original burial place, and one of the holiest sites in Anglo-Saxon England. There's an award-winning museum, which holds the 'Viking raiders' stone, depicting the attack that destroyed Lindisfarne's first religious foundation in AD 793.

The priory was founded by the Bishop of Durham 190 years later, and shows its age: the mellow red sandstone is deeply weathered. Inside, its columns are patterned with zig-zags and chequers. The remaining rib of the crossing, known as the rainbow arch, shows that it once had a strong tower. Part of the cloister remains, but there is not much more, except a gatehouse and defensive walls.

VISIT THE MUSEUM
Lindisfarne Centre
lindisfarne-centre.com
Marygate, TD15 2SD | 01289 389004
You can only marvel at the artistry displayed in the virtual pages of the vividly coloured digital copy of the famous *Lindisfarne Gospels* that has pride of place here. The book, painstaking illuminated with brush and pen, is a marvel of Anglo-Saxon religious art. It was made by the monks of Lindisfarne towards the end of the seventh century and the original is in the British Library.

The Centre also has a mini-cinema which shows a re-creation of the devastating Viking raid of AD 793. It's hard to suppress the feeling that it must have been more fun to be

a Viking that a sleep-deprived, half-starved, celibate holy man living in a chilly stone cell.

SEE A LOCAL CHURCH
Church of St Mary the Virgin
Church Lane, TD15 2RX

Pilgrims still come to Lindisfarne's Church of St Mary, where the story of Christianity in the northeast began. Built on the site of the monastery founded by St Aidan in AD 635, and dating from between 1180 and 1300, the parish church is the oldest building on the island (older than the ruined Norman priory that stands next to it), though a round-headed arch in the chancel, and a strange high-level doorway above it, are certainly Saxon. The chancel and its lancet windows are from the 13th century, and the priest's door and a low side window in the south wall remain intact inside a new vestry. The round arches of the north arcade are from the late 12th century, and the south

▼ Lindisfarne Priory

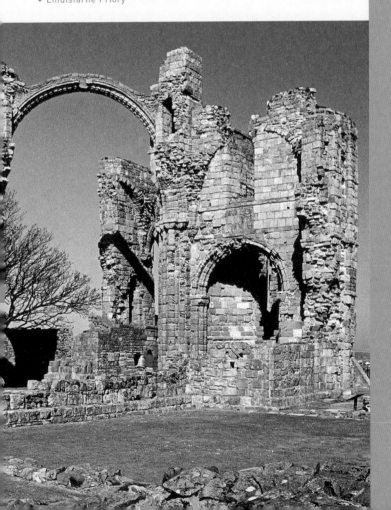

arcade, together with the original windows of its aisle (now blocked), is from around 1300.

The west end is capped by a typical Northumberland bellcote – perhaps of the same 1754 date as one of the bells – and the little 19th-century north vestry once served as a mortuary for drowned sailors.

GO ON A WILD GOOSE CHASE
**Lindisfarne National
Nature Reserve**
lindisfarnennr.blogspot.co.uk
01289 381470
You don't have to be an anorak

to enjoy the dunes, marches, tidal mudflats and of the Lindisfarne National Nature Reserve, which embraces the island's shoreline and a swathe of the coastal mainland. But wellies and binoculars will definitely enhance your visit.

At Budle Bay you can see sky-darkening flocks of waterfowl such as barnacle, brent and pink-footed geese, wigeon and other ducks and many waders, especially in autumn when they fly in from the Arctic in huge numbers. Look (and listen) for grey seals too – they gather to bask on

▼ The priory church

sands at low tide, and in the mating season they're quite vocal. A sandbar covered with randy seals sounds like a good party in full swing.

WALK IN ST CUTHBERT'S FOOTSTEPS

St Cuthbert's Island

Splash through the shallows at low tide – being sure to check the tide tables before you go – to St Cuthbert's Island. Just offshore, it was where the saint when he needed to spend time in prayer and meditation, in total solitude. A simple cross marks the site of his private chapel.

EAT AND DRINK

Pilgrims Coffee Shop

Front Street, TD15 2SJ

01289 389109

In the heart of the village, Pilgrims is more Continental coffee shop than English tea room, but has great sandwiches made with its own freshly baked bread. Try the local crab sandwiches, and some great cakes, too. Eat in the walled garden when the sun shines.

5 northern saints

▶ **Aidan**
Invited by King Oswald to preach Christianity to the Northumbrians, the Scots missionary Aidan founded the first monastery on Lindisfarne in AD 635.

▶ **Cuthbert**
Northumberland's patron saint (AD 634–686) ended his days as a cave-dwelling hermit. His bones are buried in Durham Cathedral (see page 112)

▶ **Edwin**
Northumbria's first Christian king was sainted after his death in battle.

▶ **Bede**
Jarrow-born Bede (AD 672–735) is renowned as the author of the first history of Christian England.

▶ **Wilfrid**
The noble-born Wilfrid (AD 633–709), bishop of Northumbria, was devout, disputatious, and – unlike his ascetic contemporaries – a bit too fond of his creature comforts.

▶ Housesteads

english-heritage.org.uk

Housesteads Roman Fort, Haydon Bridge, NE47 6NN | 01434 344363

Open Apr–Sep daily 10–6, Oct–Mar Sat–Sun 10–4 (Feb 17–25 daily 10–4)

It's easy to see why Housesteads – Roman Vercovicium – is the most visited fort on Hadrian's Wall. It's worth going for the site alone, but the remains of the ancient fort are in surprisingly good shape, considering that almost 2,000 years have rolled over them. It also has access to one of the best parts of the wall.

You won't be alone here, and you should avoid summer weekends to dodge the crowds. Visit the museum first to get the big picture and admire archaeological treasures. Then climb to the remains of town buildings by the South Gate. These buildings still show the grooves that once held shutters, so they may have been shops or taverns, and you can imagine Roman legionaries unwinding over a pint here after a hard day's Pict-bashing.

The gate itself was rebuilt as a bastle in the Middle Ages for a family of horse-thieves. Through it, to the right, you can visit the 12-seater latrines. There was clearly no sense of privacy in the Roman military.

The Romans built everything to a standard plan, and Housesteads followed the standard square pattern, with the headquarters in the centre and the commanding officer's house south of it. You can also see the remains of the hospital, complete with operating theatre, and the granaries.

The fort was built to protect Knag Burn, one of the wall's weak points, and the North Gate has huge foundations on the crag above the burn. Climb it for a classic wall view, then walk westwards along the wall westwards to Milecastle 37 or, to really stretch your legs, as far as Steel Rigg, where you can see how the massive military structures of Rome have been absorbed into the Northumbrian landscape.

◀ Fort Vercovicium

▶ Kielder Water

You'll find Europe's largest artificial lake and Britain's largest forest at Kielder, hard by Hadrian's Wall and the Scottish border. Kielder Water has 27 miles of shoreline, and it's surrounded by more than 153,140 acres of woodland. It's an entirely man-made environment, dedicated to commercial timber growing and managed by Forest Enterprise. Three quarters of the forest is Sitka spruce, which is well suited to harsh upland environments. It comes from Alaska, so it can handle even the harshest English winter. Other alien tree species here include Norway spruce and lodgepole pine, and they far outnumber native larch, Scots pine and broadleaf trees such as birch and beech. But more deciduous trees are being planted, and the aim is to increase the proportion of hardwoods to eight per cent by 2020.

If you're just visiting, though, this hardly matters. Kielder may not be pristine wilderness, but it is one of Britain's biggest nature reserves. Its hills, rivers, woods and forest glades shelter as many as 6,000 roe deer, along with red squirrels.

Kestrels are seen regularly, sparrowhawks are common, and there is always a chance of seeing merlin, peregrine or goshawk. Bakethin Reservoir attracts ospreys as well as sizeable numbers of wildfowl and gulls at all times of the year. In the main conifer forest, the elusive crossbill flits through the tree canopy, and the broadleaf woods of the North Tyne Valley attract pied flycatcher and redstart.

There are more than 372 miles of streams and rivers in the forest and otters are on the increase here, with signs that they are using all the major waterways in the area.

The remarkable diversity of Kielder is shown in the fact that here there are no fewer than nine Sites of Special Scientific Interest. Embracing some 18,500 acres, this represents 4 per cent of the total SSSI area in England alone, and sites include ancient woodland, fossil trees, geological sites, moorlands and the extensive Border Mire peat bogs. Access to part of the mires has been improved by the completion of a boardwalk, which just happens to surround one of the best ponds for dragonflies in Northumberland.

On the lake, Kielder's tranquil beauty is complemented by sailing and other watersports, fishing and ferry cruises. You can explore the fringes of the lake and the forest glades on foot (the best way of seeing shy wildlife) by bike or on horseback.

▼ Kielder Water

PLAN YOUR VISIT
Kielder Castle Visitor Centre
visitkielder.com
Kielder, NE48 1ER | 01434 250209
Open daily 9.30–5

Kitschy Kielder Castle, with its mock-medieval fortification, was built in 1775 as a hunting lodge for the Duke of Northumberland and looks more like a film set than the real thing – you expect Robin Hood or the Sheriff of Nottingham to turn up any moment.

The focal point for visitors to the forest, the Castle is now the main visitor centre for the national park and houses a series of exhibitions about birds, wildlife, history and the daily working of the forest. Next to it stands the Minotaur Maze, a labyrinth made of glass and basalt. There are also picnic sites in the grounds, along with a children's playground, walking trails, and cycling routes.

EXPLORE BY BIKE
The Bike Place
thebikeplace.co.uk
Kielder Village, NE48 1ER
01434 250457 | Open
daily 9.30–5.30
1 King Street, Bellingham, NE48 2AX | 01434 220120 | Open Mon–Sat 10–5.30

Rent a bike from The Bike Place, with branches in Kielder Village and Bellingham. They'll give you useful tips on where to ride. Trails range from the easy 7-mile Borderline circuit to the challenging 9.5 mile Deadwater route and the long-distance Lakeside Way.

MEET THE RAPTORS
Kielder Water Birds of Prey Centre
kwbopc.com
NE48 1AX | 01434 250400
Open daily 10.30–4.30; flying demonstrations three times daily, weather permitting

Encounter all our native owl species at Kielder Water Birds of Prey Centre, along with hawks, eagles and other owls and birds of prey from all over the world. With more than 60 birds from almost 30 species, this is one of the largest and most fascinating collections of birds of prey in the north of England. Weather permitting, flying demonstrations take place three times a day.

GET STEAMY
Leaplish Indoor Pool and Sauna
visitkielder.com
Leaplish Waterside Park, Kielder, N48 1BT | 01434 251000
Open daily 8–6

You're not allowed to swim in Kielder Water, and anyway only the brave would be tempted to take a dip in its chilly waters. Happily, there's an alternative – you can do a few laps at the heated Leaplish Indoor Pool, and if you're feeling a bit stiff after a long day you can steam away any aches and pains in its sauna. The Waterside Park also offers family activities ranging from archery to fencing, boules and miniature golf.

ENTERTAIN THE FAMILY ON KIELDER WATER

Leaplish Waterside Park

visitkielder.com

N48 1BT | 01434 251000

Open daily 8–6

Kielder Water has some fine specimens of brown trout. Hire a boat from the Leaplish Waterside Park, or cast a fly from the bank. Permits are sold at Leaplish Waterside Park and Tower Knowe Visitor Centre

You can also take a trip on the *Osprey*, a 60-seater lake cruiser which sails four times a day in each direction between Leaplish Waterside Park, Tower Knowe Visitor Centre and Belvedere. You can take bikes on board, so it's the ideal way to explore different parts of Kielder Forest and the Lake shore without having to pedal all the way.

▼ Sailing on Kielder Water

SPECIAL NEEDS

Kielder Water and Forest Park

calvert-trust.org.uk/kielder

NE48 1BS | 01434 250232 | Open daily 9.30 – 4.30

People with special needs and their carers can enjoy a whole range of exciting activities at the Calvert Trust in Kielder Forest. The centre offers orienteering, climbing walls, sailing, canoeing, zip wires and laser clay shooting (quieter, cheaper and more friendly than the real thing) and more, all purpose-built to be accessible to wheelchair users, people with visual and hearing difficulties, and others. Purpose-built accessible accommodation is also available, and the centre is staffed by fully trained carers. You don't have to be living with a disability to use the centre's canoes, kayaks, sailing dinghies

and motor boats – day visitors can rent these from the centre's boathouse at Matthew's Linn.

LEARN TO WATERSKI
Merlin Brae Waterski Club
merlinbraewaterski.co.uk
Shilling Pot, Kielder, 1 mile from Tower Knowe Visitor Centre
01434 250037 | Open Apr–Oct Sat–Sun 10.30–5.50
Day visitors are welcome at Merlin Brae Waterski Club on summer weekends, when novices can learn the basic skills of waterskiing and wakeboarding and experienced enthusiasts can show off their techniques. Hire of equipment, including boards, boat and wetsuits, is available.

MESS ABOUT IN BOATS
Leaplish Waterside Park
www.nwl.co.uk
N48 1BP | 01434 251000 | Pleasure boats are available Sat–Wed 12–5, Jul–Aug, subject to weather conditions.
Pack a picnic and set off to explore Kielder Water on your own with a motor boat rented from Leaplish Waterside Park.

WATCH THE SKIES
Kielder Observatory
kielderobservatory.org
Black Fell, Shilling Pot, Kielder, NE48 1EJ | 07805 638469
Open Mon nights 8–11 and for special events
If you're afraid of the dark, steer clear of Kielder on winter nights. If you love stargazing, though, this is a great time to be here, because the skies above Kielder are the darkest in England. There are few villages and no big towns nearby, so light pollution is minimal and on a clear, frosty night with no cloud the view overhead can be breathtaking – looking up at a sky full of stars, it's impossible to believe that we're alone in the universe. Somebody else must be out there somewhere.

Kielder Observatory's scopes are open to visitors, and local astronomers hold special events and sky-watching classes.

EAT AND DRINK
The Pheasant Inn
thepheasantinn.com
Stannersburn, NE48 1DD
01434 240382
In the early 17th century, agricultural workers drank at this ivy-clad country inn which now finds itself where the Northumberland National Park meets the Border Forest Park. It's well positioned for cycle tracks, a sculpture trail, an observatory, endless walks and wildlife watching.

Most spaces in the two bars have been filled with historic Northumberland memorabilia, and on the exposed stone walls that support the blackened beams are photos of yesteryear's locals working at forgotten trades like blacksmithing and coalmining. The restaurant, with terracotta-coloured walls and furnished in mellow pine, looks out over the countryside.

▷ Kirknewton

Use Kirknewton village as a jumping-off point for walks in the Cheviot Hills (see page 92), or in the nearby valley of the College Burn. But take time out to explore the village, too. Huddled below the Cheviots, it's a cluster of stone houses and the village church is a lot older than it seems. At first glance, it looks Victorian, but inside is an unusual chancel with a stone roof that curves to the floor like the hull of an upturned ship. By the arch leading to the chancel is Kirknewton's other treasure – a 12th-century carving of the Wise Men visiting the infant Jesus and his mother. It is carved roughly and has an almost cartoon-like quality, but is a fascinating and moving glimpse into a world that existed nearly 1,000 years ago.

▷ PLACES NEARBY

Yeavering Bell

Slog to the twin summits of this hill in the Cheviots to discover, 1,184ft (362m) above sea level, the remnants of a hill-fort built by the Votadini, the Brythonic nation who held the lands between Hadrian's Wall before the Romans came, and after they left. The Votadini, or Gododdin, were sometimes allies and sometimes enemies of Roman but were never conquered. After the Romans left, they became a major power north of the border and great enemies of the Anglo-Saxons. Yeavering Bell is a tribute to their strength and their skill as fortress-builders. In its way, it's every bit as impressive as the Roman forts along the Wall or the castles built by medieval kings and earls. The top of the hill was wrapped round by a stone rampart that was some ten feet thick. Inside it was an inner keep, partly built into the living rock of the summit. All around are the remains of stone houses, and there are many burial barrows in the surrounding area, showing that Yeavering Bell was a place of importance, perhaps even a royal capital, in its day.

▷ Lindisfarne

see **Holy Island,** page 143

▷ Marsden Bay

Come to Marsden Bay for sea views, to visit a historic lighthouse, and to eat and drink in a unique grotto. The coast of Durham south of the Tyne was long renowned for its smugglers, and the natural caves at the base of the cliffs of Marsden Bay provided hiding places for illicit activity.

GO UNDERGROUND
Marsden Grotto
marsden-grotto.co.uk
Coast Road, South Shields, NE34 7BS
0191 4556060
In the 1790s a quarryman known as Jack the Blaster used explosives to increase the size of one of the caves and provide steps from the cliff top, setting up home there with his wife and selling refreshments to visitors – including, it is said, to the local smugglers. In the 19th century an underground ballroom was created here, and in the 1930s a lift was installed. It's now a pub, and it's well worth the price of a pint for look inside the only cave restaurant in Europe.

GET OUTDOORS
Souter Lighthouse and The Leas
nationaltrust.org.uk
Coast Road, Marsden | SR6 7NH
0191 5293161 | Open Sat–Thu 11–5
The red-and-white striped Souter Lighthouse was erected in 1871 to protect ships from the notorious rocks called Whitburn Steel, just off the coast. It was the first light in the world to be electrically powered. Originally it was nearly a quarter of a mile from the sea, but erosion has brought the cliff edge much nearer. Farther inland, walkers can discover two windmills – the first near Marsden retains its sails, but another in Cleadon is now a ruin. The Leas, a 2.5 mile stretch of grassland and sea-carved limestone cliffs, is a good place for bracing walk and a breath of fresh sea air.

Marsden Rock
Looking offshore, you can see clouds of seabirds – kittiwakes, fulmars, cormorants and guillemots – flying around a cluster of seastacks. These pillars have been formed as North Sea waves grind away at their soft limestone rock. The process is ongoing – in 1996, the natural arch that linked the largest and famous stack, Marsden Rock, with its smaller neighbour, collapsed. The remains of the smaller stack were demolished for safety reasons, which was surely erring on the side of caution, and Marsden Rock is nowhere near as impressive as it was.

EAT AND DRINK
Marsden Grotto
marsden-grotto.co.uk
Coast Road, South Shields, NE34 7BS
0191 4556060
The famous cave is now a popular pub and quirkily decorated eating place called the Marsden Grotto. The fish and chips is well known. It was once owned by the Vaux brewery and it has an appropriately wide choice of tasty ales. There's posher seafood on the menu too, and a good wine list.

▶ Matfen

There's not a lot to see and do in Matfen itself, but it's a charming little place and well worth a short visit if you're in the neighbourhood. Planned and built as a model village in the 18th century, it's laid out around a village green and all in all it really belongs on a picture postcard. The Black Bull, in the centre of Matfen, is a classic village pub. If you fancy posher dining, head for nearby Matfen Hall. To get your adrenaline levels up, make a trip to Go Ape! with its crazy treetop zip wires and Tarzan ropes.

WALK THE HIGH ROPES

Go Ape! Matfen

goape.co.uk/matfen

Matfen Hall Hotel, NE20 0RH

0845 6439215 | See website for opening times and availability

Go Ape! has more than 800yds of zip-wires and ropes at treetop height – the highest point is 36ft above the ground. This was the first Go Ape! course to be set in the grounds of a country house hotel, and it nestles within one of the UK's most unspoilt areas of natural beauty. If you can't summon the courage to try out its giddy crossings, you can enjoy a less challenging stroll through Matfen's 300 acres of historic parkland.

PLAY A ROUND

Matfen Hall

matfenhall.com

NE20 0RH | 01661 886400

Open daily

A 27-hole parkland course set in beautiful countryside with many natural and man-made hazards. The course is an enjoyable test for players of all abilities but it does incorporate challenging water features in the shape of a large lake and a fast-flowing river. The dry stone wall presents a unique obstacle on several holes. The 4th, 9th, 12th and 14th holes are particularly testing par 4s, the dog-leg 16th is the pick of the par 5s but Matfen's signature hole is the long par 3 17th with its narrow green teasingly sited just over the river.

EAT AND DRINK

Matfen Hall, Golf and Spa ◉◉

matfenhall.com

NE20 0RH | 01661 886500

Ancestral home of the Blackett family, Matfen was opened as a luxury spa hotel in 1999, so all may now enjoy its 300 acres of parkland, its grand public rooms, and the majestic, book-lined library with its ornate mouldings, panelling and magnificent views now forms the hotel's fine dining restaurant, where. The kitchen explores the modern British repertoire for inspiring stalwarts such as smoked haddock and pea risotto, king scallops with black pudding, and main courses such as seared salmon on lemon-crushed potatoes in dill beurre blanc, or roasted beef fillet with thyme and garlic rösti and Jerusalem artichoke purée. Desserts bring on plenty of fruity creations, along the lines of lime cheesecake with mango sorbet and passionfruit jelly, or apple sponge with blueberry parfait and honeycomb. As well as the Library, Matfen Hall has three more places to eat. The Conservatory and Keepers Lodge overlook the golf course and offer gastro-pub style food in casual surroundings, while the Juice Bar offers snacks, light meals, freshly pressed juices and smoothies.

▶ Middleton-in-Teesdale

You can still imagine throngs of miners crowding the streets of Middleton. In its heyday, it was the centre of the dale's lead-mining industry, and nine out of ten of its workers were employed in the mines. The London Lead Mining Company opened its North of England headquarters here in 1815 and developed the town rapidly. Owned by Quakers, it provided homes for its workers, schooling for their children, a town library and a brass band.

The company was just as obsessed with the state of its workers' souls as with their material well-being – perhaps even more so, as lead poisoning must have ruined the health of many mine workers. Chapel attendance was almost compulsory, and every boy who wanted a job had to have a course of religious instruction. By the early 20th century local lead extraction was being undercut by cheaper foreign imports, and the company went bankrupt in 1905.

Most of Middleton's stone houses date from the 19th century, but its earlier history can be appreciated from the little bell-tower of 1567, like a garden summerhouse, in the corner of the churchyard, away from the Victorian church. The London Lead Mining Company's Middleton House, with its fine clock-towered stable, is up the hill to the northwest, and the company's housing estate, Masterman Place, to the east of the town, is approached through a grand archway. You can see the jolly cast-iron fountain given to the town by the company superintendent, Mr Bainbridge, in Horsemarket.

You'll find England's highest waterfall, High Force, not far from town, and the country's longest cascade, Cauldron Snout, nearby at Langdon Beck. There are spectacular basalt cliffs in the narrow valley below, and rare Arctic plants on the sugar limestone of Widdybank Fell.

▲ Waterfall at Bowlees, Upper Teesdale

GET OUTDOORS
Bowlees Visitor Centre and Gibson's Cave

northpennines.org.uk
Newbiggin, DL12 0XF
01388 528801 | Open Jun–Oct daily
9–6, Oct–Nov 10–4, Nov–Feb
Fri–Sun 10–4

Get out of town and explore the wild landscapes of Upper Teesdale. Upstream from Middleton the River Tees becomes increasingly spectacular. The Visitor Centre at Bowlees, three miles northwest of town, provides an excellent introduction to the geology, archaeology, flora and wildlife of Upper Teesdale. Picnic at the nearby site, and walk to Gibson's Cave, where you can hide like Rob Roy or Robin Hood behind a 20ft waterfall, Summerhill Force, which has formed a hollow in the soft rock.

▶ **PLACES NEARBY**

Wynch Bridge

Cross the Tees by this, Europe's oldest suspension bridge. Built for miners in the 1740s, it was rebuilt in 1828, which is comforting to know, as there's quite a drop from the narrow bridge – only two feet wide, but 70 feet long – into the river below. Just above the bridge is Low Force, a series of picturesque waterfalls, but the big attraction is High Force, 1.5 miles further on, reached by a path through woods opposite the hotel. There's a picnic area here, so if you're feeling lazy you can drive and park nearby. White water thunders over the Great Whin Sill, plunging into the gorge creating a drop of 70ft, the highest single-drop waterfall in England.

Eggleston Hall Gardens

egglestonhall.co.uk

DL12 0AG | 01833 650230

Visit this walled garden for a spring and summer blaze of colour from azaleas, rhododendrons, rock roses and other hardy herbaceous plants which thrive in the local microclimate. Espaliered pear and plum trees grow around the walls, and an alphabetical apple walk is an eye opener – who knew there were 26 varieties?

▶ **Morpeth**

Morpeth is a pleasant enough little market town. Being just off the A1, it's a good place to stop for a break on a longer north–south drive. There are some fine old buildings in the town centre, including the Town Hall by Vanbrugh, rebuilt after a fire in the 19th century, and the 17th-century Clock Tower, in the middle of Oldgate. The 19th-century bridge used to carry the Great North Road across the River Wansbeck into the town, until Morpeth was bypassed by the new A1. The bypass was a mixed blessing – heavy traffic no longer thunders through the town centre, but on the other hand the new road deprived Morpeth of its passing trade, as most drivers now hurtle by without considering that the town might be worth a detour.

Up to a point, they're right, because it doesn't have a lot of knock-your-eye-out sights. In 1261 King John burned down Morpeth's first castle, which stood on Ha' Hill near St Mary's Church, along with the rest of the town, and the castle was not rebuilt. Only a gatehouse on Castle Walk and some bits of wall remain of a second, 15th-century castle. Nearby in Carlisle Park is the Courthouse, once the gateway to the gaol. The bridge chapel, the Chantry, holds the town's Bagpipe Museum.

Take a peek into the 14th-century St Mary's Church to see the best stained glass in the whole of Northumberland. Unlike many of the windows in other churches in the region,

the glass is not a later 18th- or 19th-century addition but contemporary with the church. The churchyard has a watchhouse where a guard kept an eye open for 'resurrection men'– body-snatchers who supplied 19th-century anatomists with fresh corpses for dissection. The churchyard also contains the grave of suffragette Emily Davison, who died when she threw herself under the hooves of George V's horse at the 1913 Derby meeting.

There are some more notable religious buildings near Morpeth. St James's Church, 0.75 miles north, is a superb Victorian neo-Norman building. Newminster Abbey was one of the richest Cistercian abbeys in the north until Henry VIII's dissolution, owning vast swathes of the Cheviot Hills. Little remains today except part of the Chapter House, set among grass, wild flowers and brambles. Mitford, west of Morpeth, has a fine church in woodland and the remains of a castle.

VISIT THE MUSEUM

Morpeth Chantry
Bagpipe Museum

experiencewoodhorn.com/
  morpeth-bagpipe-museum
Bridge Street, NE61 1PD
01670 624455 | Open Mon–Sat
9.30–5 and Sun in Aug
Morpeth Northumbrian Gathering
is normally held first weekend after
Easter. See northumbriana.org.uk
for dates

Learn about Northumberland's very own instrument, the small pipes or Northumberland pipes, at this unusual museum. It may come as a surprise to discover just how many different kinds of bagpipe there are, and where they come from. Places as diverse as Bulgaria, Greece, Galicia and Brittany have their own versions, and of course Highland emigrants and the kilted regiments of the British Empire took the pipes all over the world. As a result, there are pipe bands from Canada to China, by way of Pakistan and India. Visit during the Morpeth Northumbrian Gathering to hear the small pipes being played.

MEET THE MEERKATS

Whitehouse
Farm Centre

whitehousefarmcentre.co.uk
North Whitehouse Farm, near
Morpeth, NE61 6AW
01670 789998
Open May–Aug daily 10–5,
Sep–Dec Tue–Sun 10–5, Jan and Nov
Sat–Sun 10–4

Pick up a meerkat, a cuddly bunny or even stroke a (non-poisonous) snake. There are less exotic but equally charming farm animals too, including lambs, goats, and pigs, as well as trampolines or an inflatable castle. Get lost in the willow maze or drive a pedal tractor or a go-kart.

◀ Courthouse and gardens, Carlisle Park

GET OUTDOORS
Scotch Gill Wood Nature Reserve
Mitford Road, NE61 1RG
01670 506789 | Open any reasonable time
In spring, banks of bluebells and snowdrops make Scotch Gill Wood Nature Reserve, near Morpeth, a lovely place for a stroll through woods and along the river bank. In summer, it's loud with birdsong.

WE HAVE LIFT OFF
Alba Ballooning
albaballooning.co.uk
5 Primrose Gardens, Carrington, Midlothian, EH23 4LP | 01875 830709 | Flights normally Apr–Sep, selected dates | see website for info.
Take to the skies on a hot air balloon flight with Alba Ballooning, which flies from Longhorsley. Which part of Northumberland you drift over will depend on the wind, but it's a great way to see the Northumberland Park, stretches of Hadrian's Wall, the Pennines and the coast, laid out like a patchwork quilt.

PLAY A ROUND
Macdonald Linden Hall, Golf and Country Club
macdonaldhotels.co.uk/lindenhall
NE65 8XF | 01670 500011
Open daily
Set in the Linden Hall Estate on a mixture of mature woodland and parkland, established lakes and burns provide interesting water features to match the peaceful surroundings.

Percy Wood Golf and Country Retreat
percywood.co.uk
Coast View, Swarland | NE65 9JG
01670 787010 | Open daily
A parkland course set in mature woodland with scenic views. There are seven par 4 holes in excess of 400yds. A good challenge for all levels.

EAT AND DRINK
The Chantry Tea Room
9 Chantry Place, NE61 1PJ
01670 514414
It is always a pleasure to find a place like The Chantry, where you are assured of a warm welcome and attentive service. There are 11 blends of tea available, including a 'Northumbrian' blend, to accompany the sandwiches, scones, cakes and light meals on the menu. Once you've settled in, look around at the original paintings and photos, many of which are for sale.

Eshott Hall ◉
eshotthall.co.uk
Eshott, NE65 9EN | 01670 787454
An elegantly proportioned Georgian property, its facade hung with wisteria, Eshott Hall is surrounded by gardens and woodlands. A magnificent stained-glass window looks over the entrance, and, in winter, expect open fires in the grandly appointed public rooms, including the dining room, with its soothing décor, pillars, moulded plasterwork and candelabra on crisply clothed tables. On the menu,

look for seasonal game and fresh fish among the variety of other excellent and imaginative dishes.

Extras like canapés are appreciated, and to finish there may be Yorkshire rhubarb cheesecake.

▶ Newbiggin by the Sea

In the early 20th century (before we all started taking our buckets and spades to the Costa Brava), this little fishing village with its long sandy beach was a favourite holiday destination for families from the northeast looking to get away from city or the mines for a breath of fresh sea air. But Newbiggin got hit by a double whammy – many of its visitors deserted it for cheap package holidays in the sun, and, as if symbolically, its sands were gradually washed away by the North Sea waves.

Something had to be done – and in 2007, something was done. A long breakwater was built to stop erosion, and 500,000 tonnes of sand was imported from Skegness (which presumably has sand still to spare), a stylish new beach promenade – the longest in Northumberland – was built, and Newbiggin is once again a lively spot in summer.

VISIT THE MUSEUMS AND GALLERIES

Newbiggin Maritime Centre

newbigginmaritimecentre.org.uk
Church Point, NE64 6DB
01670 819251 | Open Wed–Sat 10–4, Sun 11–4 (daily in school hols)

Get a glimpse of Newbiggin's past as a fishing village at this lively heritage centre. There are photos of fisher-folk and their ships, piles of lobster pots and other paraphernalia, and pride of place goes to two hands-on exhibits, the RNLI lifeboat *Mary Joicey* and the fishing coble *Girl Anne*.

These open wooden cobles evolved to land their catch on sandy beaches, and going to see in one of these seemingly fragile boats must have required a great deal of courage.

The Newbiggin by the Sea Art Trail

visitnewbiggin.com
Front Street, Newbiggin by the Sea, NE64 6NJ | 01670 817029

You can track down more than 50 quirky works of art on this free outdoor trail, created by local artists' group KEAP Creative. Among the most impressive is the larger than life *Couple* sculpture, created by artist Sean Henry and standing on the seafront breakwater. Allow around two hours to find all the sculptures scattered along the promenade and around the village.

Newcastle upon Tyne

Newcastle has had its ups and downs but (like its neighbour Gateshead (see page 123), just across the Tyne) it keeps on bouncing back and reinventing itself. To its natives, it's just 'the Toon' (and supporters of its football team are the 'Toon Army') The northeast's biggest city make a lively contrast with the medieval castles, ruined abbeys and wide open spaces of the northeast's hinterland. It gets its name from the New Castle built in 1080 by Robert Curthose, eldest son of William the Conqueror, but the city as it stands today is overwhelmingly a creation of the industrial age – with some notable 21st-century additions.

M Metro station

LLC

The original castle is long gone, and little remains of the second castle, built a century later by Henry II, except for its keep. You could do worse than start exploring the city by visiting it and climbing to the roof of the keep for a great view of the city, the River Tyne and the bridges that are Newcastle's signature landmarks. Queen Victoria is said to have kept the blinds down while her royal train passed through Newcastle on the way to and from Balmoral – she favoured sweeping, romantic views of Scottish bens and glens over the new industrial grandeur of the age of steam. So she missed the view of the bridges and the river, and passed up the chance to visit a place of vibrant energy, then and now, and one of the friendliest of northern cities. She would certainly not have been amused by the antics of the skimpily clad young revellers enjoying the notoriously raucous nightlife of the city's Bigg Market.

Victorian railway builders cut ruthlessly through the medieval castle ward, so its medieval entrance, the Black Gate, is now separated from the keep. A picturesque brick house (c. 1620) perches on top of its 13th-century lower floors. The railway goes into Central Station, a masterpiece of Newcastle architect John Dobson. The huge curved train shed, supported by slender iron columns, was much imitated. From here you can connect with the Metro system, which is still the most convenient way of getting around Newcastle. The hub of the Metro system is Monument Station, just by the column to Earl Grey, the 19th-century local grandee and parliamentary reformer.

Grey Street, lined with elegant, columned buildings, curves down towards the Tyne. Near the top, the lively Theatre Royal, northern home of the Royal Shakespeare Company and of the National Theatre, adds a punctuation mark with its elegant portico.

◀ Previous page: the Tyne Bridge; Newcastle upon Tyne Castle

Bessie Surtees House, nearer the river, is a survivor from an earlier Newcastle, and has a half-timbered front with a vast array of small-paned windows. From one of them – marked with blue glass – Bessie, the daughter of a Newcastle banker, eloped with her lover John Scott; although from relatively humble beginnings, he later rose to become Lord Chancellor of Great Britain.

The river near here is crossed by four of Newcastle's most famous bridges. Each one is a tribute to the skills of local builders and engineers. Robert Stephenson's High Level Bridge was finished in 1849, with twin decks for trains and cars. The Swing Bridge was built 25 years later by another firm of engineers from the northeast, Armstrongs, and was driven by their hydraulic engines. The semicircular Tyne Bridge is the bridge that reminds exiled Geordies all over the world of home. Much more recent is the graceful Millennium Bridge which opened in time to welcome in the 21st century. It leaps over the river from the Quayside, where a famous Sunday morning market is held, and you can hop on a river cruiser here for

▼ The Millennium and Tyne bridges

a trip on the Tyne. The Quayside is also a focus of Newcastle's youth culture, with pubs and clubs jostling with each other in the streets around.

Two church towers dominate this part of Newcastle. Classical All Saints – now deconsecrated – has a fine spire attached to a very unusual elliptical body. The Cathedral of St Nicholas, with its splendid tall crown, was threatened with destruction from Scottish cannon fire during the Civil War, but mercifully the firing ceased when the Mayor decided to fill the cathedral with Scots prisoners.

Newcastle has more than its fair share of excellent museums, and several of them are among the best in Britain for families. The Great Northern Museum, with its fine Roman artefacts, is the principal museum for Hadrian's Wall, and also houses John Hancock's magnificent collection of birds, as well as geological exhibits, making it one of the finest collections in the country. Newcastle Discovery tells the city's story. Stunning Victorian paintings can be seen at Laing Art Gallery, including several by local visionary artist John Martin.

There is horseracing at High Gosforth Park, north of the city. The Northumberland Plate meeting in June, a valuable 2-mile handicap, is known as 'The Pitmen's Derby' because all the collieries closed for the day so that miners could attend.

TAKE IN SOME HISTORY
The Castle Keep and the Black Gate
www.castlekeep-newcastle.org.uk
Castle Garth, NE1 1RQ
0191 2327938 | Open Mon–Sat 10–5, Sun 12–5

Unless you know it's there, the castle is easy to miss. Much of the castle has been destroyed, including the Great Hall, which was demolished in 1809, and what's left is concealed by newer (and not very pretty) buildings.

The one splendid building that has survived is the keep, its 12th-century walls rising tall and proud over the bustle of the modern city. It is built of sandstone, and the walls are generally between 15 and 18ft thick and 65ft high. In its day,

it was one of the most important medieval castles in northern England. It was huge, and was surrounded by great walls and ditches. Several towers added strength to the site, including the Black Gate, which had its own drawbridge, passage with gates, a portcullis, and a terrifying number of arrow slits.

Within the keep, there are five floors, although the upper one is mainly a wall gallery. One room contains a well which is 100ft deep and lined with cut stone, and basins and pipes suggest that water flowed from here to the lower parts of the building. That was pretty sophisticated stuff for the middle ages. There is also a chapel with some fine moulded arches.

VISIT THE MUSEUMS AND GALLERIES
Great North Museum
twmuseums.org.uk
Barras Bridge (Haymarket Metro), NE2 4PT | 0191 2226765 | Open Mon–Fri 10–5, Sat 10–4, Sun 11–4

This century-old natural history museum is a great place to take kids on a rainy day. It may be a venerable institution, but its galleries and displays are bang up to date. It's close to the centre of Newcastle, just five minutes' walk from the nearest metro stop, and it's free.

There's a comprehensive collection of some of the most important finds from sites

◀ Grey's Monument at dusk

along Hadrian's Wall. Young would-be naturalists and time-travellers will enjoy close encounters with resident creepy-crawlies and sensational galleries that show them tantalising glimpses of the animal kingdom and the powerful and often destructive forces of nature, an angle that makes the museum highly relevant in our age of climate change. There are prehistoric bones, fossils from the age of dinosaurs, and just for variety, there are ancient Egyptian mummies too.

5 farmer's markets

The region has plenty of farmers' markets, selling local produce. They include:

▶ Barnard Castle
First Saturday of each month, all year

▶ Durham
Third Saturday of each month, all year

▶ Alnwick
Last Friday every month, all year

▶ Hexham
Second and fourth Saturday of each month, all year

▶ Newcastle
First Friday of each month, all year

For a comprehensive programme, visit the North East England Farmers' Markets site, neefm.org.uk

Discovery Museum
twmuseums.org.uk
Blandford Square, NE1 4JA
0191 2326789 | Open Mon–Fri 10–5, Sat 10–4, Sun 11–4

Discovery Museum is another family-pleaser. For children, it will be an eye-opener, revealing the breathtaking speed of technological progress over just a few generations. The big ticket is the *Turbinia*, with a gallery all of her own. When she was launched in 1894, this liner, designed by Charles Parsons, was the first steam-turbine driven ship, and the fastest ever. With a measured top speed of 34.5 knots, *Turbinia* still stacks up well against 21st-century vessels. Cunard's flagship liner, *Queen Mary 2*, launched in 2004, does just 30 knots.

Other displays cover military history – including the weapons of mass destruction devised by local engineer and founder, William Armstrong, whose breech-loading guns served the British Empire well from the mid-19th century until the 1920s. Maritime splendours, scientific curiosities and local history are also covered.

Segedunum Roman Fort, Baths and Museum
twmuseums.org.uk
Buddle Street, NE28 6HR
0191 2369347 | Open Apr–Oct 10–5, Nov–Mar 10–3

No other Roman fort in Britain has been dug up and reconstructed as thoroughly as Segedunum. In a way, the fact that it's in the middle of a major city, not stuck out in the wilds, makes it all the more interesting.

Wallsend is just an undistinguished part of Newcastle now, but in its day it must have been quite a place. You'll have guessed by the name that this was the eastern terminus of the great Roman barrier that crossed Britain from sea to shining sea. Not all the legionaries and auxiliaries landed in Dover, then tramped up the great north road to their garrisons on the Wall. Quite a few of them – more as the Roman Empire grew older and came to depend on mercenaries from beyond its borders – came to Britain from the low, marshy lands around the mouths of the Rhine and the Scheldt. They would have disembarked here, and for many of them this would have been their first taste of the power of Rome. You can imagine, too, hardened Roman professionals – the empire's equivalent of today's elite special forces – setting off by sea from Wallsend on long-range reconnaissance patrols, travelling up the coast and deep into the heart of Pictland.

Segedunum served as a garrison for 600 soldiers until the collapse of Roman rule around AD 410. This major historical venture shows what life would have been like during this period, using artefacts, audio-visuals, reconstructed buildings and a 112ft-high viewing tower.

ENTERTAIN THE FAMILY
Life Science Centre
life.org.uk
Times Square, NE1 4EP
0191 2438210
Open Mon–Sat 10–6, Sun 11–6
Highlights at Life include the 4D Motion Ride, the northeast's biggest planetarium, live theatre shows and the exhibit-crammed Curiosity Zone. This is an exciting and award-winning science centre where science comes alive in a fun environment, aiming to inspire curiosity and helping visitors uncover new things about life, whatever their age. There's a special area just for under-7s, and a changing programme of exhibitions and events.

From November to February, Life hosts an outdoor ice rink.

GET OUTDOORS
Jesmond Dene
Lord Armstrong presented this landscaped valley to the city of Newcastle in 1883 as a free public park, and it has been much loved and visited ever since.

The millionaire arms magnate and local benefactor spent a small fortune to turn Jesmond Dene into a personal oasis around his stately home. His house has gone, but the walks and bridges laid out for him remain in this unusual park, where swans paddle on the pools and a waterfall tumbles over rocks.

CLIMB THE WALLS
Newcastle Climbing Centre
newcastleclimbingcentre.co.uk
285 Shields Road, Newcastle upon Tyne, NE6 2UQ | 0191 2656060
Open Mon–Fri 10–10, Sat–Sun 10–8
Learn the ropes at Newcastle Climbing Centre, where would-be climbers from five years old can have a go at bouldering, climbing on roped walls almost 50 feet in height, inside a former church. Experienced climbers can sharpen their skills too.

READ ME A STORY
National Centre for Children's Books
sevenstories.org.uk
30 Lime Street, NE1 2PQ
0845 2710777
Open Mon–Sat 10–5, Sun 10–4
If you're a parent who worries about your kids rejecting reading in favour of mobile devices and games, take them to the National Centre for Children's Books, where they will enjoy live events including story-telling, exhibitions, and the opportunity to try their hand at writing a story.

GO TO THE THEATRE
Theatre Royal
theatreroyal.co.uk
Grey Street, NE1 6BR
08448 112121
You can see ballet, contemporary dance, drama, West End musicals and pantomime on stage at the elegant Theatre Royal, which is the northern home of the Royal Shakespeare Company and of Britain's National Theatre.

CRUISE THE TYNE
River Escapes
riverescapes.co.uk
Quayside, NE1 3DX
01670 785666/785777
Scheduled cruises all year call for timetables
Board a river boat at the Quayside to take a trip up or down the Tyne. There's no better way to see the river and its landmarks – including the Tyne and Millennium bridges, BALTIC contemporary arts centre, Sage Gateshead and the skyline of the city. A guide narrates the city's history, and refreshments are available on board.

EXPLORE BY BIKE
The Cycle Hub
thecyclehub.org
Quayside, NE6 1BU
0191 2767250 | Open Mon–Fri 9–5, Sat 10–6, Sun 10–5
'It's all about the bike' is the slogan of The Cycle Hub, which rents bikes of all shapes and sizes from its friendly base on the Quayside. There's a nice cafe, too, where you can carbo-load before setting off or top up when you get back with a healthy appetitite. It's right by the river, so you can pedal on the flat as far as you like. The Cycle Hub offer pick-up and drop-off to the start and end points of various recommended cycle rides in and around Newcastle.

SEE A FOOTBALL MATCH
St James' Park
nufc.co.uk
NE1 4ST | 0844 3721892
Contact club for fixtures and tours
Take a tour of St James' Park, ancestral home of Newcastle United since the 1880s. Smell the testosterone in the changing rooms, feel the pitchside excitement, and find out how TV presenters, radio commentators and sports correspondents cover matches from the media suite. Or just join the Toon Army when the lads are playing at home and the sweet smell of victory is in the air. Or not, as the case may be.

PLAY A ROUND
Northumberland Golf Club
thengc.co.uk
High Gosforth Park, NE3 5HT
0191 2362498
Open daily
Predominantly a level heathland style course, the firm, fast greens are a particular feature. Selected as an Open 2014 Regional Qualifying Course in 2013.

Westerhope Golf Club
westerhopegolfclub.com
Whorlton Grange, Westerhope, NE5 1PP | 0191 2867636
Open daily
Attractive, easy walking parkland with tree-lined fairways. Good open views towards the airport.

EAT AND DRINK
Blackfriars Restaurant ◉
blackfriarsrestaurant.co.uk
Friars Street, NE1 4XN
0191 2615945
The Dominican friary at the heart of medieval Newcastle is an integral part of the city's heritage, and a thriving modern restaurant has arisen on the site where they began serving food to the monks in 1239. Plenty of natural wood, exposed stonework and medieval artefacts establish the venerable tone, but the clientele is more mixed these days, with students and tourists mingling with football supporters fortifying themselves early, before setting off to St James' Park. The brasserie classics of today are given some productive twists, as in a dish of hand-rolled pasta with Northumberland oxtail in sage butter, or peppered mackerel with goats' cheese and chive soufflé and horseradish cream.

Pan Haggerty Restaurant ◉
panhaggerty.com
21 Queen Street, NE1 3UG
0191 2210904
A regional dish of potatoes and cheese, plus a few other ingredients, the constituents of which may well depend on whose granny you choose to believe, Pan Haggerty is also a thriving restaurant in an iconic Tyneside address. There is a local flavour to the menu, but this is bright, modish cooking that catches the eye. It's a great

room with exposed brick and a lively buzz, and the service team keeps it all ticking along nicely. Spiced cauliflower soup with cauliflower bhaji and curry oil shows the modern British aspirations of the team in the kitchen, and there's a 'British Classics' section to the menu, too, which might deliver that pan haggerty with pan-fried black pudding, crispy quail's egg and smoked bacon.

Hotel du Vin Newcastle ⊛⊛

hotelduvin.com

Allan House, City Road, NE1 2BE

0191 2292200

The Newcastle offshoot of the HdV chain conforms to the brand's values with its stylish reworking of a character-laden old building, in this case the red-brick Edwardian warehouse of the Tyne Tees Steamship Company. The riverside location puts it in pole position for shopping and taking in the city's arts and cultural attractions, with glorious urban landscapes along the Tyne to the iconic arching bridge as a backdrop. True to house style, the restaurant sports the trademark retro French bistro look, while the kitchen hauls in Northumberland's fine produce as the basis of its please-all modern brasserie repertoire – slow-cooked duck leg with wild mushrooms and Puy lentil jus, or roast cod with chorizo, butter beans, chilli and lemon are typical main course ideas. As is always the case in a Hotel du Vin, you can bank on a superb wine list of intelligently chosen bottles that casts its net wide for quality drinking, with an expert sommelier on hand.

David Kennedy's Food Social ⊛

foodsocial.co.uk

The Biscuit Factory, 16 Stoddart Street, Shieldfield, NE2 1AN

0191 2605411

There's a lot of creativity going on at the Biscuit Factory, a venue packed with contemporary art and workshops, plus, in the shape of Food Social, a restaurant that fits the bill. You get a sense of the industrial heritage of the building in the space, with its pictures, exposed brickwork and ducting, and the relaxed, cheerful mood of the place only

adds to its appeal. On the menu are lots of local goodies, sourced with care and attention, and treated with respect. It's a little bit modern, a little bit rustic, and the kind of stuff you want to eat. Rillette of slow-cooked pork with a black pudding fritter and red wine dressing to start, for example, followed by fillet of North Sea cod with creamed salsify and cod Kiev, or a chargrilled 10oz rib-eye steak. Finish with treacle tart with lemon curd.

Jesmond Dene House @@@
jesmonddenehouse.co.uk
Jesmond Dene Road, NE2 2EY
0191 2123000
In a leafy residential area of the city (the centre of which seems a world away but is actually easily accessible), Jesmond Dene House is an Arts and Crafts townhouse in a woodland setting that makes a good impression. It's a boutique hotel with an appealing combination of designer chic and a pleasing lack of stuffiness. Food-wise, what isn't grown in the grounds comes from carefully chosen suppliers, a good deal of whom are from hereabouts. Smoked eel stars in a first course with chorizo, pickled oysters and potato salad, and vegetarians will find happiness in the form of roasted figs with pickled celery and Colston Bassett salad. The outstanding quality of the produce is evident in main-course roast loin of venison with pancetta, parsley

▼ Newcastle quayside

roots, chanterelle mushrooms and bitter praline. There's a tasting menu if you fancy going the whole hog, and a wonderful vegetarian version which must surely be the best for miles around. The wine list, like everything here, is a class act.

Café 21 Newcastle ⊛
cafetwentyone.co.uk
Trinity Gardens, Quayside, NE1 2HH
0191 2220755

Still delivering on its promise of providing a great urban metropolis with great urban buzz, Terry Laybourne's spacious, bustling brasserie in the refurbished quayside area of the city sails majestically on. Multiple windows let the Geordie light shine in on the grey-walled, dark-floored space, and the kitchen is open to view from the bar area. A large brigade turns out a seasonally rotating menu, with daily specials keeping it fresh, and southern European culinary references abounding. A platter of Basque charcuterie and pickles encourages friendly commensality from the word go, or you might like to dunk sole goujons into a sweet-sour dipping sauce. Mains may encompass the familiar – smoked haddock and poached egg, or duck confit with Lyonnaise potatoes – but there is also room for delightfully tender roast Northumberland venison with sour cherries, grapes, bacon and walnuts in juniper sauce with spätzle.

Dessert might offer counterpointing textures in the shape of apple parfait with cinder toffee.

Malmaison Newcastle ⊛
malmaison.com
104 Quayside, NE1 3DX
0844 6930658

In a former warehouse on the lively quayside, Newcastle's 'Mal' enjoys a prime location on the River Tyne with views of the blinking Millennium Bridge. The trendy boutique hotel chain's set-up works a treat here, with the public areas decked out in the multi-textural tones of deep reds and purples. Moody lighting in the bar sets the scene for a cocktail or something from the impressive wine list, taken seated at a purple velvet bar stool or tucked away in a velvet booth. The brasserie is typically relaxed and informal with the closely-packed tables leading to a happy hum, especially in the evening. Straightforward classics make the most of Northumberland's fine larder; Scotch quail's egg and bacon salad with piccalilli vinaigrette is one way to start, followed by Herdwick mutton masala with pilaf rice and naan bread, or, from the grill, lobster with garlic butter, herb aïoli and fries. Baked New York cheesecake and blueberries is a fitting finish.

▶ Norham

Scotland is just a stone's throw from Norham, and it was troubled by incursions from the other side of the Tweed for much of its history.

Norham isn't a big place, but like so many towns in the northeast it has experienced more than its fair share of history. In 1209 the Scottish king, William the Lion, agreed to pay tribute money to King John here. That didn't stop his successor, Alexander II, besieging the castle five years later. The 40-day siege failed to starve the defenders into submission. The English Edward I – later to be known as the 'Hammer of the Scots' – declared himself paramount ruler of Scotland at Norham, setting in train the long and bloody Scottish War of Independence which culminated in a great Scots victory at Bannockburn in 1314. The Scots returned to Norham in 1513. They were more successful than in 1214 and the great red sandstone keep was battered into surrender before the Scots set off to be slaughtered at the Battle of Flodden.

The Marmion Gate is a reminder that Sir Walter Scott set his poem about the battle here. The romantic ruin was also a favourite subject of the 19th-century artist J M W Turner, who often painted its tumbledown ramparts.

Norham Castle, which guards an important ford across the Tweed into Scotland, was built about 1158. It was the Bishop of Durham's chief northern stronghold – the area was known as Norhamshire and was part of County Durham, not Northumberland. In the village, St Cuthbert's Church shows the rich and enduring influence of the Durham Bishops, with a chancel of about 1170 and Norman nave arches like part of Durham Castle. The 17th-century vicar's stall and pulpit were once in Durham Cathedral (see page 112). The cross set on the village green has a medieval base and 19th-century top. Norham Station (open by appointment) has a working signal box, a good model railway and a fine collection of Victoriana.

TAKE IN SOME HISTORY
Norham Castle
english-heritage.org.uk
TD15 2JY | 01289382329
Call for opening times

The most imposing feature at Norham is the huge rectangular keep, its thick walls still towering up to 90ft in places. It originally had three floors (including the vaulted basement), and most of this was completed after 1158 by the Prince-Bishop of Durham, who held the castle for many years. It passed to the Crown in 1173, and King John may have been responsible for the building of the Sheep Gate. In the 15th century, a further two floors were added. Norham was so close to the Scottish border, and changed hands between Scots and English lords so often, that local masons were kept busy patching it up almost constantly from the 12th to the 16th century. The first building, founded by Flambard, Bishop of Durham in 1120, survived only 20 years before it was destroyed by the Scots. King James IV of Scotland was a big fan of artillery, the cutting-edge superweapon of the middle ages. His heavy cannon bombarded the castle in 1513, destroying parts of the newly renovated Great Tower and forcing the garrison to surrender just a few days before James was killed at the Scottish defeat at the Battle of Flodden Field.

SEE A LOCAL CHURCH
Church of St Cuthbert
norhamdeanery.org.uk
Church Lane, Norham, TD15 2LF
01289 382325
You can tell from its architecture, proportions and interior decoration that this church – which is surprisingly grand for its location in this now-sleepy community – was a

▼ Norham Castle

project driven forward by the Prince-Bishops of Durham. It shares many of the design features and motifs of Durham Cathedral. St Cuthbert's was built in 1165, although most of the existing building was reconstructed in a harmonious neo-Norman style in the 19th century, after many years of neglect. Many Anglo-Saxon carvings show that there was a ninth-century church here, beneath it or to the east, where a raised section in the graveyard suggests a former building. Notice the very fine late Norman chancel arch, the south arcade of the nave, pillars on the north side, and the foundations of the side wall. The church contains some attractive 19th-century stained glass and late 17th-century 'Bishop Cosin' woodwork

brought from Durham Cathedral – note especially the large carved timber coat of arms of Charles II in the tower archway.

▶ PLACES NEARBY

Chain Bridge Honey Farm

chainbridgehoney.co.uk
Horncliffe, TD15 2XT
01289 386362 | Open Easter–Oct daily 10–5, Nov–Easter Mon–Fri 10–5

Life is sweet at Chain Bridge Honey Farm, where the Robson family have been raising bees since 1948. As well as fine honey, you can buy propolis, soaps, skin care products and beeswax polish here, but for many people the fun part is the collection of vintage farm and commercial vehicles, including Caterpillar tractors and a veteran London bus.

▶ North Shields

Try as you might, it's hard to find anything kind to say about North Shields. It's Newcastle's (see page 166) ferry and freight port, and there are many who would argue that the best view of this gritty industrial district is from the stern of a ferry departing for Ijmuiden, or headed across the Tyne to South Shields (see page 209). If you're really into ecclesiastical history, there are two historic churches here.

SEE A COUPLE OF LOCAL CHURCHES

Christ Church

Preston Road, on the junction of Albion Road, NE29 0LW

Christ Church was built in the 1650s and 1960s, in the plain style of a Presbyterian preaching house, with four arms of equal length and a

pulpit in the centre. The church soon had to be expanded to accommodate the growing congregation, and by 1793 the four corners had been extended, the walls raised and galleries built above the north and south aisles. In 1869 the chancel was also expanded.

St Columba
United Reformed Church,
Northumberland Square,
NE30 1PW

Standing out from the rest of the buildings in the square, St Columba's is the rather grand permanent home to several Presbyterian and Congregational chapels, the first founded in Howard Street in 1662 by early Dissenters.

Built in 1857, the present church – the 'Square Pres' – has a two-storey central block, built of ashlar sandstone under a slate roof in the Palladian style. Above the arcaded first floor is a dentilled cornice and balustrade parapet, and there are sandstone chimneys at both ends. The central door is raised up three steps and recessed under a canopy. The brick wings look very domestic in comparison with the central block, being built slightly later.

Light-filled and quite spacious, the interior has galleries on three sides, standing on iron columns. Their original wooden pews are still in place.

▶ *Northumberlandia*

northumberlandia.com

Off the A1 near Cramlington, NE23 8AU | 0191 2846884 | Open daily from dawn to dusk; park is staffed Wed–Sun 9.30–4

Known as the 'Lady of the North' (or, rather less elegantly, 'Slag Alice') *Northumberlandia* is a unique piece of public art, set in a 46-acre community park. This enormous land sculpture in the shape of a reclining female figure was created as part of the re-development of the adjacent open-cast coal mine at Shotton, a rather more creative solution than returning the excavated material to the surface mine when operations cease, as is usually the case.

Designed by American landscape architect Charles Jencks, the figure is made of 1.5 million tonnes of rock, clay and soil. She's 112ft high and 1,312ft long, and is claimed to be the largest land sculpture in female form in the world. Rather than being a rigid manicured art form, *Northumberlandia* is a living part of the countryside, maturing over time and changing with the seasons. Opened in August 2012, it's hoped that she'll encourage an additional 200,000 visitors a year to come to Northumberland. An extra bonus is that if you climb to the top, you can see right into the Shotton Surface Mine. A particular attraction for fans of big machinery. And let's face it, who's not a fan of big machinery?

▶ Hills at Yeavering Bell in Northumberland National Park

▶ **Northumberland National Park**

There aren't that many places in this increasingly crowded
country where you can really get out into the wilds on foot, by
car, on a bike or on horseback. This expanse of green hills
where flocks of Cheviot sheep graze, remote curlew-haunted
moorland and steep-sided river valleys is one of the best
places in England to get away and recharge your batteries.

The Northumberland National Park covers almost 400
square miles in a long, fairly narrow salient between the
Cheviots and the Scottish border, and it takes in the most
spectacular and historically interesting parts of Hadrian's Wall.
It has had National Park status since 1956 and attracts more
than a million visitors each year, but has a resident population
of only around 2,500. There are no major towns, and only a few
villages of any size. Only Ingram, Alwinton, Kirknewton and
Elsdon have more than a cluster of houses. Wooler

(see page 237), Rothbury (see page 202), Bellingham (see page 74) and Haltwhistle (see page 129), all natural entry points and good bases for exploring, are outside its boundaries.

The only tourism hotspots are along Hadrian's Wall, but as long as you try to avoid Housesteads fort (see page 150) on a sunny bank holiday, you're unlikely to feel crowded. Visit the remoter parts of the park in winter (when you should wrap up warm and equip yourself with good footwear, a reliable map and a mobile phone) and you're likely to meet no more than a handful of people and an incurious sheep or two.

National Park status doesn't change the ownership of the land – 60 per cent of the Park is privately owned, mostly by farmers who struggle to make a living in the difficult uplands. The Right to Roam legislation means that much of the moorland is open for access – indeed, much of it has been open for many years, thanks to agreements negotiated with landowners by the National Park Authority. However, landowners still have the right to close land sometimes, so look out for signs, and only wander on access land.

The National Park Authority runs visitor centres, organises walks and publishes guides and leaflets. It also supports the local farmers and offers grants for conservation purposes, such as mending stone walls and managing traditional woodland, helping them to deal with the pressures that even the most careful visitors inevitably cause.

Another 20 per cent of the park consists of the Forestry Commission's extensive conifer plantations, many of which are open for walkers – some also have designated biking trails. But you should keep a sharp eye open for the red flags that show you may be straying near to one of the Army's live-firing ranges. The Ministry of Defence was here long before the National Park was created and still owns around 20 per cent of

▲ Hadrian's Wall on Cuddy's Crag

its area. The Army and Air Force use large areas for training. Some people think the training areas, where live firing occurs and where tanks or camouflaged soldiers may materialise at any moment, are inconsistent with National Park status. Others argue that the presence of the Forces has helped to preserve the wildness of the area. Certainly some birds, butterflies and wild plants which still thrive on the moors, untroubled by the sound of gunfire, might otherwise have been driven out by tractors and agricultural chemicals.

From Wooler (see page 237), a pleasant, work-a-day place, full of local farmers and visiting walkers and fishermen, there is easy access to the great Cheviot massif (see page 92) lying immediately to the southwest. Evidence of early settlements can be discerned all over the area, and the historic Battle Stone beside the A697 to the north of the town is a reminder of the fighting between the Scots and the English at **Humbleton Hill**.

To the south of the town are two beautifully wooded valleys, **Happy Valley** and **Harthope Valley**, which was formed by

Harthope Burn flowing through a fault in the hills. You can drive through Earle and the delightfully named Skirl Naked as far as **Langleeford**, and from here it is real walking country. The slog to the boggy summit of the Cheviot ends in anti-climax but the climb up to the 1,184ft (362m) summit of Yeavering Bell (see page 156) rewards you with fine views from the remains of Northumberland's most spectacular Iron Age fortress, with its massive rubble wall, which was once 10 feet thick. Part of it has been reconstructed to show what it was like then. More than 130 timber buildings – the largest 42ft across – occupied the 13.5-acre site. The hill was occupied on and off for centuries, and the remains of the Anglo Saxon King Edwin's palace, **Ad Gefrin**, was discovered lower down the hill in the 1950s. A monument by the road marks the place. St Paulinus baptised local people in the River Glen to the north in AD 627, and probably preached in Ad Gefrin's most unusual feature, a wooden theatre like an open-air university lecture hall, perhaps built in imitation of a Roman theatre, for the Saxons still lived among relics of Roman Britain that were much more intact in their time than they are in ours, after centuries of carting away of Roman stones by local builders.

The narrow **Breamish Valley** is one of the greatest joys of the National Park, and **Ingram**, sited on the Park border, is a fine gateway to it. The small village church (with its large Georgian rectory) is actually more interesting inside than its frowning exterior might suggest – bits of it may be pre-Norman – but most visitors come to Ingram for the scenery. There are car parks and picnic sites along the valley both east and west of the village, and a comprehensive Visitor Centre that holds discoveries from archaeological digs in the Cheviots.

Excellent walking from the village can take you right up to the Scottish border – and beyond. There are Iron Age hill-forts and deserted medieval villages in the valley, too – look out for the earthworks as you walk, especially if the sun is low. **Linhope Spout**, 3 miles west of Ingram, is one of the county's best waterfalls, reached by a riverside path from Linhope.

The Simonside Hills (see page 209), easily reached from Rothbury, contrast with the rounded summits of the Cheviots. They have crags and bogs, and much of the area is heavily planted with conifer forest. There are fine views from many of the summits – try the panorama from **Dove Crag** for a marvellous taste.

The western edge of the National Park is, if anything, wilder than the east. You can get a taste of the landscape by taking a walk around **Tarset Burn**. The southern edge of the park is bounded by well-preserved parts of Hadrian's Wall.

PLAN YOUR VISIT
Northumberland National Park Centres

northumberlandnationalpark.org.uk
Northumberland National
Park Headquarters, Eastburn South
Park, Hexham, NE46 1BS
01434 605555
The main headquarters for
the Park is at Hexham, outside
the Northumberland National
Park. There are also visitor
centres in the Kielder Water
and Forest, which is within
the park boundaries (see
page 151). There are seasonal
visitor centres at Ingram,
Rothbury and Once Brewed; for
opening times and contact
details consult the official
Northumberland National
Park website.

▼ Dove Crag

▶ Old Bewick

You're almost within sight of Scotland here, just off the B6346 in one of the quietest and most isolated little communities in Northumberland, and in one of the most beautiful parts of the northeast. Old Bewick's name may come from a combination of the Norman French *beau* (for beautiful) and the Saxon *wick* (Saxon for village). If so, it's an interesting hybrid. Others derive from the Anglo-Saxon for 'bee farm'. On the hillsides around Old Bewick are many boulders carved with the incredibly ancient 'cup and ring' petroglyphs that are the work of some of the northeast's very earliest dwellers. They were made at around the same time as the Pyramids of Egypt.

SEE A LOCAL CHURCH

Holy Trinity Church

Look first for the Celtic cross at the entrance to the lane that leads to Old Bewick's Holy Trinity Church. It's the only clue to the location of this serene little place of worship. At the right of the churchyard entrance gate, the first thing you see is a charming *pouslinia* (gardener's hut), which originally provided a bed, pen and ink, and a prayer book for any passing pilgrim; then you are brought up short by the sight of the small basilica. Holy Trinity was built between the 12th and 14th centuries and restored in 1695 and again in 1866–7. It has an externally concealed eastern apse containing three windows, and medieval grave slabs built into the fabric of the south porch. On the north side of the chancel, a stone effigy of a lady seems to embody the spirit that resides in this isolated place.

EAT AND DRINK

The Tankerville Arms

tankervillearms.com
Eglingham, NE66 2TX
01665 578444

In the heart of a quiet village – pronounced 'Egglin–jum' – the Tankerville Arms has some good real ales and an excellent menu, which changes every month. You can eat in one of several cosy areas, surrounded by old prints, listening to the talk of local farmers.

▶ Otterburn

Near Otterburn is the site of that rare thing, a Scots victory over the English. The Battle of Otterburn was fought on 19 August 1388. Leading the Scots, the Earl of Douglas. In the English corner, Harry 'Hotspur' Percy, later immortalised by Shakespeare. The clash spawned more than one ballad, and sources differ as to what actually happed and where, but it seems to have been a night action in which Douglas was killed in his moment of victory and Hotspur captured by the Scots (he was later ransomed). Many of the dead were buried at Elsdon church. The Percy Cross, in a plantation located northwest of the village, is traditionally said to mark the spot where Douglas died. Don't be alarmed if you hear the sound of weapons fire in the distance: modern soldiers have practised firing on the Ministry of Defence's Otterburn Ranges, north of the village, for more than a century. There is public access on certain days along rights of way and roads, but not when the red flags are flying. Check locally (or call Range Control on 01830 520569) and don't stray or pick anything up in case it goes bang.

EAT AND DRINK

Otterburn Castle Country House and Hotel
otterburncastle.com
Otterburn, NE19 1NS
01830 520620
Otterburn Tower is a hotel in a battlemented castle that dates back to the Middle Ages and is now a luxurious place to stay. You can take a traditional afternoon tea in the Garden Room, in the panelled dining room or, in good weather, on the terrace or the lawn. Afterwards, walk it off in the 32 acres of pretty grounds that include a stretch of the River Rede and, at the right time of year, a bluebell wood.

▼ Otterburn Tower, Northumberland

▶ The Pennine Way

nationaltrail.co.uk/pennineway

This is one for walkers and lovers of wide open spaces, fresh air and exercise (though it has to be said that happily there are plenty of great pubs along the way). The Pennine Way was the first of Britain's National Trails, and plenty of people still think it's the best, despite the appearance of rival long-distance trails elsewhere. It starts in Edale in the Peak District and tramps along the spine of England all the way to the Scottish border. The trail crosses into County Durham and the North Pennines near Bowes, then wanders through the northeast (with a westward detour towards Cumbria), passing through Middleton-in-Teesdale (see page 159) and **Alston** before winding up in Scotland at Kirk Yetholm, not far from Wooler (see page 237) in Northumberland.

If you can't spare the week or so that it takes to traverse the whole northern stretch of the Way, plan a shorter walk along the stretch between Middleton and Greenhead (see page 129), where the trail strikes Hadrian's Wall. Leaving Middleton, the Pennine Way takes you upstream along Teesdale, over the North Pennines moors, then down to Greenhead. While you traverse some of the wildest stretches of wide open country in England, consider that the Romans on Hadrian's Wall had wilderness at their back as well as to their north. They weren't just guarding a completely civilized province – there was turbulent tribal country on both sides of the Wall. After you reach Greenhead, the Pennine Way roller-coasters you eastward along the Wall, through Housesteads (see page 150), before it finally turns north through Wark and Redesdale to **Byrness**. This final stretch tests your stamina – but if you haven't fallen by the wayside by now, the previous days' walking will have toughened up your leg muscles for the Border Ridge traverse to Kirk Yetholm.

Take it easy

You can walk the Pennine Way with only a light day pack by using one of the specialist self-guided walking tour companies which provide a route plan, pre-booked accommodation (mostly in cosy bed and breakfast rooms and village inns), and a luggage transfer service to deliver your heavy bags to your accommodation each day along the way. They include Contours (contours.co.uk) and Mac's Adventure (macsadventure.com).

▶ The Pennine Way towards Stoodley Pike

EAT AND DRINK

Full steam ahead and damn the calories – walking the Pennine Way makes you appreciate the simple pleasures of a pie, a pint (or several) and a cosy bed. Fortunately, there are plenty of places that will provide all three and send you on your way the next day with a good breakfast inside you.

The Tan Hill Inn

tanhillinn.co.uk

Reeth, DL11 6ED | 01833 628246

This isn't strictly in the northeast, but it has a Durham postcode, so let's not be pedantic. Anyway, it's the highest pub in Britain, at 1,732ft above sea level, so if you start from here heading north you can kid yourself that it's going to be downhill all the way. The bar serves at least six real ales, the menu features proper no-nonsense pub food, and you can stay in cosy bed and breakfast rooms, hostel bunks, or – if you're hardy enough – you can bring your own tent.

Strathmore Arms

strathmoregold.co.uk

Holwick, Middleton-in-Teesdale, DL12 0NJ | 01833 640362

You can sink a few pints of Strathmore Gold, the signature golden ale of the Arms, with relative impunity. The custom made brew is tasty, but comes in at only 3.6 per cent alcohol by value, so it's a great thirst quencher that won't knock you out. They bake their own bread, too. Breakfast is substantial, and there's a fairly wide lunch and dinner menu, including traditional English favourites such as chicken balti. Four en suite double and twin rooms are on the small side but comfortable.

Langdon Beck Hotel

langdonbeckhotel.com

Forest-in-Teesdale, DL12 0XP

01833 622267

There's no TV in the bedrooms here because there's no TV signal. What a blessing. However, if you must catch what's going on in the world, there's WiFi. The bar-restaurant serves stick-to-the-ribs pub grub and award-winning ales from the Jarrow Brewery and the tables outside have great views of the hills.

The Black Bull

blackbull-wark.co.uk

Main Street, Wark, NE48 3LG

01434 230239

Wark is only 15 minutes from Hexham, from where there are frequent trains and buses to Newcastle and Carlisle, so it's a convenient place to drop out of the Pennine Way trek if your feet have had enough. The Black Bull, in the centre, serves a mainstream pub menu, but tries to use local produce wherever it can. The full English breakfast is generous, and all the rooms are en suite. Parts of the building go back to the Middle Ages, and several rooms have period fireplaces.

The Redesdale Arms Hotel

redesdale-arms.co.uk
Horlsey, NE19 1TA | 01830 520668

After a while you begin to suspect that some eating places along the Pennine Way do rather trade on the fact that at the end of a long day's walking their guests are more interested in a no-fuss, filling meal than in fancy dishes and presentation. There's only so much steak and ale pie you can eat in a week without wishing for something different. The Redesdale Arms Hotel in Horsley, near Otterburn, fills this gap with a menu that is still no-nonsense but shows a bit more sophistication than some of the competition.

The last pitch of the Pennine Way heading north from Byrness to Kirk Yetholm is an initimidating 27 miles, with nowhere to stay on the way (when this book was researched). Cleverly, two walker-friendly inns in Byrness village offer minibus transfers to the halfway point of this last stretch. Purists may say that's cheating. Do you care?

Byrness Hotel

thebyrness.com
Byrness, NE19 1TR | 01830 520231

Cosy is the best way to describe the this converted 17th-century farmhouse, which offers affordable rooms and has a cafe for light meals as well as serving evening meals. It is licenced, so you can enjoy a restorative whisky in front of the open fire or a glass of wine with dinner. The Byrness Hotel will also supply you with a packed lunch.

Forest View Walkers Inn,

forestviewbyrness.co.uk
7 Otterburn Green, Byrness, NE19 1TS | 01830 520425

Also in Byrness, the Forest View is aimed squarely at Pennine pilgrims, with a free drying room for boots and other gear, a restaurant that has a better than average range of vegetarian choices, a sun lounge and a bar with an outstanding selection of locally brewed cask ales. Choose from single, double, twin and triple rooms.

Border Hotel

theborderhotel.com
The Green, Kirk Yetholm, TD5 8PQ
01573 420237

You're now in Scotland, where the Border Hotel on Kirk Yetholm's village green offers just a touch of luxury to reward you for completing a long and demanding walk. This former 18th-century coaching inn has five big en suite rooms – one of them a family triple – all with large beds and perks including flat-screen TVs and tea- and coffee-making kit. There are two bars and a restaurant, plus a beer garden and patio for summer evenings.

▶ Peterlee

A working class hero is something to be, said John Lennon. Peter Lee was one of the archetypal heroes of the proletarian struggle. Born in 1864, he went to work underground at the age of 10. Throughout his life, he fought for workers' rights, becoming general secretary of the Durham Miners Association and, before his death in 1935, president of the radical Miners International Federation. Britain's first (and most idealistic) post-World War II Labour government built this new town in 1950 to offer decent housing to workers in the nearby coalfields and their families, and a hub for the surrounding villages. The town was named in his honour.

At a time when the new towns built in the 1950s and 1960s are held as examples of a failed dream, Peterlee stands as a monument to what they tried to be. It can claim to be the most attractive of the northeast's new towns (not that there's strong competition for that award). Lying in gently rolling countryside only two miles from the North Sea, the characteristics of the site were fully exploited by the planners, who created attractively grouped housing which is well segregated from the industrial areas.

Peterlee quickly established its own character and, despite the decline in mining, has succeeded in attracting new industry. Visit it if only for a glimpse of what the socialist utopians of the second half of the 20th century hoped to achieve. It didn't work out the way they hoped, but at least they gave it their best shot.

▶ Preston Tower

prestontower.co.uk

NE67 5DH | 01665 589227 | Open daily, daylight until sunset or 6pm

For more than three centuries after it was built by Sir Robert Harbottle, a noted local warlord and trusted friend of Henry IV – who made him Sheriff of Northumberland and Constable of Dunstanburgh – Preston Tower changed hardly at all. It was one of 78 pele towers listed in 1415, but unlike many of the northeast's defensive towers it did not grow into a great house through the addition of ever grander and more comfortable wings.

Robert Harbottle was a contemporary of the fiery Harry 'Hotspur' Percy and fought alongside him at Battle of Otterburn in 1388 (a rare away win for the Scots). A display in the Tower illustrates life during those turbulent times. Another Harbottle, Guiscard, was one of six knights killed at Flodden Field in 1513 in hand-to-hand combat with King James IV of Scotland. The Flodden Room in Preston Tower tells the story of Guiscard's part in the battle, and of Flodden's grievous impact on the history and literature of Scotland and the north.

When the crowns of England and Scotland were united by James I and VI in 1603 and the borderlands of the northeast became less fraught with dangers, Preston Tower was partially demolished. Stones from two of its towers were used to build adjoining cottages and farm buildings, and the surviving Tower gradually decayed for the next 250 years. It was not until 1864 that Henry Baker Cresswell, whose family bought the Tower in 1861, came to the rescue. He removed the agricultural additions and built up its rear wall to make it weatherproof. He also added the clock, which he made himself. His home was the Georgian house next door, and part of the Tower was made to hold tanks of water for it, pumped from a nearby spring. His descendants still own and live in Preston Tower.

There are pleasant walks through wooded, landscaped gardens with exotic and native trees.

▸ **PLACES NEARBY**
Doxford Hall Hotel & Spa ◉◉
doxfordhall.com
Chathill, NE67 5DN | 01665 589700
A continuous programme of investment and generous dollops of TLC in recent years have brought food and rooms fully up to 21st-century spec at Doxford. Entered through a classic period portico, the late-Georgian pile is framed in ten acres of landscaped grounds (including a maze) just a short drive from the Northumbrian coast. For those intent on pampering and rejuvenation, there's a classy spa and leisure club, the elegant restaurant features a huge stone fireplace, white linen, burnished wood panelling and full-length windows. Fresh, local and seasonal are clearly buzz words, and the kitchen takes a gently modern approach that sits comfortably alongside tried-and-tested classics. Casserole of pheasant served with steamed suet and leek pudding, thyme and pancetta impresses with the quality of produce and power of its flavours, and warm pear and almond tart with pistachio ice cream is a good way to finish.

▸ Prudhoe Castle

english-heritage.org.uk
NE42 6NA | 01661 833459 | Open Apr–Sep Thu–Mon 10–5
In the late 12th century, Scotland was arguably a greater power in the north of Britain than was Norman England. William the Lion, King of Scotland, had great ambitions to push his nation's borders deep into Northumbria. In 1173 and again in 1174 he drove south, ravaged the northeast, and successfully assaulted

many of its castles. The unassuming earthworks of Prudhoe's first castle were the only stronghold in Northumberland which successfully defied the Scots.

In 1175, Henry II of England rewarded Prudhoe by ordering the building of a more imposing stone castle here. Prudhoe's square keep was one of the first great towers to be built in Northumberland. At the same time, or a little later, a gatehouse was added, along with stone curtain walls. Prudhoe was provided with a moat and drawbridge, two barbicans and a stronger gatehouse in the 13th century. A fine vaulted basement was built under the gatehouse, and a chapel was added on the first floor. The chapel had a beautiful oriel (bay) window that is thought to be one of the earliest of its kind in any English castle. In 1381 Prudhoe passed into the hands of the influential Percy family.

▶ PLACES NEARBY

George Stephenson's Birthplace

nationaltrust.org.uk
Wylam, NE41 8BP | 01661 853457
Open Mar–Oct Thu–Sun 12–5
Birthplace of the world-famous railway engineer, this small stone tenement was built around 1760 to accommodate mining families. The furnishings reflect the year of Stephenson's birth here in 1781, his whole family living in one room.

Churches of St Peter and St Andrew

Bywell, NE43 7AD
This private village, consisting of a castle, hall and estate cottages, must certainly be the only village in England with two surviving Saxon churches. They were built by rival orders – the Church of St Peter, in AD 800, by the Benedictines or 'Black Monks' of Durham and the Church of St Andrew by the Dominicans or 'White Monks'.

Don't read too much into these soubriquets. They do sound a bit like something from a role-playing game, but regardless of the colours of their habits, both orders felt themselves to be on the side of the Lord. St Peter's, like so many contemporary churches in these parts, has Roman stones in its walls, which may indicate that it stood on a Roman site. The north wall of the nave and west parts of the chancel are the oldest existing parts of the church, and some foundations also remain from this early structure. Discovered in the wall of the tower, and now placed inside the church, is an ancient cross-shaft carved with a Crucifixion scene, which may date from the seventh century.

After being destroyed by fire, the church was rebuilt in the 13th and 14th century and now consists of a nave, south transept, chancel, north vestry and a west tower. The

▲ Prudhoe Castle

tower is plain and square and, with walls 16ft thick, it is thought to have been built for defence.

Well-carved medieval grave slabs are inside and out, and although most of the church is 13th century, there is Victorian remodelling in the vibrantly coloured stained glass, a splendid reredos and a tiled mosaic floor.

▶ Raby Castle

www.rabycastle.com

DL2 3AH | 01833 660202

Open May, Jun and Sep Sun–Wed, Jul–Aug Sun–Fri 11–5

The Neville family were a big noise in northern England in their heyday, and for almost three centuries Raby Castle lay at the heart of a web of violence and intrigue as the Nevilles jockeyed for position against other great lords of the north – most notably, the Percy dynasty of Northumberland.

The intensely romantic building you see today was begun in the 14th century. Romance was not, of course, its purpose. When the Neville family built Raby there were constant threats from Scotland, and the surrounding landscape was harsh and unwelcoming. The 30ft curtain wall is long gone, but the huge feudal castle, which grew gradually through the generations, can still give you the shivers. It was here that Richard III's mother, Cicely Neville, 'The Rose of Raby', was brought up by her father, the first Earl of Westmorland.

The royal connection did not help the treacherous sixth Earl, who led the Rising of the North in 1569. That plot to overthrow the Protestant Elizabeth I and put her Catholic cousin Mary, Queen of Scots on the throne of England failed. Neville fled, first to Scotland, then to the Spanish Netherlands, where he raised a small rebel company that hoped to return to Scotland with the Spanish Armada. Well, we all know what happened there. The invasion fleet was defeated and England was saved. Neville eked out a poor living on a pittance from the King of Spain until his disappointed death in 1601, two years before the death of the Queen he hated, and the accession to the English throne of a member of the Scots royal house that the Nevilles had fought for centuries.

Meanwhile, Raby and all the Neville lands were forfeit to the Crown. After more than 50 years of neglect, the castle it was sold to the Vane family. There seems to have been sedition in the water supply, though. The first Sir Henry

▶ Raby Castle

Vane deserted his patron for the Parliamentary cause at the start of the Civil War. His son, the second Sir Henry Vane to live at Raby, also served Parliament and was executed in 1662 by a vengeful Charles II. But the Vanes were survivors, and under later monarchs eventually became Barons Barnard, Earls of Darlington and Dukes of Cleveland. The last duke died in 1891, and Raby is now owned by Lord Barnard.

Approached through the gatehouse is the awesome bulk of Clifford's Tower, built in about 1378. Other reminders of the original castle are Bulmer's Tower and the perfect 14th-century kitchen, with its ox-sized fireplaces, and the servants' hall. The spectacular Neville Gateway leads to the cobbled Inner Court. The long tunnel was created by John Carr when he restored and reshaped the castle in the 1760s.

The magnificent contents of the castle were all collected after the first Lord Barnard, furious at his son's marriage, sold everything in 1714. A favourite of many visitors is the statue of a Greek slave girl by Hiram Powers.

▶ **PLACES NEARBY**
Church of St Mary
stmarysstaindrop.org.uk
Front Street, Staindrop, DL2 3NJ
01833 660237
Richard Neville, 16th Earl of Warwick, AKA 'the Kingmaker' is the best known scion of the powerful Neville family. In the treacherous decades of the Wars of the Roses – a real-life inspiration for George R R Martin's *Game of Thrones'* series of novels – he was the

most devious warlord of the lot, until he fell at the Battle of Barnet in 1471. But the Nevilles were a big name in these parts long before he earned his nickname, and you can see the tombs of several generations of these powerful aristos within this once-humble Saxon church. Ralph Neville, lord of nearby Raby Castle and 1st Earl of Westmorland, altered and enlarged it at the end of the 14th century, and memorials to the Lords of Raby have accumulated over the centuries. The ceiling of the choir is decorated with the Neville arms, the 15th-century font carries the arms of Ralph's son Edward, and many effigies lie in state on carved chest tombs. The elaborate stained glass windows are much later additions, dating from 1893.

▸ Rokeby Park

rokebypark.com

Rokeby, DL12 9RZ | 01833 695692

Open 5 May, 26 May–1 Sep, Mon–Tue 2–5

So many of the northeast's stately homes have dark histories as warlike medieval strongholds. And their roots often show. Try as their later owners might, the original fortified keep remains the core of many mansions, especially those close to the Scots border. Rokeby Park makes a welcome change. If its name is famous for one thing, it must be Velasquez's painting of the goddess of love, known as *The Rokeby Venus*, which hung in the castle's grand saloon until it went to the National Gallery in London.

This ochre-painted house is a villa in the purest Palladian style; a poised composition of a tall central block and lower, retiring wings, all with pyramid roofs, following in its wake. The house was designed by Sir Thomas Robinson, for himself, on the site of the old Robinson mansion – some distance from the still-surviving medieval tower of the Rokeby family, from whom the Robinsons bought the estate during the Civil War. 'Long Sir Tom' was the son-in-law of the Earl of Carlisle, for whom Vanbrugh was building the baroque Castle Howard, but Robinson's taste was for the neoclassical style. Rokeby was to be both a home and a show place.

Like so many of his rakish contemporaries, Sir Tom had a taste for the high life and found it hard to live within his means. He was nearly always in debt because of his high living, and spent a period of time as Governor of Barbados to escape his creditors. If you think that sounds like an easy gig, bear in mind that, at the time, a posting to the fever-ridden West Indies was regarded as not far from a death sentence. When in London he was a director of entertainments at Ranelagh Gardens, and he appears both in Hogarth's picture *The Beggar's Opera* and in Fielding's novel *Joseph Andrews*. He sold Rokeby to John Sawrey Morritt, whose family still lives here. It was Morritt's son who acquired *The Rokeby Venus*.

The lower ground-floor rooms are not lofty, but each has its characteristic decoration, especially the breakfast room, enlivened with cut-out 18th-century prints. But it was on the piano nobile – the main floor – that Robinson expended most of his talent and money. The music room is a fitting introduction to the grandeur of Rokeby's principal rooms. The full height of the house, the Saloon should be filled with the music of Handel for full effect, for it is of the same stately richness, from its gilded ceiling to the marble fireplaces and the doorways, surrounded by columns and crowned with triangular pediments.

▶ **PLACES NEARBY**

Thorpe Farm Centre
thorpefarm.co.uk
Thorpe Farm, Greta Bridge,
DL12 9TY | 01833 627242

Animal paddocks, children's play area (free), heritage woodland bistro and shops, plus a campsite mean there's plenty for all the family here.

▶ Rookhope

Walk a short distance from unassuming little Rookhope to discover a medieval mining industry marvel. Just west of the village, you could easily assume the Rookhope Arch, with its two stone channels, is just another tumbledown old bridge. It's much more. It's what is left of a conduit that was built to carry toxic fumes from Rookhope's lead and silver ore-smelting works up to the hills above, where the worst of the noxious smoke would be blown away. But it had a dual purpose. The fumes cooled as they rose up the flue, and lead and silver residue condensed out in the funnel itself, and at its mouth, where they could be painstakingly recovered. For its time, this was quite sophisticated technology.

Rookhope means 'valley of the rooks' and is today a small, remote Weardale village. But it has a long and fascinating history. By 1153, when King Stephen granted a licence to mine for lead and iron, it was known as Rykhup. In the 14th century the local farmers combined agriculture with searching out the lead on the stream banks. The Rookhope farmers were generally free from the cattle raids that plagued their counterparts further north, but a famous raid of 1569 into Weardale ended with the

raiders cornered in the Rookhope Valley, where a
pitched battle resulted in victory for the Weardale men.
Their exploits were recorded in the 24-verse ballad
Rookhope Ryde.

▶ Rothbury

One of the main tourist centres of Northumberland, Rothbury,
the capital of Coquetdale, is an attractive town, with stone
buildings spreading outwards from an irregularly shaped green
and a medieval bridge over the River Coquet.

The town suffered from William Wallace's army in the 13th
century, and proclaimed the Old Pretender as James III in the
18th, but since the 19th century it has developed a robust
reputation as a holiday centre.

The parish church suffers from its Victorian restoration,
which destroyed a Saxon tower and left very little of the rest,
but it is worth visiting for a glimpse of the font – its bowl dates
from 1664, but stands on part of the ninth-century Rothbury
Cross, decorated with vigorous Celtic-inspired designs.

WALK ALONG THE RIVER

Cross the bridge east of
Rothbury to the Thrum,
where the Coquet rushes
through a narrow gorge.
The river powers through a
channel that in places here is
no more than five feet wide,
scouring the sandstone
riverbed into contorted shapes
and powering Thrum Mill's
undershot waterwheel.

West of Rothbury, near the
tiny and picturesque village of
Holystone, is the Lady's Well, a
stone-lined pool amid trees,
where St Paulinus is alleged
– probably wrongly – to have
converted and baptised 3,000
locals in AD 627. Like a lot of
similarly-named pools and
springs throughout Britain, it
was almost certainly a pre-
Christian place of worship
dedicated to a local water

goddess. An 18th-century
statue of the saint stands
beside the well.

PLAY A ROUND

Rothbury Golf Club
rothburygolfclub.com
Whitton Rd, NE65 7RX
01669 621271
Open daily
Scenic, flat parkland course set
alongside the River Coquet,
surrounded by Simonside Hills
and Cragside Hall.

EAT AND DRINK

Harley's Tea Rooms
harleystearoom.co.uk
Bridge Street, Rothbury, NE65 7SE
01669 620240
In the heart of the bustling
village of Rothbury, this is a
traditional family-run cafe
housed in an old stone building.
Harley's can provide you with a

full afternoon tea, as well as light snacks and full meals – all of them homemade and tasty.

▶ PLACES NEARBY

Cragside

Cragside (see page 97), east of Rothbury, is one of Northumberland's major tourist attractions, but with more than 900 acres of country park and gardens, even in high summer it is usually easy to find a quiet corner.

Built for the first Lord Armstrong by the architect Norman Shaw, it is a fantastic Victorian creation, a cross between an English manor house and a Bavarian schloss. It hangs over the wooded gorge of Debdon Burn in a sea of trees and its interior is full of heavy, late-Victorian atmosphere, though parts are quite dark and cramped. Spectacular exceptions include the fine library and the drawing room, with its huge alabaster fireplace.

Harwood Forest

forestry.gov.uk
Harwood, near Rothbury, NE61 4LF
01434 250209

This is definitely one for the anorak and binocular brigade. On the southeast fringe of the Northumberland National Park, it's a spread of serried spruce and other conifers that can seem boring but create a habitat for some birds that are hard to see elsewhere. You can expect to add crossbills to your life list here, and other conifer-loving birds including siskins and lesser redpoll are not unusual. On the downside, some urban locals seem to like walking their dogs here, and don't feel responsible for the results. Mind where you put your feet.

▶ Seaham

There is no better place than Seaham to reflect on the rise and fall of the northeast in the industrial and post-industrial era. The church that stands near the edge of Seaham's limestone cliffs is late Saxon. There are Roman stones in its walls and its font dates from the 12th century. But from the cliffs, there are stunning views over the harbour built by Lord Londonderry in 1828 to ship coal from his nearby mines to the rest of England, and beyond. Seaham, like so much of the northeast, has suffered from the decline of the Durham coalfields and no pits now work here. The seafront has been cleaned up and new 'natural' landscapes created where pit slagheaps dominated the landscape until the 1980s.

To the north of the town is the 18th-century Seaham Hall, a white mansion, now a hotel, where Lord Byron stayed after his marriage to the heiress, Anne Millbanke, in 1815. As he separated from her the following year and left England for ever, this may account for his jaundiced comment that the coast here was dreary. It may have been a bit unromantic in his time, but one major benefit of the passing of the age of coal has been cleaner air and a cleaner coast. The Durham shoreline is no longer blackened by the residue of the pits.

▼ Blast Breach near Seaham

EAT AND DRINK

Seaham Hall Hotel

seaham-hall.co.uk
Lord Byron's Walk, SR7 7AG
0191 5161400

Seaham Hall is quite a pad. It was saved from rack and ruin back at the turn of the century to be reborn as a rather magnificent five-star hotel. There are two restaurants, the Blunos Sea Grill, where you can try classical dishes in a totally lavish, contemporary setting; and the flame-coloured Ozone Restaurant, which serves up some impressive Pan-Asian food in a cool and chilled-out setting. There's an open kitchen, views over the rounds (especially good from the terrace) and a menu packed with great flavours. Sharing and grazing is the best way to approach things. Main course deep-fried sea bass comes with tamarind sauce, Thai herbs and jasmine rice, or go for crispy pork belly with pak choi, green beans, shiitake mushrooms and a garlic and soy sauce.

The Seaton Lane Inn

seatonlaneinn.com
Seaton Lane, SR7 0LP
0191 5812038

With a traditional bar area as well as a stylish restaurant and lounge, this boutique inn offers four real ales to keep the regulars happy, served from the central bar. The menu proffers many pub favourites – hot sandwiches such as the traditional BLT are served with chunky chips; pasta dishes, tortilla wraps and warm salads are all here as well as a good selection of main courses. A sample evening menu features braised shoulder of lamb on champ mash with rich minted jus; salmon marinated in teriyaki sauce with onions, peppers and tomatoes; and chunky beef cottage pie. Bedrooms are modern, spacious and smartly furnished.

▶ Seahouses

Seahouses is a pretty wee place these days. In 1858, a Victorian visitor called it 'a common-looking town, squalid in places'. But the Victorians worshipped their version of progress, and this old fashioned community probably didn't fit into that. The fisher-folk cottages around Craster Square strike most visitors as rather cute. The harbour was built in the 18th century, to serve the North Sea fishing boom. The fishing industry grew even more in the 19th century, and the harbour was expanded still further. There are fewer fishing boats now, but Seahouses harbour is the place to get boat trips to the Farne Islands (see page 117). Walk north or south and you're into great beachcombing territory on long sweeps of North Sea sands.

A mile south of Seahouses is Beadnell, with an 18th-century church and a pub – the Craster Arms (see page 71) – with a large carved coat of arms on its front wall and the remains of a medieval tower at the back. Above the harbour – the only one on the east coast that faces west – is the site of the medieval St Ebba's chapel and a group of lime kilns which date from 1798.

EXPLORE THE DEPTHS

Sovereign Diving

sovereigndiving.co.uk.

The Olde School House, 17 North Lane, NE68 7UQ | 01665 720760

Diving all year round, call or see website for scheduled trips; boats also available for private charter. PADI or BSAC Sports Diver qualification required. Tank fills (air and nitrox) available, but no other equipment provided.

Dive with seals and see puffins and guillemots swimming underwater around the Farne islands on a scuba trip with Sovereign Diving. Sailing from Seahouses, the Sovereign team know their way around the undersea world of the Farnes – 26 islets that rise steeply from the seabed, creating spectacular walls and gullies infested with fish, nudibranchs and crustaceans. Half a dozen wrecks create yet more havens for marine life.

RIDE THE SANDS

Slate Hall Riding Centre

slatehallridingcentre.com

South Lane, Seahouses, NE68 7UL

01665 720320 | Open daily

There's a special sort of thrill to riding along the long sweep of coast by Bamburgh Castle, with Lindisfarne and the Farne Islands off to the east. It makes you feel like a Saxon warlord, a Viking jarl or a Norman conqueror. Riding here is a very different experience from hacking across the moors of the Northumberland hinterland. Saddle up with Slate Hall Riding Centre for a great day out – they have ponies and horses for beginners, novices and experienced riders, but beach rides are for experienced riders only.

EAT AND DRINK

The Olde Ship Inn

www.seahouses.co.uk

9 Main Street, NE68 7RD

01665 720200

Set above the bustling old harbour of Seahouses, The Olde Ship is a stone-built residential inn. Built on a farm around 1745, it has been in the present owners' family for over 100 years, and has a long-established reputation for good food and drink in relaxing surroundings. Lit by stained-glass windows, the main saloon bar is full of character, with its wooden floor made from ships' decking. It offers whiskies as well as a selection of real ales, such as Farne Island and Nel's Best. The inn's corridors and boat gallery are an Aladdin's cave of antique nautical artefacts, ranging from a figurehead to all manner of ship's brasses and dials. Bar foods include locally caught seafood and home-made soups.

In the evenings, starters like chicken liver pâté, and venison and pork terrine are followed by chilli bean stew, trio of mixed grilled fish, and steak-and-ale pie. The bedrooms have en suite bathrooms and are tastefully decorated; some have views of the Farne Islands.

The Bamburgh Castle Inn
bamburghcastleinn.co.uk
NE68 7SQ | 01665 720283
With its prime location on the quayside giving wraparound sea views as far as the Farne Islands, this is surely one of the best positioned pubs anywhere along Northumberland's stunning coast. Dating back to the 18th century, the inn has been transformed in more recent times to offer superb bar and dining areas plus seating outside. A beer festival is held in the garden every year, children and dogs are welcomed, and pub dishes of locally sourced food represent excellent value. Typical of these are venison and chilli pâté, homemade fishcakes, and Moroccan lamb steak.

▶ Sedgefield

Sedgefield is famous (or infamous, depending on where you stand) for two things. 'Racing from Sedgefield' conjures up images of peaceful, rural England, but don't be deceived. This may look at first sight like typically Tory shireland, but Sedgefield is within the proudly class-conscious proletarian hinterland of the northeast. As such, it repeatedly elected Tony Blair as its member of parliament until he stood down in 2007, and even in the post-Blair years it still looks like a safe Labour Party constituency. If you're after a flutter, you'll find the famous racecourse just southwest of the village.

At the heart of Sedgefield is the church, with its grand 15th-century tower. It's surrounded by tall trees and old gravestones, Georgian houses and pantiled cottages. Inside is woodwork – hearty Gothic pinnacles and luscious carving – given by Bishop Cosin's son-in law, rector here from 1667 and later Dean of Durham.

An archway by the Hardwick Arms leads to Hardwick Hall Country Park. Its first owner spent so much on the garden buildings that he couldn't afford to build a house, but now most of them are in ruins, or have vanished altogether. An exception is the gateway, which is a classic English wealthy landowner's folly – it was built to look like a romantic ruin in the first place, and ironically it has survived in better shape than most of the park's other buildings.

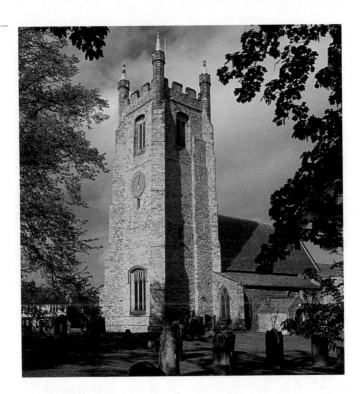

▲ St Edmund's Church, Sedgefield

PLAY A ROUND
Knotty Hill Golf Centre
knottyhill.com
Sedgefield, TS21 2BB
01740 620320 | Open Tue–Sun
and BHs
The 18-hole Princes and
Bishops Courses are situated in
mature parkland with
strategically placed water
hazards and bunkers, along
with tree-lined fairways,
making accuracy a premium
and the courses rewarding for
all standards of play. The
Academy Course is ideal for
aspiring golfers and those
seeking more leisurely play.

EAT AND DRINK
Dun Cow Inn
duncowinn.co.uk
43 Front Street, Sedgefield, TS21 3AT
01740 620894
In 2003, when he was
Prime Minister and MP for
the town, Tony Blair brought
US President George W Bush
to Sedgefield. Since he
stepped down, there are
fewer men in black lurking
and helicopters hovering
around the village, but you can
still eat very well at the Dun
Cow. It's a charming building
with several different eating
areas – fish is a speciality (try
the sea bass in olive oil with
roast tomato if it's listed) as
well as local specialities.

▶ Simonside Hills

The summit plateau of Simonside, with its chopped-off, craggy edges is recognisable from as far south as Newcastle and parts of County Durham. The Simonside Hills are not the highest in Northumberland, but they are undeniably the most distinctive. The taller Cheviots and hills of the North Pennines present a rounded, soft face to the visitor, so that it is often difficult from a distance, to distinguish one from another, but the rough-edged Simonsides look very different.

People have lived here for an almost unimaginably long time. At many sites, most notably Lordenshaws, where the Simonside ridge tails off to the roadside, there are traces of human activity reaching back for many millennia. Rocks here show 'cup and ring' carvings dating from neolithic times. If you want a taster, have a look at rockart.ncl.ac.uk. The Bronze Age is represented by 4,000-year-old cairns and burial mounds, while the top of the hill is dominated by an Iron-Age earthwork built around 350 BC. More recent remains, dating back only a few centuries include walls, old tracks and the spoil heaps of 19th-century lead prospecting.

▶ South Shields

Close to the mouth of the Tyne, South Shields has great North Sea views and beaches. It's a residential suburb of Newcastle (see page 166) now, but there are plenty of relics of its identity as a community in its own right. Signs welcome you to 'Catherine Cookson Country', and you can get a real taste of how grim life in South Shields was less than a century ago, as depicted in many of her books, by following the Cookson Trail around town and visiting a reconstruction of the author's childhood home in the local museum.

The history of South Shields starts with the Romans, who built a fort at the place they called Arbeia, as a supply base for Agricola's invasion of Caledonia. Jarrow, now part of South Shields, has a long and distinguished history. One of the first places to be invaded by the Vikings, who eventually colonised the northeast, it was also the home of the Venerable Bede: scholar, monk and writer, known as the Father of English History. Bede received his education from the age of seven at St Paul's monastery, which was founded in AD 682 by Ceolfrith, an Anglo-Saxon abbot and saint. Its superb library, assembled by Benedict Biscop on his travels to Rome, soon turned it into the cradle of English art and literature.

Amazingly, the church Bede knew – dedicated in April 685, as we are told on its dedication stone – still survives and its nave has now become the chancel of the present building. The ruins found to the south of the church are from a later Benedictine monastery. Across the park, the Bede's World Museum contains some finds from the site and has reconstructions of Anglo-Saxon timber buildings.

Much more recently, Jarrow became famous for the 'Jarrow Crusade' of 1936, when starving shipyard workers, unemployed after the closure of the shipyard that was the city's biggest employer, walked to London to protest at their plight. They were led by Jarrow's Labour MP, 'Red' Ellen Wilkinson – one of the first women to win a seat at Westminster. The march is still remembered as an iconic moment of working-class protest. What is usually forgotten is that the Conservative-dominated coalition government of the time responded only by cutting their unemployment pay for the days they had spent on the road.

▾ South Shields coastline

GO BACK IN TIME
Arbeia Roman Fort and Museum
twmuseums.org.uk/arbeia
Baring Street, NE33 2BB
0191 4561369 | Open Apr–Sep
Mon–Fri 10–5, Sat 11–4, Sun 2–5
This is what you come to South Shields to see. Arbeia was in use from the second century to the fourth century, when it was first a supply base for Agricola's thrust into Caledonia, and then for troops serving on Hadrian's Wall. Since the 1980s, volunteer archaeologists have painstakingly recreated full-size

reconstructions of the West Gate, a barrack block and part of the commanding officer's house, a herb garden and museum of site finds and you can watch them at work throughout the summer. The west gate, as rebuilt, was clearly designed to awe the natives with the magnificence of Rome – and to remind the legions, far from home, of what they stood for. The commander's residence does the same thing in a cosier way: here, high-ranking Roman officers could still enjoy a Mediterranean lifestyle, complete with central heating, on the northernmost fringe of the empire. The brightly coloured paintwork and furnishings bring the past vividly to life in a way that the time-worn stones of the other sites along the wall do not. It's so easy to think of the past as a monochrome place, so these are useful reminders that the world along the wall was probably much more vivid than we imagine.

PLAY A ROUND
South Shields Golf Club
ssgc.co.uk
Cleadon Hills, NE34 8EG
0191 4568942
Open Mon-Fri and BHs
A slightly undulating downland course on a limestone base, ensuring good conditions underfoot. Open to strong winds, the course is testing but fair. There are fine views of the coastline.

Whitburn Golf Club

whitburngolfclub.co.uk
Lizard Lane, NE34 7AF
0191 5292144 | Open Mon–Sat and
BHs, Sun in winter
Parkland with sea views.
Situated on limestone making
it rarely unplayable.

▶ **PLACES NEARBY**

Bede's World

bedesworld.co.uk
Church Bank, Jarrow, NE32 3DY
0191 4892106 | Open Feb–Dec
Mon–Sat 10–5, Sun 12–5
Bede's World is an ambitious
stab at time travelling into the
misty margins of the early
medieval world. You may find it
hard to get your 21st-century
head around the fact that
during Bede's lifetime there
was no such place as England.
But there was a greater,
broader place called
Christendom, and Bede was a
part of that intellectual world
from an early age.

He was schooled in Latin
– which was the most
widespread written language in
the world of his time. He could
also read the Greek of the early
eastern scholars, both
Christian and pagan. All of this
hints that he was born into a
noble Anglo-Saxon family and
given over to Christianity as a
boy – perhaps by parents who
had themselves recently
accepted the Christian faith.

We know he was born near
Jarrow in AD 673 and entered its
monastery at the age of ten.
From the standpoint of that
early monastic foundation, he
must have observed the
internecine struggles between
Anglo-Saxon, native British,
Scots and Pictish kings and
princes.

Before his death in 735, he
managed to pull together an
amazing variety of sources
which he compiled to create the
Historia Ecclesiastica – the first
history of the Christian faith in
the Anglo-Saxon world.
Meanwhile, his letters to
monastic scholars the length
and breadth of Christendom
undoubtedly brought the
long-benighted lands of
England back into the
broadening world of a Europe
emerging from the Dark Ages
that followed the fall of Rome.

Church of St Paul

stpaulschurchjarrow.com
Church Bank, Jarrow, NE32 3DZ
This church is all that remains
of the monastery of St Paul at
Jarrow, where Bede lived,
studied and wrote. Bede's
writings became so celebrated
in the eighth century that they
made the monastery famous in
its time, but all that remains
are some ruins at the south
side of the church. The
dedication stone, set above the
chancel arch and facing you as
you enter the west door,
declares the date of AD 685,
making it the oldest such stone
in England.

As you pass into the chancel,
you will see an Anglo-Saxon
window on the south side, inset
with a circular pane holding
fragments of seventh-century

stained glass, the oldest in the world. Sharing this space are 20th-century windows by the artists John Piper and Leonard Evetts, which somehow make the great age of the chancel, the oldest part of the building, even more palpable.

In the north aisle you can see the Saxon Cross, excavated by the Victorians when digging the foundations for a nave to replace the Saxon-Norman nave, which had collapsed. You can also see some fine early sculptured stones here. Another modern piece, a wonderful sculpture of the risen Christ, carved from a single tree, seems to soar above the nave, with no visible means of support.

The monastery at Jarrow was twinned with another foundation at Wearmouth, seven miles away on the River Wear near Sunderland, which was founded 13 years earlier than Jarrow. Both monasteries were destroyed by the Danes in about AD 860 and it is thought they were probably abandoned by the end of the first century, ending a golden age of early Christian scholarship.

▶ Stanhope

The market town of Stanhope is known – perhaps pompously – as the 'Capital of Weardale'. Among its claims to fame are a fossilised tree stump, next to the entrance to the churchyard. It's reckoned to be 250 million years old.

Stanhope has an open-air swimming pool, and there are stepping stones set across the Tees to riverside walks. The Durham Dales Centre combines craft shops and a tea room with the Tourist Information Centre.

On the first weekend in September at Wolsingham, 6 miles west, the oldest agricultural show in England is held. Killhope Lead Mining Centre (see page 51) is nearby.

▼ Stepping stones across river Wear

▶ Stockton-on-Tees

Like so many towns in the northeast, Stockton went very quickly from medieval rags to industrial riches in the age of coal and steam. It was created by the Bishop of Durham in the 12th century, and until the Middlesbrough Transporter Bridge opened, further downriver in 1911, it was the lowest crossing point on the Tees, which gave it a natural edge. There are few relics of its medieval past, apart from the surpisingly splendid Church of St Mary the Virgin, set in a very pretty churchyard in the town centre.

From the 17th century, it was an important shipbuilding port, and it also got in early on metal-bashing and coal. Local industrialists smelted iron and lead and Stockton colliers shipped coal up and down the coast from the local mines. The central landmark, standing by the river, is the grand, red-brick Town Hall. Built in 1735, it seems to symbolise the town's sense of self confidence and prosperity at that time.

But what you think of first (if you think about Stockton at all) is the world's first passenger railway. Designed and built by George Stephenson and opened in 1825, it ran right across Teesside and Durham to Darlington, carrying passengers at then unheard-of speeds. Sometimes trains topped 20mph.

VISIT THE MUSEUMS
Preston Park Museum and Grounds
prestonparkmuseum.co.uk
Yarm Road, Eaglescliffe, TS18 3RH
01642 527375 | Open Tue–Sun 10–4
and BHs
Shipping nabob Robert Ropner bought Preston Hall from its impecunious owners in 1882 and set out to transform it into a palatial home worthy of a self-made Victorian grandee of the industrial age. Walking through its salons now, you can see that he did himself proud. Ropner added a ballroom, a billiard room, and drawing rooms, bedrooms and kitchens galore – plus, of course,

◀ Stockton-on-Tees Town Hall

quarters for an army of maidservants, manservants, nannies, valets, grooms, butlers, cooks, cleaners, gamekeepers, gardeners...you get the picture. It must have been a great old life while it lasted, but Ropner's decendants, like so many other grand families, couldn't afford the upkeep. By 1949 Preston Hall ended up in the possession of the borough council. It's been a museum and public park since 1953.

These days you can get a glimpse into what it was really like to be one of the servants emptying chamber pots and scrubbing pans at a real life Downton Abbey. There's fun stuff for children too in the surrounding park, but the best part of the museum has to be the recreation of Stockton's Victorian High Street, complete with a blacksmith's, a printer's workshop, grocer's and draper's store – all staffed by folk in period costume – and a tearoom.

PLAY A ROUND
Teesside Golf Club
teessidegolfclub.com
Acklam Road, Thornaby, TS17 7JS
01642 616516 | Open daily
Flat, easy walking parkland.

▶ Sunderland

Sunderland, at the mouth of the River Wear was a 19th-century boomtown that prospered on shipping coal and building ships until both those industries collapsed. That happened within living memory, and you can tell that the city is still battling gamely to find a new role for itself. It's not a natural destination for the casual visitor, but does its best to promote itself as a place worth visiting.

The Museum and Winter Garden in Burdon Road, Sunderland, displays the lustreware pottery for which Sunderland was once well known. The Victorian buildings at the Engines Museum, at Ryhope, south of Sunderland, house enormous pumping engines built in 1869 that are still in working order. Across the river is the North East Aircraft Museum, and not too far away, Hylton Castle, built around 1400, has fine battlements and a resident ghost. Modern arts and crafts are on display at the Reg Vardy Arts Foundation Gallery at Sunderland University, and at the Northern Gallery for Contemporary Art. From the north end of the Wearmouth Bridge it is but a short walk to reach the Greek-style Monkwearmouth Station Museum, built in 1848 and preserved as it was at the turn of the 20th century. Transport and travel in the early 1900s are recorded here, with a look behind the scenes of the booking offices and guard's van.

▼ Wearmouth rail and road bridges

VISIT THE MUSEUMS AND GALLERIES

National Glass Centre
nationalglasscentre.com
Liberty Way, SR6 0GL
0191 5155555 | Open daily 10–5
Watch expert glass-blowers turn a glowing blob into beautiful glasswork, while wincing at the thought of what might happen if they breathe in by mistake. The National Glass Centre is a centre for culture and learning, dedicated to exploring ideas through glass and providing opportunities for people to get creative and be inspired. A varied programme of changing exhibitions shows international glass, contemporary art, craft and design.

Located in an innovative glass and steel building beside the River Wear, NGC houses the UK's largest art glass-making facility and is home to the University of Sunderland Glass and Ceramics department.

Sunderland Museum and Winter Gardens
twmuseums.org.uk/sunderland
Burdon Rd, SR1 1PP
0191 5532323 | Open Mon–Sat 10–5, Sun 2–5
Sunderland isn't the most welcoming of towns in winter, but it's almost worth coming here in the colder months to marvel at the Victorian ingenuity of the Winter Gardens. In this horticultural wonderland, exotic plants from around the world grow to their full natural height in a spectacular glass-and-steel rotunda, ignoring the bitter North Sea weather outside. It's a bit like being in a steam-era spaceship, designed by Wells or Verne. Back down to earth, an award-winning attraction with wide-ranging displays and many hands-on exhibits covers the archaeology and geology of Sunderland, the coal mines and shipyards of the area and the spectacular glass and pottery made on Wearside. Other galleries show the changes in the lifestyles of Sunderland women over the past century, works by artist LS Lowry, and wildlife from all corners of the globe.

Monkwearmouth Station Museum
twmuseums.org.uk/monkwearmouth
North Bridge Street, SR5 1AP
0191 5677075 | Open all year, Mon–Sat 10–5, Sun 2–5
Time stands still in this beautifully restored Victorian station. Travel and transport in the early 1900s are recorded with a look behind the scenes of the booking offices and guard's van. The 'Play Station' activities area has been designed for young visitors, with regular organised events for children.

SEE A FOOTBALL MATCH
Stadium of Light
safc.com
SR5 1SU | 0871 9111224
All tours start at 2; call 0871 9111224 to book
Meet the 'Black Cats' of the

past, present and maybe future too – on a tour of the iconic Stadium of Light. Sunderland AFC's home, which opened in 1997, was a beacon of hope for a town in the doldrums, and by hosting world class music artists, as well as the beautiful game, it has helped put Sunderland back on the map.

Tours take you through every area of the stadium, and on the way you'll see what is claimed to be the oldest painting of a football match in the world, Thomas Hemy's *Aston Villa vs Sunderland*, painted in 1895.

PLAY A ROUND
Wearside Golf Club
wearsidegolfclub.co.uk
Coxgreen, SR4 9JT | 0191 5342518
Open daily
Open, undulating parkland rolling down to the River Wear beneath the shadow of the famous Penshaw Monument. Built on the lines of a Greek temple it is a well-known landmark. Two ravines cross the course presenting a variety of challenging holes.

GET KARTING
Karting North East
kartingnortheast.com
Warden Law Motorsport Centre, SR3 2PR | 0191 5214050
Open Mon–Fri 9–10, Sat–Sun 10–8
This is one for petrolheads, *Mad Max* wannabes and fans of *The Hunger Games* too. Karting North East lets you put the pedal to the metal with 390cc karts. You'll be on the track alongside up to 30 other drivers. You can also learn to handle ferocious off road Rage buggies on a challenging off-road circuit, and the menu of other activities includes archery (minimum group size six people) and a whole bunch of other stuff guaranteed to get the testosterone pumping.

▶ **PLACES NEARBY**
Herrington Country Park
Houghton le Spring, DH4 7EL
0191 5348526
This was once the site of Herrington Colliery, which closed in 1985. At that time the colliery waste-heap was the largest in the northeast – some 11,000,000 cubic metres of shale. Nowadays the park has cycle routes, a boating lake, cycle/skate park, large amphitheatre created from graded grassed embankments and features numerous sculptures/art works. During the transformation, only coal left the site and useful minerals like sandstone and red ash were retained – the sandstone for the sculptures and the red ash for the paths.

On top of Penshaw Hill, overlooking the park, sits the Earl of Durham's Monument, a 70ft-high replica of the Temple of Hephaestus in Athens. Looked after by the National Trust, it's one of Wearside's most beloved landmarks, appearing on the badge of Sunderland AFC.

▶ Tynemouth

It doesn't take long to get away from the industrial dreariness of North Shields (see page 181) and find instead the bright and breezy seaside of Tynemouth. The name's a bit misleading, because Tynemouth is just a bit beyond the mouth of the river, and its sandy beaches face east. In Victorian and Edwardian times, its North Sea breezes were considered bracing, and sea bathing was quite the thing. Now that we've all been spoilt by holidays in the sun, the only people who routinely take the plunge here are windsurfers and kiteboarders, protected from the chill by wetsuits. The appropriately named Longsands is Tynemouth's longest sandy reach, stretching almost three quarters of a mile towards Cullercoats, north of the town. At its southern end, what was once an outdoor, all-weather tidal swimming pool has been turned into a haven for seals and other hardy sea creatures.

A medieval priory is the town's other major landmark, but fans of Italian revolutionary history may like to seek out the plaque on the wall of a house on Huntingdon Place which recalls Giuseppe Garibaldi's brief stay in Tynemouth in 1854.

TAKE IN SOME HISTORY

Tynemouth Priory and Castle

english-heritage.org.uk

Pier Road, NE30 4BZ

0191 2571090 | Open Apr–Oct daily 10–5, Nov–Mar Sat–Sun 10–4; Gun Battery access limited, ask site staff for details

This is one of the very earliest Christian sites in England. It was founded in the early seventh century, and was so revered that two early Anglo-Saxon royal converts – Oswin, king of Deira, who was murdered in AD 651 and Osred, king of Northumbria, who was killed in 792, are buried here. Both died through treachery. It was hard to know who to trust in the many centuries of shifting loyalties as the Dark Ages drew to a close. As the Danes became more of a menace in the late eigth century, the monks of Tynemouth made some attempt at fortifying their home. However, the Danes came again, and after a final raid in AD 875 the priory was destroyed.

Even so, the site was a natural stronghold, so in the mid-11th century Tostig Godwinson, Earl of Northumbria, took it as his seat. Tostig died at Stamford Bridge in 1066, fighting his brother Harold for the throne of England.

The next few centuries are a bit confused, but by the late 13th century Tynemouth had become a combination of castle and monastery, with battlements commanding the entrance to the river. It went on being a castle long after Henry VIII's dissolution, and as late as

World War II there were coastal defence guns emplaced here. You can see traces of the history of the priory and castle today, from the underground magazines beneath the 20th-century coastal battery to the priory arches and the sturdy remains of medieval walls.

MEET THE SEALIFE
Blue Reef Aquarium
bluereefaquarium.co.uk
Grand Parade, NE30 4JF
0191 2581031 | Open daily from 10

If you are burdened with offspring, take them to the Blue Reef Aquarium, which is a great place, whatever the weather. Watch seals looping endlessly and effortlessly underwater in the outdoor lagoon, dabble in touchpools where local denizens of the North Sea shallows swim, crawl and scrabble, and gaze through glass at more exotic beasties such as seahorses, poison arrow frogs, sharks and stingrays. A transparent tunnel takes you deep into a world where fish swim all around you. There are informative and entertaining talks and feeding displays throughout the day, and the Amazing Amazon section takes you into a tropical rainforest complete with reptiles, monkeys and fearsome river fish.

PLAY A ROUND
Tynemouth Golf Club
tynemouthgolfclub.com
Spital Dene, NE30 2ER
0191 2574578 | Open Mon, Wed–Fri; Tue and Sun afternoon only

Well-drained parkland course, not physically demanding but providing a strong challenge to both low and high handicap players.

▶ Vindolanda
vindolanda.com
Vindolanda Trust, Bardon Mill, NE47 7JN | 01434 344277
Open Apr–Sep daily 10–6, Feb–Mar and Oct daily 10–5. Limited winter opening, please contact site for details

Civvy street, Roman style – this is one site along Hadrian's Wall that you really must not miss. Agricola built a turf fort at Vindolanda around AD 80 to guard the Stanegate, one of the strategic Roman highways that were still being built to subdue Britain. You can still see part of the paved road here, as well as a Roman milestone. Another fort was built at Vindolanda before Hadrian's time, and when the wall was constructed, the fort was rebuilt in stone. It was almost totally rebuilt 100 years later, still keeping to the standard rectangular plan that the Romans used for all their military bases. The layout of the headquarters and parts of the gates are clearly visible.

Vindolanda also has the biggest civilian settlement that can be seen on the wall. Visit the *mansio* (an inn for travellers) with

▲ Vindolanda

its bathhouse, and the large 'corridor' house, part of which was a butcher's shop. Other buildings, long, thin 'strip houses', had their narrow ends to the street to avoid high taxes. The town bathhouse was frequented by women and children as well as men – hairpins and a child's sandal were found in the drains. You can still see some of the pink waterproof plaster that lined the walls and floors.

Children visiting Vindolanda usually make straight for the reconstructions of sections of Hadrian's Wall, based on archaeological evidence. The Turf Wall shows what the original, Cumbrian part of the wall was like before it was rebuilt in stone. Here it has a timber gateway, as may once have been found at the milecastles. More impressive is the Stone Wall, nearly 23ft high, with battlements, turret and ditch.

Bardon Mill (see page 65) is nearby, as is Housesteads Roman Fort and Museum (see page 150).

VISIT THE MUSEUM
Roman Army Museum
vindolanda.com
near Greenhead, CA8 7JB
01697 747485 | Open Apr–Sep 10–6, Feb–Mar and Oct daily 10–5; limited winter opening, please contact site for further details
Vindolanda's waterlogged soil has helped to preserve many details of daily life – the museum shows some of them, including leather shoes, textiles and ornaments. There is also a replica of a Roman kitchen. Most important are the wooden writing tablets, with gossip, party invitations, letters requesting new underwear, and accounts of food stores,

bringing the Romans and their neighbours vividly to life.

One of the best-known tablets records an invitation to a birthday celebration. It was sent by Claudia Severa, wife of the commander of the fort at Briga, to Sulpicia Lepidina, wife of Cerialis, who was the commander at Vindolanda. She wrote a message warmly inviting her friend to come and help her make sure that the day of her birthday was one of celebration. Other high points include the 3D video 'Edge of Empire' which gives a real (and sometimes, if you are imaginative, scary) idea of what it was like to be a soldier of Rome on its most remote and dangerous frontier.

▶ Wallington

nationaltrust.org.uk

NE61 4AR | 01670 773600 | House open Mar–Oct Mon–Fri 1–5, Sat–Sun 11–5; grounds all year dawn–dusk; walled garden Apr–Sep daily 10–7, Jan–Mar & Oct–Dec 10–4

Wallington is a place of history and historians. A medieval castle here was owned by the Fenwicks until 1688 – the last was Sir John, executed for plotting to assassinate William III. Parts of the castle still survive in the cellars of the present plain, square house, built in 1688 for Sir William Blackett and altered around 1745 by his son, Sir Walter Blackett. These changes transformed the inside with a new grand staircase and wonderfully delicate plasterwork, most elaborate in the high Saloon, where Reynolds' portrait of Sir Walter hangs, and wall cabinets display part of Wallington's famous china collection. In addition, there is fine Chippendale and Sheraton furniture, 18th-century needlework and a collection of dolls' houses.

The Trevelyan family owned Wallington for almost 200 years and one of them married the sister of historian Lord Macaulay, whose library is now here. Lord Macaulay's great nephew was another historian, George Macaulay Trevelyan; it was his brother who gave Wallington to the National Trust in 1941.

Wallington shone brightest in the 19th century, when Sir Walter Trevelyan and his wife Pauline entertained writers, scientists and artists – Swinburne, the poet from nearby Capheaton, and the painter Millais among them. It was at Ruskin's suggestion that the courtyard was roofed, creating an attractive Italianate central hall with two levels of open arches. Murals of Northumbrian history by William Bell Scott include *The Descent of the Danes*, with Pauline as a woman crying during a Danish raid, and *The Building of Hadrian's Wall*, with Newcastle's town clerk as a centurion, but best of all is *Iron and Steel*, showing the modern industries of Newcastle.

▶ PLACES NEARBY

Belsay Hall, Castle and Gardens

english-heritage.org.uk

NE20 0DX | 01661 881636

Open Apr–Sep daily 10–6, Oct daily 10–4, Nov–Mar Sat–Sun 10–4; also Feb half-term hols

Amazingly well preserved – considering the region's violent past – the yellow sandstone walls and sturdy battlements of the 14th-century tower-house of the Middleton family still seem ready to repel the Scottish invaders who made its construction and fortification necessary in the first place. Even the Great Hall's painted wall decorations, looking just like tapestries, are well preserved.

The 17th-century manor house next to it was rebuilt during the 19th century, then abandoned when Sir Charles Monck built his startling new house nearby. Born a Middleton, Sir Charles changed his name in honour of his maternal grandfather after inheriting from him. This was not uncommon at the time.

Sir Charles was mad for ancient Greece (also not uncommon at the time) and

▼ Wallington Hall

commissioned Belsay Hall in Greek Revival style. As a result, it is severely plain and symmetrical. Inside, it's even grander. The central hall is two storeys high with a glazed roof, and is surrounded by columns. Yet, despite its perfect proportions, you can't help feeling it was never very cosy.

Next to the Hall, the Quarry Garden – created by Sir Charles and his descendants from the pit from which the Hall's foundations were dug – has an abundance of exotic trees and flowering shrubs, a rose terrace and magnolia garden.

8 famous locals

▶ **Harry 'Hotspur' Percy**
Dashing, hot-blooded scion of the Percy dynasty, this famed 15th-century warrior was immortalised by Shakespeare in Henry IV.

▶ **Grace Darling**
Fearless lighthouse-keeper's daughter who rescued survivors of the shipwrecked *Forfarshire*.

▶ **Emily Davidson**
The suffragette who died beneath the hooves of King George V's horse at the 1913 Derby is buried at St James's Church in Morpeth.

▶ **John Fenwick**
The border chief was executed in 1684 for his part in a plot to assassinate William III; his castle at Wallington was forfeit to the Crown.

▶ **Robert Curthose**
Eldest son of William the Conqueror, who founded 'New Castle' in 1080.

▶ **Ellen Wilkinson**
Fiery Labour MP 'Red' Ellen Wilkinson led shipyard workers on the famous 'Jarrow Crusade' against unemployment in 1936.

▶ **Tony Blair**
The controversial former prime minister and former MP for Sedgefield.

▶ **Peter Mandelson**
Tony Blair's urbane master of the political dark arts seems an unlikely match with gritty Hartlepool, but Peter (now Lord) Mandelson was a popular MP.

▶ Wark

You can use this unassuming, quiet village as a base for visiting nearby Hexham (see page 137) and exploring the countryside. It's worth walking to the flat top of Mote Hill, just south of the village, to see what happens when a medieval castle is completely side-tracked by history. There was a Norman stronghold here in the 12th century. It was built on the 'motte and bailey' pattern of early Norman castles in Britain, so it was little more than a wooden stockade surrounded by a ditch. But there's nothing here to show that it ever existed. That's what happens when you don't build in stone. Or, perhaps, if you're lucky enough to live somewhere that neither invaders nor defenders think is strategically important.

EAT AND DRINK

Battlesteads Hotel and Restaurant

battlesteads.com

NE48 3LS | 01434 230209

Outstanding green credentials, including a carbon-neutral heating system, account for some of the awards picked up by Richard and Dee Slade's hotel, restaurant and pub. Standing just a few miles north of Hadrian's Wall and close to Kielder Forest it was converted from an 18th-century farmhouse and is utterly charming – from the flower tubs and hanging baskets to Gilroy the cat, who long ago adopted the place as his home. Renowned for superb food, there are three dining options: a relaxed bar area, where Durham Magus and other regional real ales are on tap; the conservatory, with views of the secret walled garden; and the main restaurant where dark wood furnishings, low lighting and old British Railways travel posters create a more formal setting.

The food is all sourced either from the two-acre gardens and polytunnels, or from no more than 25 miles away from the village. The style is primarily modern British, with seasonal game, Cumbrian beef, Northumbrian lamb, and fish and seafood from North Shields. There are more than 25 organic, Fairtrade and biodynamic wines to choose from.

▶ PLACES NEARBY

Chipchase Castle

chipchasecastle.com

NE48 3NT, 2 miles southeast of Wark
01434 230203 | Open afternoons in Jun, other times by arrangement

If you look north from the line of Hadrian's Wall you can see Chipchase Castle, high on its plateau above the North Tyne. It's a magical mix of medieval, Jacobean and Georgian, reflecting both the turbulent history of the area and the vicissitudes of its ownership. Like many of the great Northumbrian houses, it began life as a defensive pele tower against the Scots' frequent raids – and against the neighbours and authorities, too, for the Heron family, who owned Chipchase from 1348, were a quarrelsome lot.

How long the tower stood alone is unclear, but by 1541 a stone manor house was joined to it. It was from here that the Herons, as Keepers of Tyndale, set out on Scottish raids, sometimes in defiance of their overlords. The entire history of the family seems to have consisted of skirmish, capture and bloodshed. In 1537 John Heron was accused of murder, but was later pardoned. His son, Sir George, was killed by the Scots at Carter Bar. The Heron estates, which were considerable, were inherited by Cuthbert Heron in 1591 when he was only six. The castle's E-shaped south-east front makes it one of the north's best buildings of its time, with its four great bow windows – Victorian restorations, but very much in keeping – and the fanciful cresting over the porch tower.

Yet within 60 years of Cuthbert's confident gesture in building a new home, there was almost nothing left of the Heron fortunes. Mortgages and dowries, as well as the difficult political climate of the 17th century, had taken their toll. The family struggled on at Chipchase until 1727, when they were forced to sell. Ownership changed several times until it came to John Reed in 1734.

Reed obviously found the Jacobean house dark and gloomy, for he added sash windows and put false windows on the pele so that the south-west side of the house is symmetrical – if you can make the mental effort to ignore the turrets on the medieval tower.

▼ Chipchase Castle

He transformed the interiors at Chipchase, too, with elegant plaster ceilings and fine doorcases, particularly in what is now the billiard room, where there is also a superbly carved wooden overmantel, a survivor from the previous house.

Barrasford Arms ⦿

barrasfordarms.co.uk

NE48 4AA | 01434 681237

Sitting proudly at the heart of village life in this North Tyne valley hamlet, the Barrasford is a Victorian inn that hosts quoits tournaments and darts matches, like pubs did in the era before video games and Sky Sports. It enjoys a symbiotic relationship with the local community, its decor of fishing rods and shotguns reflecting the region's country pursuits, and Northumbrian produce naturally informs the bulk of Tony Binks's culinary output. Up-to-the-minute country pub dishes are big on flavour and accuracy of rendition, as witness breadcrumbed veal escalope topped with tomato and Mull Cheddar, served with buttery Charlotte potatoes, as well as grilled mackerel jazzed up with lively dressings of tomato and chilli salsa and citrus crème fraîche. A well-rendered chocolate fondant is properly molten in the centre, made with rip-roaring chocolate, and sauced with espresso custard.

▶ Warkworth

Shakespeare set parts of his *Henry IV* here. One of his characters calls Warkworth Castle 'this worm-eaten hold of ragged stone'. Hardly fair, especially since Shakespeare had no more been to Warkworth than to Bohemia, Verona or Venice. In fact, this huge fortress is one of the most spectacular in a part of England that is studded with awe-inspiring castles.

Set in a loop of the River Coquet on the site of the original motte, its plan is a cross superimposed on a square. It stands to its full height, thanks to a 19th-century restoration by the Duke of Northumberland. The original 11th-century structure was replaced by a stone castle before 1158 and in 1174 was sacked – like pretty much everything with a wall and a tower – by the Scots, who were on one of their rampages at the time. The Great Gate Tower, guarding the south approach, was built around 1200, as was the Carrickfergus Tower to the west.

The Percys lived at Warkworth until they moved to more comfortable Alnwick (see page 53) in the 16th century, and the Lion Tower carries their crest.

▶ Warkworth Castle by the River Coquet

The Percy Lion is also carved on the keep wall that dominates the little town, where the medieval street plan is still evident. Georgian and Victorian houses lead down the hill to the church and the fortified bridge. In 1715, Northumbrian sympathisers of the Jacobite Cause proclaimed the exiled James Stuart James III of England and VIII of Scotland in Warkworth, then dined at the Masons' Arms. In the church a Catholic chaplain said prayers. But it all came to nothing. James never even left France, his supporters in Scotland shillied and shallied, and the rebellion fizzled out.

The church has a 14th-century spire but inside it is almost all Norman, with a nave more than 90ft long and an unusual stone-vaulted chancel, its roof ribs highly decorated with sharp-cut zig-zags. This now-peaceful church was the scene of a massacre in 1174, when the Scottish army slaughtered most of the population of Warkworth, seeking refuge within its walls.

TAKE IN SOME HISTORY
Warkworth Castle and Hermitage
english-heritage.org.uk
Castle Terrace, NE65 0UJ
01665 711423 | Castle open Apr–Sep daily 10–5, Oct daily 10–4, end Feb to end Mar Sat–Sun 10–4, mid-Feb Mon–Fri 10–4; Hermitage temporarily closed due to operational issues with access

It's hard to believe that William the Lion's easy conquest of Warkworth in 1173 was said to be because the castle was 'feeble in wall and earthwork'. That could be English propaganda, of course. Maybe they just didn't want to admit that Scots were better fighters at the time – after all, they took almost every other castle in Northumberland on that campaign.

Whatever the reason, subsequent lords of Warkworth deemed it prudent to strengthen its defences, and as you see it today it is one of the most potent strongholds in northern England.

The unusually-shaped keep was raised by the Earl of Northumberland in around 1390. It is basically square, but has towers projecting from each of its four sides. One tower contained an elegant chapel, and there were comfortable living quarters in some of the others.

Rainwater was collected on the roof and channelled to holding tanks in the basement, permitting a constant supply of clean water to many of the basins and latrines – a great luxury in a medieval castle. The Earl, wishing his castle to reflect his powerful status, ordered separate living quarters in the keep to divide him and his family from the rest of the garrison.

It was probably this same earl who ordered a (never

completed) fine chapel in the courtyard, the foundations of which can still be seen.

The Earl and his famous son, Hotspur, are perhaps the most renowned residents of the castle, for it was they who fought so hard to put Henry IV on the throne in 1399, and to force the rightful king, Richard II, to abdicate. Four years later, these two men fought equally hard to wrest the crown from Henry once more. The King promptly marched to Warkworth and blasted its walls with cannon fire until the castle surrendered.

The King then gave Warkworth to his brother, later the Duke of Bedford, although it was restored to Hotspur's son in 1416. The Percys' political favour continued to wax and wane during the 15th century, and in 1572 Sir Thomas Percy was executed for his part in a plot against Elizabeth I. With his death, this great fortress began to decline in importance.

Abutting onto the Percys' keep were walls that formed a large enclosure containing several buildings, now mostly ruins, although the Lion Tower (named after the Percy lion) and the Grey Mare's Tail Tower, with its massive fan-tailed crossbow loops, still stand.

A short walk from the castle is a small rock-hewn chapel and stone-built outer chamber: the Hermitage. The inner part comprises a chapel and a smaller chamber, both with altars. There is an altar-tomb with a female effigy in the chapel. It's probably 14th century, and the traditional story of the origin of the hermitage is told in Bishop Percy's ballad *The Hermit of Warkworth* (1771). The chapel was in fact built as a chantry, and occupied by a series of clergy from 1489 to 1536. It's usually open in the summer.

SEE A LOCAL CHURCH
Church of St Lawrence
11 Dial Place, NE65 0UR

Although there was an important Saxon church here, the present building dates mainly from the 1130s. This includes the whole north side of the nave and much of the vaulted chancel, which originally had a mysterious high-level chamber, perhaps a treasury or a relic house. The church survived the Sack of Warkworth by the Scots in 1173, when hundreds of villagers were slaughtered inside it.

The west tower dates from around 1200, but the belfry and spire were built around 1350. The rather grand 15th-century south aisle, and its two-storeyed south porch, are a rarity in Northumberland but can be explained by the patronage of the powerful Percy family and the proximity of their castle.

▶ **PLACES NEARBY**

The Cook and Barker Inn

cookandbarkerinn.co.uk

Newton on the Moor, Felton, NE65 9JY | 01665 575234

Enjoying outstanding views of the Northumberland coast and the Cheviot Hills, The Cook and Barker is a traditional stone-built inn clad in creepers and flower baskets. A long-established family business that goes way beyond providing 'pub grub with rooms', thanks to expert front-of-house and skilled kitchen teams. As the owneralso runs Hope House Farm, 8 miles away, they have no trouble sourcing the organic beef, lamb and pork that feature on the wide-ranging bar and restaurant menus. These offer modern European cuisine focusing on seafood and 'forest and field' with the occasional oriental influence. The cosy en suite bedrooms are smartly furnished, some with traditional features such as exposed wooden beams.

Washington

Amazingly, a few score American visitors turn up every year in this blandly modern, slightly depressed new town, created by mashing a bunch of villages together in the mid-20th century. They are, of course, looking for the ancestral home of America's first president, the eponymous George. His ancestors, the pretentiously-named de Wessyngtons, sensibly sold up and left for foreign parts in 1613.

Coal from Washington's mines was transported to the River Tyne along the Bowes Railway, which is now preserved at Springwell Village. The world's only standard-gauge, rope-hauled railway, it was begun by George Stephenson in 1826. You can take a ride on a steam-hauled train, follow a historical trail and visit a fascinating exhibition.

The Wildfowl and Wetlands Trust, east of Washington, was founded by the naturalist Sir Peter Scott. Its 114 acres of parkland are home to flamingos, swans, geese and ducks, as well as to flocks of migrating waders and wildfowl. Hides let you see the shyer species, and picture windows in the Visitor Centre give wide-ranging views even in bad weather.

Each July Washington hosts the two-day Sunderland International Friendship Festival, when kite-makers and -flyers from around the world meet for the UK's biggest event of its kind. This lively event includes street theatre, music and activities for children.

Art-lovers could sample Washington Arts Centre, a converted farm building that houses an exhibition gallery, artist studios and a community theatre.

Dominating the landscape from its hilltop southeast of Washington is the Penshaw Monument, a soot-blackened half-size replica of the Temple of Theseus in Athens. It was built by local subscription as a tribute to the first Earl of Durham, 'Radical Jack' Lambton, a great local benefactor who became the first Governor of Canada. Nearby is another example of historical copying – the Victoria Viaduct, which is a replica of the Roman bridge at Alcantara in Spain.

TAKE IN SOME HISTORY
Washington Old Hall
nationaltrust.org.uk
The Avenue, Washington Village, NE38 7LE | 0191 4166879
Open Apr–Oct, Sun–Wed and Easter 11–5; garden 10–5; tea room 10–4
Washington Old Hall, a delightful 17th-century manor incorporating parts of an earlier medieval home, was the home of George Washington's ancestors from 1183 to 1613. It was from here the family took their name.

The house has been restored and filled with period furniture, and contains displays about George Washington and the history of American Independence. Most of this historic building dates from around ten years after George Washington's ancestors, the de Wessyngtons, sold up in 1613.

The house is furnished in the 17th-century style, with polished oak furniture, pewter plates, and some fine Jacobean panelling. There is, of course, a bust of George Washington, and a family tree that traces his ancestry to King John.

Celebrations here perpetuate the American connection by marking Washington's Birthday in February, as well as US Independence Day on 4th July and Thanksgiving in the autumn.

MEET THE BIRDLIFE
Washington Wetland Centre
wwt.org.uk
NE38 8LE | 0191 4165454
Open summer 9.30–5.30, winter 9.30–4.30
Waders, curlews, oystercatchers, and ducks of all kinds are to be expected in these parts. But the Washington Wetland Centre confronts you with some unexpected exotics in its wetland and woodland enclosures, where as well as the usual seabird suspects you can see Chilean flamingos, Eurasian cranes and other unfamiliar species.

Whitley Bay

Whitley Bay is, undeniably, slightly seedy. It was a classic seaside boomtown, but since the 1970s it's been all downhill. That said, it has a great location which attracted the attention of a famous English admiral and an equally famous dramatist-turned-architect.

TAKE IN SOME HISTORY
Seaton Delaval Hall
nationaltrust.org.uk
The Avenue, Seaton Sluice,
NE26 4QR | 01912 379100
Open May–Oct

Never one for tame classical copying, Sir John Vanbrugh used his commission from Admiral George Delaval to build a house on this windswept northern coast to indulge his taste for the dramatic.

By the time Vanbrugh came to design his masterpiece at Seaton Delaval he had already produced both Castle Howard and Blenheim Palace. As a former playwright, Vanbrugh knew how to utilize scenery for impressive effect, and the north-facing entrance front of his main block – strangely, it largely ignores the sea – is hugely powerful, almost aggressive, with its towers and turrets and the enormous columns casting sinister shadows that dwarf the central doorway. Even the garden front is monumentally and magnificently intimidating.

From the outside, the hall looks whole and complete, but the Great Hall of the central block is semi-ruinous, open to the roof and still bearing the marks of the fire that swept

through it in 1822. Blackened statues stand in their niches and a delicate iron gallery, now restored, gives access to vanished floors. In the Mahogany and Tapestry Rooms on the north side there is a display of family portraits and mahogany panelling survives, while the vaulted basement could have held supplies for an army.

In the west wing, open only by special appointment, the former kitchen is now the entrance hall, and in this and the other habitable rooms are furniture and paintings that were rescued from the blaze, as well as items from Melton Constable in Norfolk.

Over in the opposite wing, Vanbrugh's fine stables, like a pagan temple, still have the horses' names above the classical niches holding their mangers. The stalls have their original finely moulded timberwork and paved floors.

SEE A LOCAL CHURCH
Church of Our Lady
The Avenue, NE26 4QS

Hidden behind Seaton Delaval Hall, this tiny, unassuming Norman church can be reached by a short walk down a country path. Built at the end of the

5 top walks and rides

▶ **Bamburgh Coast**
Beachcomb along Bamburgh's sandy beach, then loop inland through rolling countryside.

▶ **Coquet Gorge**
You'll need watertight boots and a fair level of fitness to explore the gorge of the River Coquet, which carves its way through the Cheviot Hills near Otterburn.

▶ **Druridge Bay**
Take a shoreline stroll through a nature reserve where coastal lakes attract many migrant birds.

▶ **Hadrian's Wall and the Stanegate**
Leave the car at Once Brewed and get on your bike for a 12-mile ride that takes you along the line of Hadrian's Wall.

▶ **Kielder Water and the Tyne**
Starting at the east end of Kielder Water, you can cycle for miles along forest trails and along the banks of the River Tyne.

11th century by Guy de Laval, the nephew of William the Conqueror, it was the private chapel of the Delaval family for over 700 years.

Above the entrance is an ancient window, carved from one piece of stone for the original 14th-century east window, and now filled with Victorian glass. Inside, the church is sparse by modern standards, with stone floors, plaster walls and high-backed wooden pews at either side of a central aisle. Closer inspection reveals the magnificent Norman chancel, choir and nave, which are separated from each other by two beautiful arches, perfectly carved with the zig-zag pattern typical of Norman design. On the nave and west walls hang six funeral hatchments (coats of arms), of which there are only 50 in the whole of Northumberland. There is a Norman piscina used for washing the Communion vessels on display, and the two remaining aumbries (wall safes) show off the depth of the walls.

Even more striking, the effigies of a Delaval Crusader knight and his lady lie in the crypt beneath the altar, though he might have been part of a tomb chest that stood where the altar is now. Although they are badly damaged and worn, and retain no traces of the bright colours with which they must once have been adorned, they are powerful reminders of 900 years of history.

▶ Wooler

You wouldn't go out of your way to make a special visit to
Wooler, but this unassuming town is a good base for exploring
the Northumberland National Park or setting off to walk all or
part of the Pennine Way or the St Cuthbert's Way between
Melrose in Scotland and Holy Isle. The town seems to have
been quietly prosperous since its foundation in the early
Norman era, and it also appears to have escaped most the
sacking and pillaging that went on during the seemingly
endless wars between England and Scotland that ended only
in the early 17th century.

PLAY A ROUND
Wooler Golf Club
woolergolf.co.uk
Dod Law, Doddington, NE71 6AN
01668 282135
Hilltop, moorland course
with spectacular views over
the Glendale Valley. Nine
greens played from 18 tees.
A very challenging course
when windy with one par 5 of
580yds. The course is much
under used during the week so
is always available.

EXPLORE BY BIKE
Wooler Cycle Hub
wooler.org.uk
Haugh Head Garage, NE71 6QP
01668 281316
Hire bicycles to venture
into the Northumberland
National Park, along the
remote College Valley, or –
for the fitter and perhaps
younger – into the rugged
trails of the Harthope Valley.

▼ Cycling around Wooler

Riding
Mill

Country Park Whickh...

A694

Whitley
Chapel

Slaley

Rowland's Gill

Gibside

Burnopfield

Tanfield
Railway

Beamish
Hall

243

A68

Ebchester

244

Beamish Museum
Stanley

B

A692

Leadgate

Annfield Plain

A693

Derwent
Reservoir

Consett

Blanchland

Edmundbyers

River Derwent

Castleside

Lanchester

A691

Diggerland

A68

Rookhope

Stanhope

A689

Tow Law

Crook

A690

Brandon

Spenny

Wolsingham

240

Witton
le Wear

Binchester
Roman Fort

DURHAM

Hamsterley
Forest

River Wear

A68

Witton
Castle Lakes

Auc

Bowlees Visitor Centre
and Gibson's Cave

Newbiggin

Toft Hill

Bishop
Auckland

Shild

Woodland

West
Auckland

A6072

Middleton-
in-Teesdale

Mickleton

Eggleston

Copley

A688

A68

Eggleston Hall
Gardens

Romaldkirk

River Tees

Raby Castle

Staindrop

Cotherstone

A67

Gainford

A67

Pierc

Pennine Way

Barnard Castle

Eggleston
Abbey

Bowes

A67

A66

Rokeby Park

Greta
Bridge

Bowes
Castle

A66

Newsham

A66

Gilling West

Sc
Co

YORKSHIRE DALES

Langthwaite

NATIONAL

eld

Richmond

A1

PARK

A6108

Hipswell

hwaite

A6136

Muker

Low Row

Seaham

sington

*Durham
Heritage Coast*

Peterlee

A1086

A179

★ **HARTLEPOOL**

Hartlepool Bay

A19

A689

A178

Tees Bay

olviston○

○ **Billingham**

Redcar○

Marske-by-
the-Sea○

Saltburn-by-the-Sea○

River Tees

A1085

**STOCKTON-
ON-TEES** ★

A66

Brotton○

A174

MIDDLESBROUGH ○

Skelton○

Loftus○
A174

A171

○ **Eston**

● **Preston Park
Museum**

A174

A171

arm

A1044

○ **Guisborough**

A171

A19

A173

Great Ayton○

Kildale○

Stokesley○

○ Castleton

○Crathorne

NORTH YORK MOORS

A19

NATIONAL

A172

Cleveland Way

PARK

Seave Green ○

NORTH YORK MOORS

○Osmotherley

Bonchester
Bridge

A7

A68

A6088

SCOTTISH   BORDERS

NORTHUMBERLAN

Kielder

Kielder
Water

Leaplish
Waterside Park

Falsto

Newcastleton

CUMBRIA

Walltown Crags
and Turret

Gilsland

Carvoran

Greenhead

Haltwhistle

Smithfield

A6071

A69

River South Tyne

Brampton

A689

A689

M6

Wetheral

Castle
Carrock

238

Knarsdale

Cumrew

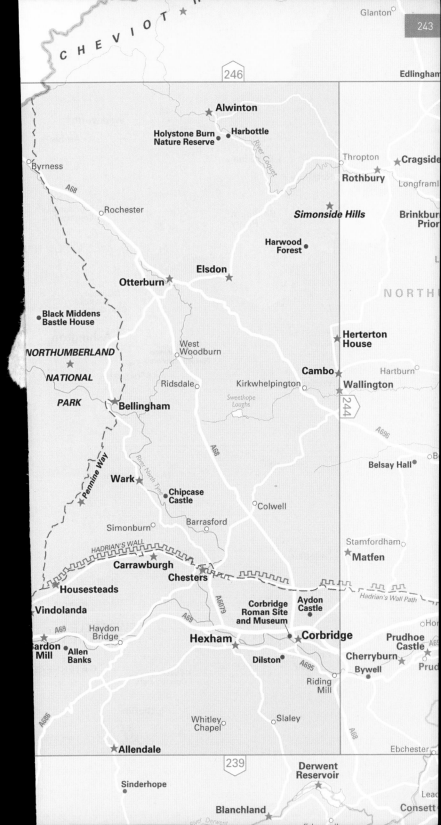

CHEVIOT

Glanton

Edlingham

Alwinton

Holystone Burn
Nature Reserve

Harbottle

River Coquet

Byrness

Thropton

Cragside

Rothbury

Longframl

A68

Rochester

Simonside Hills

Brinkbur
Prior

Harwood
Forest

Elsdon

Otterburn

NORTH

Black Middens
Bastle House

West
Woodburn

Herterton
House

NORTHUMBERLAND

Cambo

Hartburn

NATIONAL

Ridsdale

Kirkwhelpington

Wallington

PARK

Sweethope
Loughs

A244

Bellingham

A696

River North Tyne

A68

Belsay Hall

oB

Wark

Chipcase
Castle

Colwell

Pennine Way

Barrasford

Simonburn

Stamfordham

HADRIAN'S WALL

Matfen

Carrawburgh

Chesters

Housesteads

Corbridge
Roman Site
and Museum

Aydon
Castle

Hadrian's Wall Path

Vindolanda

A69

Haydon
Bridge

A6079

oHo

ardon
Mill

Allen
Banks

A69

Hexham

Dilston

Corbridge

Prudhoe
Castle

A69

Cherryburn

A695

Bywell

Prud

Riding
Mill

Whitley
Chapel

Slaley

A68

A686

Allendale

Ebchester

239

Derwent
Reservoir

Sinderhope

Lead

Blanchland

Consett

River Derwent

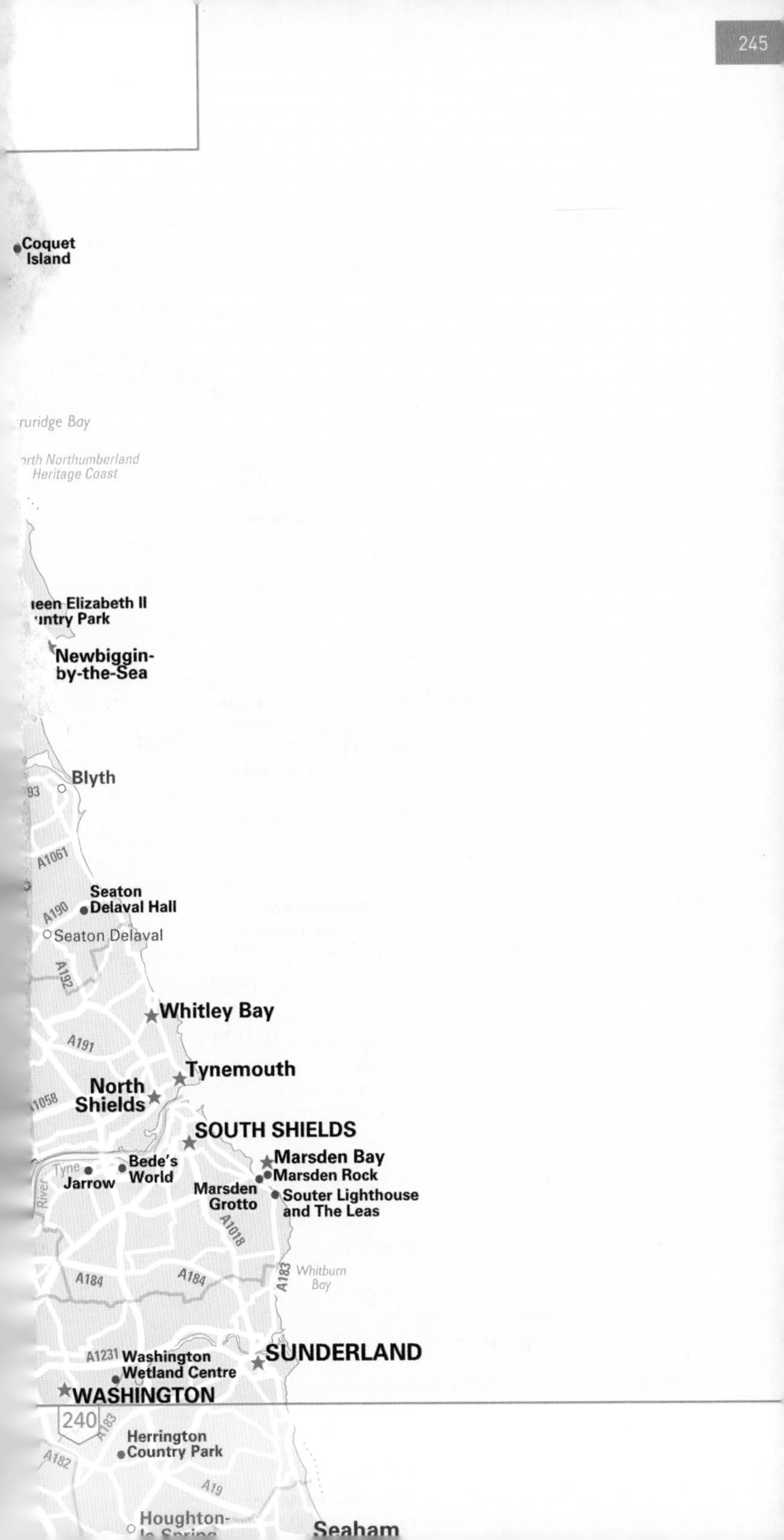

Coquet
Island

ruridge Bay

rth Northumberland
    Heritage Coast

leen Elizabeth II
untry Park

Newbiggin-
by-the-Sea

Blyth

93

A1061

A190   Seaton
       Delaval Hall
    Seaton Delaval

A192

Whitley Bay

A191

North
Shields

1058   Tynemouth

SOUTH SHIELDS

Tyne   Bede's   Marsden Bay
Jarrow World   Marsden Rock
             Marsden   Souter Lighthouse
River   Grotto   and The Leas

A184   A184   A183   Whitburn
                              Bay

A1231 Washington   SUNDERLAND
     Wetland Centre
WASHINGTON

240
       Herrington
A182   Country Park

           A19

       Houghton-   Seaham
       le-Spring

Cranshaws

Grantshouse

A1107

Coldingham

St Abbs

Eyemouth

A1

Ayton

A6112

Longformacus

Preston

Chirnside

A6105

Berwick-
upon-Tweed

Conundrum
Farm

Duns

Allanton

SCOTTISH BORDERS

Paxton House

Horncliffe

Swinton

Norham
Castle

Greenlaw

A6105

A697

Norham

A698

Ancroft

River Tweed

Hume

Eccles

A6112

Cornhill-
on-Tweed

Etal

Lowi

A6089

Ednam

A698

Coldstream

Wark

Ford
Forge

Ford

Flodden
Battlefield Trail

Kelso

Flodden

Roxburgh

A698

Milfield

River Till

Doddingto

Kirknewton

Town Yetholm

Yeavering
Bell

362

Wooler

A697

Crailing

Morebattle

NORTHUMBERLAND

NATIONAL

Pennine
Way

PARK

816
THE CHEVIOT

A68

CHEVIOT HILLS

243

Alwinton

Holystone Burn
Nature Reserve

Harbottle

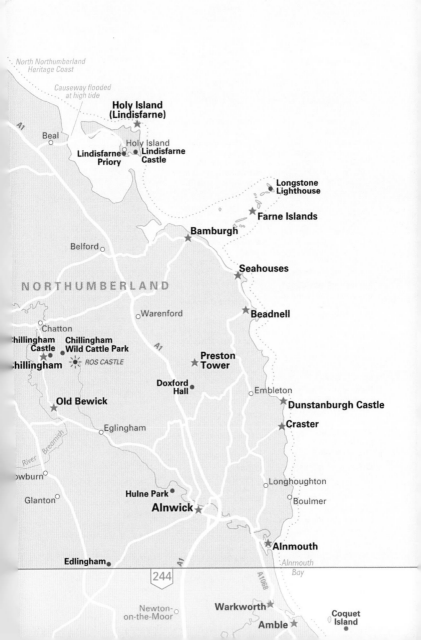

North Northumberland
Heritage Coast

Causeway flooded
at high tide

**Holy Island
(Lindisfarne)** ★

A1

Beal ○

Holy Island
Lindisfarne ● ● **Lindisfarne
Priory** **Castle**

● **Longstone
Lighthouse**

★ **Farne Islands**

Bamburgh ★

Belford ○

NORTHUMBERLAND

○ **Warenford**

★ **Seahouses**

★ **Beadnell**

○ Chatton

**Chillingham
Castle** ★ ● **Chillingham
Wild Cattle Park**

☀ *ROS CASTLE*

A1

★ **Preston
Tower**

Chillingham

Old Bewick ★

**Doxford
Hall** ●

Embleton ○

★ **Dunstanburgh Castle**

○ Eglingham

River Breamish

★ **Craster**

○wburn ○

Glanton ○

Hulne Park ●

Alnwick ★

Longhoughton ○

○ **Boulmer**

Edlingham ●

244

A1

★ **Alnmouth**

Alnmouth
Bay

A1068

Newton-
on-the-Moor ○

Warkworth ★

Coquet
Island ●

Amble ★

Index, themed

Page numbers in **bold** refer to main text entries